Anastasios Giovanidis

ARQ Protocols in Wireless Communications

Anastasios Giovanidis

ARQ Protocols in Wireless Communications

Modeling, Analysis and Optimization

Südwestdeutscher Verlag für Hochschulschriften

Imprint

Any brand names and product names mentioned in this book are subject to trademark, brand or patent protection and are trademarks or registered trademarks of their respective holders. The use of brand names, product names, common names, trade names, product descriptions etc. even without a particular marking in this work is in no way to be construed to mean that such names may be regarded as unrestricted in respect of trademark and brand protection legislation and could thus be used by anyone.

Publisher:
Südwestdeutscher Verlag für Hochschulschriften
is a trademark of
Dodo Books Indian Ocean Ltd., member of the OmniScriptum S.R.L Publishing group
str. A.Russo 15, of. 61, Chisinau-2068, Republic of Moldova Europe
Printed at: see last page
ISBN: 978-3-8381-2055-3

Zugl. / Approved by: Berlin, TU, Diss., 2010

Copyright © Anastasios Giovanidis
Copyright © 2010 Dodo Books Indian Ocean Ltd., member of the OmniScriptum S.R.L Publishing group

Zusammenfassung

Der Schwerpunkt der aktuellen Arbeit ist die Modellierung, Analyse und Regelung von automatischen Wiederholungsanfrage (Automatic Retransmission reQuest - ARQ) Protokollen, die als Teil eines drahtlosen Kommunikationssystems betrachtet werden. Die Aufgabe von solchen Protokollen ist die Detektion und Korrektur vom Fehlern. Um dies zu erreichen, informiert der Empfänger den Sender über das Ergebnis der Decodierung jedes Pakets mit Hilfe eines binären Steuersignals ACK / NACK. Das NACK Signal steuert eine Wiederholung der Übertragung für das fehlerhaften Paket an. Das ACK Signal informiert den Sender, dass das Paket korrekt empfangen wurde, woraufhin das nächste wartende Paket im Puffer für die neue Übertragung vorbereitet wird.

Eine bedeutsames Performanzmass für solche Protokolle ist der goodput, der definiert ist als die Rate der korrekt über die drahtlose Verbindung übertragenen Pakete. Typischerweise wird der goodput beschrieben als Produkt der Übertragungsrate mal der Erfolgswahrscheinlichkeit. Dieses folgt aus der Renewal-Reward Theorie, die eine feste Wahrscheinlichkeitsverteilung sowie Ergodizität des Fading-Prozesses annimmt. Alternative Masse für den goodput für Kommunikation zeitlich eng begrenzter Dauer werden vorgeschlagen, die besser geeignet sind für den Fall einer endlichen Anzahl von zuübertragenden Paketen.

Legt man die Werte für die Erfolgswahrscheinlichkeit pro wiederholter Übertragung durch a priori Auswahl der Wiedrholung-Strategie fest, kann die Entwicklung des ARQ Protokolls als success run beschrieben werden. Eine Definition für die Zuverlässigkeit der Kommunikation wird vorgestellt, die verwandt ist zur Idee der Delay-limited Kapazität. Es wird bewiesen, dass ein ARQ Protokoll dann und nur dann zuverlässig ist, wenn seine Übergangswarscheinlichkeitsmatrix ergodisch ist. Bedingung für Ergodizität und Nicht-Ergodizität führen zu einer Kategorisierung der ARQ Protokolle (und entsprechend der Leistungszuteilungs-Strategien pro Wiederholung) in zuverlässige und unzuverlässige.

Zusammenfassung

Weil bei der praktischen Übertragung die ARQ Protokolle immer zusammengeschnitten werden und ein Paketverlust auftritt, sobald die maximale Zahl an Wiederholungen erreicht wurde, untersucht diese Arbeit das Problem des optimalen Zuschnitts der Anzahl der Wiederholungen. Die Methode verwendet Argumente des optimalen Abbruchs (optimal stopping), wobei eine erfolgreiche Übertragung eines Pakets mit einer Belohnung ausgezeichnet wird, wohingegen Verzögerungen und Leistungsverbrauch als generalisierte Kosten modelliert werden. Das System vergibt außerdem eine Strafe, wenn eine Paket fallengelassen wird. Aus der sequentiellen Analyse folgt die optimale Zuschnittlänge, woraus man eine Regel erhält, die alle oben genannten Kosten und Belohnungen in eine einfache Ungleichung überführt.

ARQ Protokolle sind natürlich verwandt mit Queuing. Die Integration eines Wiederholungsprotokolls auf dem Server einer Queue verursacht eine zusätzliche Verzögerung für die gepufferten Pakete, so dass die Zuverlässigkeit der Übertragung gewährleistet werden kann. Um die Verzögerung zu reduzieren, können bestimmte Pakete durch Unterbrechung des Wiederholungsprozesses fallengelassen werden. Durch Anwendung von dynamischer Programmierung wird die optimale Abbruchstrategie hergeleitet. Die Entscheidung zum Fallenlassen hängt von dem Systemzustand ab, der das Paar aus Queue-Länge und aktuellem Aufwand für die Wiederholung bildet. Die daraus folgende Strategien sind optimal im Sinne der Minimierung des zeitlichen Mittelwerts eine Linearkombination von Queue-Länge und der Anzahl der verlorenen Pakete.

Ein nächster Schritt in der Analyse ist die Leistungssteuerung von ARQ Protokollen in einem Downlink-System. Daten, die für eine bestimmte Anzahl von Nutzern vorgesehen sind, werden an der Basisstation gepuffert. Jeder Puffer benutzt das Wiederholungsprotokoll, um Zuverlässigkeit zu erzielen, während die Basisstation ein spezifisches Gesamt-Leistungsbudget zur Verfügung hat, um dieses an alle Nutzer in jedem Zeitschlitz zu verteilen. Bei Betrachtung von festen Übertragungsraten pro Nutzer und unter Berücksichtigung von Interferenzen wird die Stabilitätsregion des Systems hergeleitet. Es wird gezeigt, dass eine Leistungszuteilungsstrategie diese Stabilitätsregion erreichen kann, und Algorithmen zur Berechnung der Leistung pro Nutzer werden angewendet und verglichen.

Die Arbeit schließt mit einer Untersuchung eines drahtlosen Ad-Hoc Netzwerks, bei dem Daten an verschiedenen Quell-Knoten eingespeist werden, die dann über die Systemknoten zu ihren Zielen geroutet werden. Fehler treten pro Hop durch Fading und Interferenz

Zusammenfassung

auf. Jeder Knoten is wieder mit einem ARQ Protokoll für Fehlerkorrektur versehen. Die Stabilitätsregion des Systems wird hergeleitet. Jeder Datenfluß wird in Beziehung gesetzt zu einer Utility-Funktion, woraus ein Netzwerk Utility Maximierungsproblem unter Stabilitätsbedingungen formuliert wird. Seine Lösung liefert die optimale Strategie für die per-Slot congestion control, routing sowie Leistungszuweisung, mit der die Summe der Utilities maximiert wird, während alle Puffer im System beschränkt gehalten werden. Die Anforderung, dass die Leistungszuweisungsstrategien in einer dezentralisierten Weise implementierbar sein sollen, kann erfüllt werden, wenn Kooperation zwischen Knoten erlaubt wird und gleichzeitig jeder Knoten Messungen durchführen kann, um die Stärke seiner Interferenz zu schätzen. Bei Anwendung der Spieltheorie und Benutzung der obigen Information, kann jeder Knoten die optimale Leistung für die Übertragung wählen.

Abstract

The focus of the current thesis is on the modeling, analysis and control of Automatic Retransmission reQuest (ARQ) protocols as part of a wireless communications system. The function of these protocols is the detection and correction of errors. To achieve this the receiver informs the transmitter over the result of packet decoding using a binary control signal ACK/NACK. The NACK triggers a retransmission of the erroneous packet, while an ACK informs the transmitter that the packet has been correctly received and the next packet awaiting in the buffer is prepared.

A significant performance measure related to such protocols is the goodput, defined as the rate of correctly transmitted packets over the wireless link. Typically goodput is expressed as the product of scheduled transmission rate times the success probability, which results from renewal-reward theory assuming fixed probability distribution and ergodicity of the fading process. Alternative goodput measures for short term communications are suggested which are more appropriate in case the number of packets to be transmitted is finite.

Fixing the success probability values per retransmission, by selecting a priori a retransmission policy, the evolution of an ARQ protocol can be described as a success run. A definition of reliability in communications is provided, which is related to the notion of delay limited capacity. It is proven that an ARQ protocol is reliable if and only if its transition probability matrix is ergodic. Conditions for ergodicity and non-ergodicity result in a categorization of ARQ protocols (and subsequently of power allocation policies per retransmission), into reliable and unreliable.

Since in practical communications the ARQ protocols are always truncated and a packet dropping occurs when the maximum number of retransmissions is exceeded, the problem of optimal truncation has been investigated. The method utilizes optimal stopping arguments where the successful transmission of a packet is related to a reward, whereas the delay and power consumption are modeled as generalized costs. The system incurs additionally a penalty when the packet is dropped. Optimal truncation length has resulted from the sequential analysis which provides a rule combining all the above costs and rewards into a simple inequality.

ARQ protocols are of course related to queuing. Incorporating a retransmission protocol at the server of a queue brings additional delay to the buffered packets so that reliability of transmission can be guaranteed. To reduce delay certain packets can be dropped by interrupting the retransmission process. Applying dynamic programming the optimal dropping policy is derived. The decision to drop depends on the system state which is the pair of queue length and current retransmission effort. The resulting policies are optimal in the sense of minimizing the time average of a linear combination of queue length and number of dropped packets.

A next step in the analysis is the power control of ARQ protocols in a downlink system. Data destined to a certain number of users are buffered at the base station. Each buffer uses the retransmission protocol to achieve reliablity, while the base station has a specific total power budget to divide among users at each time slot. Considering fixed transmission rate per user and taking interference into account, the stability region of the system is derived. A power allocation policy is shown to achieve this stability region and algorithms to compute the power per user are applied and compared.

The work concludes with an investigation of an ad hoc wireless network, where data enter in different source nodes and should be routed through the system nodes to their destination. Errors occur per hop due to fading and interference. Each node is again equiped with an ARQ protocol for error correction. The stability region of the system is derived. Each data flow is related to a utility function and a network utility maximization problem with stability constraints is formulated. Its solution provides the optimal per slot congestion control, routing and power allocation policy to maximize the sum of utilities while keeping all buffers in the system finite. The requirement that the power allocation policies should be implemented in a decentralized manner can be fulfilled if cooperation between nodes is allowed and at the same time each node performs measurements to estimate its interference level. Applying game theory and using the above information, each node can choose an optimal power to transmit.

Acknowledgment

The research for the current Thesis has been conducted in the Fraunhofer Heinrich Hertz Institute from September 2005 to September 2006, as well as the Fraunhofer German-Sino Lab for Mobile Communications from September 2006 to December 2009. The research has been funded from the BMBF Project ScaleNet (Sept. 2006 - Dec. 2008), the European NetRefound Project (Jan. 2009 - Aug. 2009), as well as industry related projects with partners Samsung (Sept. 2005 - Sept. 2006) and Alcatel (Sept. 2009 - Dec. 2009).

I would like to thank my Professor as well as the Supervisors and Project Leaders with whom I cooperated in different parts of the work within the last four years. Specifically:

- Prof. Dr.-Ing. Dr.rer.nat. Holger Boche for accepting me in his research group and trusting me to conduct research in a field which did lie very close to my interests. He has been an example of a scientist for his constant fascination for research, hard work, love in mathematics and his desire to always move a step further.

- Dr.-Ing. Thomas Haustein who introduced me to the general problems of telecommunications and for making me feel very welcome within the department.

- PD Dr.-Ing. habil. Gerhard Wunder who was responsible for the supervision of my thesis for the most of this time. I benefited a lot from his rigorousness and systematic way of approaching engineering problems, as well as his capability of using his available mathematical tools to adapt fast to new research areas.

- PD Dr.-Ing. habil. Sławomir Stańczak who supervised the work during the last year. I would like to thank him especially for his willingness to share knowledge, his friendliness and cooperation. He is a hard-working and experienced researcher with intuition in setting up and finding solutions to problems.

At this point i would also like to thank Prof. Leandros Tassiulas for accepting the responsibility to review the current Thesis and taking part in the defense commitee. This is definitely an honor for me.

Furthermore, i would like to acknowledge the help of certain colleagues. Especially Jörg Bühler for long discussions over scientific matters and for being always there to help in case i needed a second opinion. I did also enjoy very much the drinks and friendly talks. Sid Naik for the support when times where rough as well as for the exchange of ideas and life approaches. Malte Schellmann for being also a roommate for the two first years and a friend aside from a colleague. Our secretary Katharina Schweers for having always (!) the patience to listen to problems and find the best way to settle conflicts. Chan Zhou for the queueing discussions and the lunchbreaks and Moritz Wiese for the nice collaboration. The colleagues i shared the office with Michael Peter and Michal Kaliszan. I should also not forget the students i worked with for their Master's or Diploma Thesis Yosia Hadisusanto, Stoycho Stefanov and Qi Liao. There are of course many other colleagues with whom i interacted during these years and i thank them all.

Beside the research group, Berlin has been a great place to live, especially because of friends and girlfriends who made my life here very enjoyable during these years.

Above all i would like to thank my parents whose support and love was precious all this time. I had very difficult days and they where always there to motivate, calm me down and give their precious advice. Simply put, this thesis would never have finished without them.

This work is dedicated to my parents.

Table of Contents

1 Introduction   **1**
   1.1 Layered Architecture and Cross-Layer Design 1
   1.2 Errors in the Physical Layer 3
   1.3 The Retransmission Protocol 4
   1.4 General Cross-Layer Framework for ARQ 5
   1.5 Outline 11

I Single User Systems with ARQ   **15**

2 Measures of Goodput   **17**
   2.1 Some Results from Renewal Theory 17
   2.2 Alternative Goodput Measures 19
   2.3 Maximization of Goodput Measures for Channels with Outage 24

3 Protocol Stability and Reliability in ARQ Communications   **31**
   3.1 Protocols under Study 31
   3.2 ARQ as a Success Run 32
   3.3 Reliability in ARQ Communications 36
   3.4 Conditions for Recurrence and Ergodicity 38
   3.5 Recurrence for Rayleigh Fading Channels 42

4 Truncating ARQ Protocols using Optimal Stopping   **45**
   4.1 On Optimal Stopping Rules 46
   4.2 ARQ as an Optimal Stopping Problem 48
   4.3 The ARQ Stopping Problem without Cost 51
   4.4 The ARQ Stopping Problem with Cost 57
   4.5 Special Truncation Cases 61
   4.6 Applications 62
      4.6.1 Constant success probabilities $q_n = q$ 62
      4.6.2 Exponentially increasing success probabilities $q_n = 1 - e^{-\gamma n}$ 64

5 Dynamic Truncation of ARQ Protocols in a Single Queue — 67
- 5.1 A Discrete Time Markov Decision Problem 68
  - 5.1.1 Vanishing Discount Approach 72
  - 5.1.2 Existence of Stationary Optimal Policies 73
  - 5.1.3 Algorithmic Solution for Finite State Space: Value Iteration 74
- 5.2 Structural Properties of Optimal Policies 75
- 5.3 Design Rules for the Optimal Tradeoff 85
- 5.4 Optimal and Suboptimal Delay-Dropping Tradeoffs 86

II Multiuser Systems with ARQ — 89

6 Stability and Power Control in Downlink with ARQ — 91
- 6.1 The Downlink Model under Study 92
- 6.2 Notions of Stability 95
- 6.3 Downlink Stability Region with Constant Transmission Rates 98
- 6.4 Optimal and Suboptimal Power Allocation Policies 103

7 Stability and Distributed Power Control in MANETs with ARQ — 111
- 7.1 The MANET Model under Study 112
- 7.2 Network Capacity Region and Variations with Dropping 115
- 7.3 Properties of the Success Function and Maximum Goodput Function 121
- 7.4 Examples of the Goodput Region for some Simple Network Topologies .. 126
- 7.5 NUM Problem Dual Decomposition 133
- 7.6 The Scheduling Problem 135
  - 7.6.1 Relaxation 135
  - 7.6.2 Optimality conditions 137
  - 7.6.3 A Supermodular Game 138
  - 7.6.4 The Scheduling Algorithm 142
  - 7.6.5 Implementation Issues 142
- 7.7 Simulations 145

8 Conclusions — 147

Publication List — 152

Bibliography — 165

Abbreviations and Nomenclature — 167

List of Figures

2.1	Goodput vs transmission rate curves. Comparison with ergodic capacity	29
2.2	Short-term and long-term MZT and optimal rate vs power	29
4.1	Optimal truncation for $q_n = q$ vs delay cost for (a) positive, (b) zero penalty	64
4.2	Optimal truncation for $q_n = 1 - e^{-\gamma n}$ vs delay cost for zero penalty	65
5.1	Optimal and $<L, K>$ delay-dropping tradeoff for (a)$q_k \downarrow$, (b)$q_k \uparrow$.	87
5.2	Average queue length vs dropping cost for the optimal and $<L, K>$ policy.	88
5.3	Average dropping vs dropping cost for the optimal and $<L, K>$ policy.	88
6.1	The downlink power allocation model under study	93
6.2	Two User Stability Region: (a) Calculated, (b) Simulated.	99
6.3	Convex and Sigmoidal-like distribution functions $q(\rho)$	106
6.4	Price-based Power Allocation (6.22) for Sigmoidal-Like distributions.	107
6.5	Average sum of queue lengths for 4 queues: Algorithm 1 vs Brut Force.	109
7.1	An example of the wireless network with a single destination $d = 4$.	113
7.2	a. Max Goodput $g_1(\rho_1, \rho_2)$ vs power ρ_1, b. Max rate $\bar{\mu}_1(\rho_1, \rho_2)$ vs power ρ_1.	125
7.3	a. Max Goodput $g_1(\rho_1, \rho_2)$ vs power ρ_2, b. Max rate $\bar{\mu}_1(\rho_1, \rho_2)$ vs power ρ_2.	126
7.4	Two-user Rayleigh goodput region for the network of 2 T_X and 1 R_X.	127
7.5	Two-user Rayleigh goodput region for the network of 1 T_X and 2 R_X.	128
7.6	Illustration of the property (7.24)	130
7.7	Congestion control for a four node topology with two commodity flows.	146

List of Tables

1.1	Information included in the Cross-Layer design with ARQ	6
5.1	Transition probabilities $\mathbb{P}(\bullet|S_n, A)$ of the MDP under study	70
5.2	Value Iteration for Finite State Space	75
6.1	Algorithm comparison: different queue lengths and different rates	110
6.2	Algorithm comparison: constant queue lengths and different rates.	110
6.3	Algorithm comparison: constant rates and different queue lengths.	110

Chapter 1

Introduction

1.1 Layered Architecture and Cross-Layer Design

The traditional way of understanding a communications system is to divide it into layers which form a hierarchical entity. Each given layer in the hierarchy receives input from the upper one and regards the lower as a black box which provides a specific service. This way of decomposing the network architecture brings certain advantages regarding simplicity of design and understandability, while the optimization of the system can be reduced into smaller subproblems that can be treated more efficiently [BG92].

Typically in wireless communication networks with cellular infrastructure two are the main layers where the research focus has been cast on during the recent decades.

Layer 1 is called the *physical* (PHY) layer which provides a virtual link for transmitting a sequence of bits between any pair of nodes joined by a physical communications channel. The important task here is to map bits to signals at the transmitter and perform the inverse process at the receiver, in the best possible way so that, by utilizing all the degrees of freedom available, spectral efficiency can be maximized. This can be achieved by estimating the channel at either one or both ends of the communications link and using time, frequency and power allocation techniques, beamforming (in case multiple antennas are available), sophisticated receiver architectures to reduce interference (e.g. by successive interference cancellation), adaptive modulation and coding strategies etc.

Layer 2 is the *data link control* (DLC) layer whose customary purpose is to convert the unreliable bit pipe of the physical layer into a virtual error-free communication link. Important procedures performed here are the detection and correction of errors occuring in the bit pipe. In multiaccess communications however DLC is considered only as part of layer 2 and an intermediate sublayer between PHY and DLC called the *medium access control* (MAC) sublayer manages the multiaccess link to mitigate interference. Furthermore, in the case of cellular communications where the channel is a simple multiaccess channel in the uplink (i.e. from the access nodes to the base station) and a broadcast channel in the downlink (i.e. from the base station to the access nodes) the MAC sublayer deals also with problems of *congestion* occuring when users collectively demand for more resources than the network has to offer. It can then happen that packets are lost or suffer unacceptable delays. The MAC and DLC layers are therefore responsible to guarantee a required Quality-of-Service (QoS) of all participating nodes in the network. This can be done by appropriate buffer management and error control.

The Network Layer which is layer 3 in the hierarchy plays an actual role in wide area networks where all nodes are allowed to communicate with each other. Here, issues to be dealt with are related to congestion, flow control and routing. Departing from the contemporary fixed cell architecture in wireless communications and moving towards future *Mobile Ad hoc NETworks* (MANETs), the design of this layer is crucial for the performance of the system. Each node transmits packets not only of each own but also related to other users and the information flows among nodes, moving from some source to destination. The developement of distributed algorithms to coordinate geographically remote users, considering the amount of information overhead exchanged among them is here crucial.

The Transport Layer, finally, parallel to the task of multiplexing low-rate and splitting high-rate sessions is also responsible for end-to-end flow control and reliability guarantees for the Network Layer.

During the last decade the research community has started to question the optimality of the layered architecture. Many works (see [BY04], [DSZ04], [TNV04], [SRK03] and references therein) have shown that especially in the case of wireless communications there is lot in performance to be gained by approaches that jointly consider physical layer and higher networking layer issues. By combined information from different layers, the so called *cross-layer* design has already provided fruitful insights and results towards the best possible exploitation of the available communication resources and satisfaction of various Quality-of-Service requirements opening new horizons for the support of new demanding (in terms of transmission rate, latency, burstiness, reliability or security) services.

1.2 Errors in the Physical Layer

Errors are unavoidable in the bit pipe and in a way they define the limits of information transmitted over the physical channel. Wireless communications have traditionally dealt with the question of how to achieve error free communications in the presence of noise and channel fading, between points separated in space. Shannon in his well-known 1948 paper [Sha48] proved that in the presence of noise the error probability can be made as small as possible when transmitting over the link with a rate lower or equal to the capacity. The error tends to zero exponentially with the increase of codelength, while keeping the number of codewords fixed. Then channel capacity is the maximum error free information rate that can be supported by a communication link.

In the cases of wireless channels the small scale fading is a stochastic process which can be modeled by various probability density functions. The channel's stochastic nature can lead to instantaneous deep fades or high gains. To theoretically cope with such matters new notions of capacity have been introduced namely the *ergodic capacity*, which is in words the maximum transmission rate that can be supported by the channel averaged over its possible states, the ϵ-*capacity* [OSW94] equal to the maximum allowable rate supported over all channel states except a subset of probability ϵ and the *delay limited capacity* when $\epsilon \to 0$. In the situation where channel state information is known both to the transmitter and the receiver the definition of delay limited capacity is given in [HT98].

The above notions serve as theoretical limits for error free communications or communications with an ϵ-bounded percentage of errors. From a practical point of view, perfect channel knowledge at both the transmitter and receiver is not possible due to the feedback requirements, while existing modulation and finite length coding schemes will definitely result in errors on the PHY layer. Interference from simultaneously transmitting users is also a parameter that generates errors to the system. In a packet transmission level, like in the case of random access channels, simultaneous transmission from different users leads to collisions in which case all simultaneous transmissions fail to be successfully acknowledged.

Error-control schemes are thus necessary to be introduced. Their task is to detect the existence of errors at the received message and to further correct it. By means of coding, addition of parity bits with linear block codes at the original message or use of cyclic redundancy check codes makes detectability of errors at the receiver possible. Furthermore,

Forward Error Correction (FEC) codes are often applied in wireless communications which provide self correcting properties to the codewords [CJHIW98]. Detection of errors at a codeword or packet level automatically triggers *retransmission requests* which are sent via a control channel to the transmitting node. The protocol responsible for the above error correcting procedure is well-known as Automatic Retransmission reQuest (ARQ) protocol and will be explained in detail in the next section.

Error recovery using ARQ protocols can be performed in various layers of the hierarchical communication structure explained above. The DLC layer is primarily responsible for error correction occuring at the PHY. However, error recovery using retransmission protocols can as well be performed in the Network layer for the case of node failures as well as in the Transport layer where end-to-end flow control is performed. ARQ protocols are already incorporated in the TCP/IP (Transmission Control Protocol/Internet Protocol) for correction of packet failures detected at the destination nodes [JHM06], [VVTB03].

1.3 The Retransmission Protocol

The concept of ARQ protocols is to request for retransmission of information packets that are declared erroneous at the receiver DLC module. Detection of errors depends on the implemented coding scheme and detection errors can be kept at a minimum with adequate coding strategies. When an error is detected, a Not-ACKnowledgement (NACK) message is sent to the transmitter via a control channel which triggers retransmission of information. The kind of information repeated depends on the type of the protocol. The process of retransmission continues until either an ACKnowledgement (ACK) message is sent to the receiver implying that the packet is correctly received or when a predefined number of retransmissions is exceeded, in which case the packet is discarded.

There exist three major ARQ protocol types that differ especially in the way the erroneous packets are reordered for retransmission at the transmitter [CJHIW98], [LJM84], [CCJ84]. The three protocols provide different performance in delay and throughput. The most simple is the Stop-and-Wait ARQ (SW-ARQ) protocol where the sender *stops* after transmission and *waits* for the ACK/NACK response. The major drawback of the scheme is that the transmitter is idle while waiting. Go-Back-N (GBN-ARQ) protocols treat this problem by buffering N packets at the transmitter, where N is related to the roundtrip propagation and processing delays. In this scheme the protocol continuously transmits packets.

When an error occurs at some packet j, the transmitter informed "goes back" to j and resumes transmission from there. The Selective-Repeat (SR-ARQ) protocol further increases throughput by just retransmitting the specific packets which are not acknowledged, with a significant increase of buffering in both communication ends. Classical works with general performance analysis of ARQ protocols, regarding delay, queue length and throughput, include [AP86], [ASP84], [YTH93], [BM86], [MBBC86], [SR82].

Retransmissions is a simple strategy to achieve virtually error-free data transmission. The main problems are that the throughput (or 'goodput') at the receiver side is not constant, it can fall rapidly in circumstances of increasing channel error-rates and occasional error-bursts and moreover brings high latency problems to the transmitted packets. Since delay is an important issue the number of retransmissions should be kept as low as possible. This has led to the combination of FEC and ARQ techniques to provide Hybrid ARQ (H-ARQ) protocols. The main difference here is that the (re-)transmitted messages have error correcting capabilities as well. Since use of FEC codes influences the net information throughput, Type-I H-ARQ protocols vary the coding complexity per retransmission to achieve a satisfactory delay-throughput trade-off [Kal94], [KDB06a]. Here delay is understood as average number of retransmission attempts until success. The erroneous packets in both standard ARQ and Type-I H-ARQ schemes are discarded at the receiver. The idea to store those efforts in order to increase the successful decoding probability at future attempts has given rise to Type-II H-ARQ protocols. These protocols incorporate some kind of "memory" to the procedure [Sin77]. The combination of multiple packets can be seen either as a code combining [Cha85] technique where packets are transmitted adding incrementally redundancy [CT01] to the original erroneous message [LY82] or as a way of diversity combining [Sin77].

1.4 General Cross-Layer Framework for ARQ

The cross layer design of communication systems incorporating ARQ protocols for error correction is a rather complicated task where information from various layers may take part in the system optimization.

The classical cross-layer design includes information from primarily two layers, that is the PHY and the MAC. The optimization procedure, as shown in numerous existing works in the literature [YC04], [YC03], [BG02], [GKS08], [NMR03], [BW], [ZW], [BKP05], typically adapts the transmission rate to the channel and buffer conditions, retrieved from the PHY and the MAC layers respectively.

The rate μ is a function of the channel condition h and the allocated power ρ and can take the expression for the maximal error-free transmission rate, assuming infinite-length codewords per block, given by the Shannon capacity formula (here h is the Channel-gain-to-Noise-Ratio (CNR))

$$\mu(h,\rho) = \log(1 + \rho \cdot h) \tag{1.1}$$

It can also take other possible expressions for different coding schemes designed to achieve a desired or sufficiently low error probability [NMR03]. The set of possible rate values need not be continuous as is the case in real communication systems which have only a finite databank of coding schemes available and use modulation techniques for transmission. In the cross-layer design, the optimal choice of rate (or power) can further depend on the actual queue length of the system, especially when the aim is to optimize system performance, under delay restrictions. If the arrival process of the queuing system α is known as well, this information can also be used in the optimization. Then we can write the rate allocation μ as a function f of h, u and α [BG02], [GKS08]

$$\mu(h,u,\alpha) = f(h,\rho(h,u,\alpha)) \tag{1.2}$$

When errors are further considered in the analysis the following parameters from various layers can be included within the optimization framework

PHY	μ	transmission rate
	ρ	power allocation
	h	channel state feedback
MAC	u	queue length
	α	arrival process
DLC	X	ACK/NACK feedback
	Z	current retransmission effort
	Δ	dropped packets average

Table 1.1: Information included in the Cross-Layer design with ARQ

Additional information can also play an important role depending on the investigated

1.4. General Cross-Layer Framework for ARQ

system. For example in the case of random access communications, using e.g. the slotted ALOHA protocol, the information over the contention level from the Network Layer can be fed back to the transmitters. In the text we use the symbol $\mathcal{I}$ to denote the information set used from layers higher than the PHY within the optimization framework. An example could be $\mathcal{I} = \{u, Z\}$. The information set available depends once again on the specified scenario.

Since errors and their correction are taken into account for the analysis, the transmission rate is not any more equal to the reception rate. A new quantity, namely the *goodput* of the system, is defined, which is equal to the "actual" rate of correctly transmitted bits. This is the error-free rate of transmission at the DLC module. The symbol g is used for the goodput function and q for the success probability function throughout the work. The probability of error is denoted by p.

$$p := \mathbb{P}[X = 0] \qquad q := \mathbb{P}[X = 1] \qquad (1.3)$$

$$p + q = 1 \qquad (1.4)$$

where

$$X = \begin{cases} 0 & \text{if NACK} \\ 1 & \text{if ACK} \end{cases} \qquad (1.5)$$

The probability of error in detection is assumed always equal to zero. In the case of SR-ARQ as well as in the so called *ideal* SR-ARQ, the latter being a generalized ARQ protocol with instantaneous (zero delay) feedback - which brings together all three protocol types mentioned in the previous paragraph [RBZ05]- the system goodput equals simply the rate of transmission times the success probability of the channel

$$\begin{aligned} g &= \mu \cdot \mathbb{E}[X] \\ &= \mu \cdot q \end{aligned} \qquad (1.6)$$

It should be mentioned here that the above expression for goodput will be different for SW-ARQ and GBN-ARQ protocols, if the roundtrip delay is taken into account [CJHIW98].

Furthermore, the above expression, despite its simplicity and intuitive clarity, actually results from the application of the Renewal-Reward theorem [Gal96] which has been introduced in the ARQ literature to provide expressions for goodput by Zorzi and Rao [ZR96]. It silently assumes that the statistics of the random processes that influence the result of decoding remain fixed as the time $t \to \infty$. A rigorous mathematical explenation of the expression in (1.6), as well as the definition of alternative measures that can take a possible change of statistics, after a certain time, into account will be provided in Chapter 2.

The success probability q is a function of the power and transmission rate, as well as the possible available channel state information.

$$q(h,\rho,\mu) \qquad (1.7)$$

The expression for the function is not fixed, of course, but varies with the modulation and coding used, as well as the assumed channel fading statistics, that have different probability density functions (p.d.f.) depending on the number of transmitting and receiving antennas, whether line-of-sight is available or not, as well as on other parameters such as mobility and the type of communications environment (urban, suburban, etc.) considered. The function further varies for different types of ARQ protocols, depending on the correction ability of the protocol (in the HARQ Type-I case) and whether information from previous unsuccessful attempts is stored at the receiver and combined with the current effort to increase the success probability (Type-II HARQ). All the possible expressions share however certain properties (such as monotonicity and continuity (right-, or left-) on its arguements, [0, 1] range and others) which can be exploited towards a general analytical treatment.

The cross-layer design of communication systems takes into consideration parameters from layers higher than the PHY, as shown in Table 1.1. The optimal power (and/or rate) allocation rule then depends on the channel gain h as well as the higher layer information $\mathcal{I}$. This information can as well be a direct argument of the success probability function. We can then write for the goodput

$$g(h,\mathcal{I}) = \mu(h,\mathcal{I}) \cdot q(h,\mathcal{I},\rho(h,\mathcal{I}),\mu(h,\mathcal{I})) \qquad (1.8)$$

The above expression is the equivalent to (1.2) for the cross-layer design with ARQ.

1.4. General Cross-Layer Framework for ARQ

It should be mentioned here that the optimal decision on the power can depend on the choice of transmission rate and the other way round. That means that for the joint problem of rate and power allocation the solution concerning these two quantities is intertwined. A simplification could be to keep the rate fixed and control the system goodput only by varying the transmission power. The dependence is of course on the chosen μ but since this is considered a pre-defined constant it is removed as argument from the function

$$g(h, \mathcal{I}) = \mu \cdot q(h, \mathcal{I}, \rho(h, \mathcal{I})), \quad \mu = const \quad (1.9)$$

The availability or not of channel state information (CSI) (i.e. the CNR) at the transmitter is a critical issue in the cross-layer design with ARQ. Works with CSI available at the transmitter where the channel evolves as a Markov Chain, include [DKB07], [KDB06a], [KDB08], [YK05], [RBZ05], [BLZ08], [ZV05], [HGG02]. In practical systems however, due to limited resources and errors on the feedback link, this information cannot be perfect. Furthermore, the binary ACK/NACK feedback is always available in addition.

The presence of two types of feedback in such systems naturally raises questions regarding its necessity especially since feedback information definitely brings expences in system performance which are often disregarded in the analysis. The benefits in capacity increase having perfect channel knowledge at the transmitter are definitely important, they can be achieved however only through a loss in spectral efficiency by maintaining a reliable high rate feedback link at the opposite direction of transmission. The retransmission protocol on the other hand, can generally achieve the benefits of rate adaptation to channel conditions with simply binary feedback - at the cost of delay. The idea is that a transmission is initially attempted at a desired rate μ_0. As long as the channel cannot support this rate errors occur and the transmission is repeated until success after say N_{ACK} attempts. This results in an effective rate (or goodput) equal to $\frac{\mu_0}{N_{ACK}}$. In other words, the protocol adapts the transmission rate of the system to the current channel conditions in a passive way. For a comparison between link adaptation and ARQ see [URGW03] and [QCCW99]).

The ARQ control feedback can be exploited in many ways for performance increase related to link adaptation, two of which are given in the following. The first one is that the error statistics can be utilized to provide a closed-loop adaptation to errors occuring due to the imperfect channel feedback information (see [LHJL+08, pp.1343-1344] and references therein). The second is that the ARQ information can be exploited as a binary indication over the quality of the channel [Tun07] (ACK implying "good" and NACK "bad" [ZW02]) that can be used for rate and power adaptation, in cases where the channel fading is not i.i.d but has memory e.g. the Gilbert-Elliott channel. In this latter case channel state information is redundant.

Many authors optimize system performance taking expectation over the possible channel states [AB02], [AB05], [AB06], [ZW02], to avoid overly complicated control strategies. An arguement for this approach is that the average long term goodput is usually a very appropriate performance measure. Consider, for example, a channel with finite N_{ch} states with values h_i, $i = 1, \ldots, N_{ch}$ and steady state probabilities $\mathbb{P}_h(h_i)$. A rate-power pair (μ_i, ρ_i) is assigned to each channel state h_i. The steady-state average goodput is then equal to

$$g(\mathcal{I}) = \sum_{i=1}^{N_{ch}} \mu(h_i, \mathcal{I}) \cdot q(h_i, \mathcal{I}, \rho(h_i, \mathcal{I}), \mu(h_i, \mathcal{I})) \cdot \mathbb{P}_h(h_i) \qquad (1.10)$$

For other authors channel state information is not considered at all at the transmitter for the cross layer design with ARQ [BS00], [BS01], [BS06], [CT01], [HBH05]. The goodput gains in this case rely solely on the ACK/NACK feedback available without further costs in spectral efficiency due to the feedback channel. In this case goodput depends only on higher layer information.

$$g(\mathcal{I}) = \mu(\mathcal{I}) \cdot q(\mathcal{I}, \rho(\mathcal{I}), \mu(\mathcal{I})) \qquad (1.11)$$

The current work follows this line of thought, leaving CSI at the transmitter aside. In a way this is an analysis which tries to investigate the benefits and costs in a communications system focusing solely on the impact of retransmission protocols and their binary feedback. At the same time, it remains a cross-layer analysis, since the optimal power and rate allocation, as well as the system goodput is controlled by information $\mathcal{I}$ extracted from higher layers.

1.5 Outline

The current thesis utilizes the framework for cross-layer design presented in the previous section, in order to model, analyse, determine optimal design parameters and develop optimal control strategies for various systems incorporating ARQ protocols. Retransmissions and their effects are - of course - both the point of view, as well as the design and optimization objective within the system architecture. The communication systems explored within the work excibit an incremental increase in complexity and can be divided into single user and multiuser systems.

The first part of the thesis treats single user systems with retransmissions. The analysis in this part I, initiates from the isolated ARQ protocol. Chapter 2 presents measures for goodput that can be used, while stability issues of the ARQ protocol, together with conditions that guarantee non-zero goodput in case of fixed success probabilities per retransmission are presented in Chapter 3. The problem of optimal truncation of the ARQ chain under costs of delay and dropping is treated in 4. Chapter 5 analyses the delay and dropping tradeoffs in a single queue with ARQ. From this chapter on the queuing aspects are taken rigorously into consideration.

Multiuser systems are considered in the last two chapters of the thesis, which constitute part II. Chapter 6 investigates a downlink scenario with retransmissions, where power control strategies for system stability are presented, while in Chapter 7 the system is an ad-hoc network where nodes can all communicate and thus interfere with each other. In such a system the aim is the maximal satisfaction of operating users that insert data flows in a network of possibly cooperating nodes. This aim can be achieved by applying decentralized power allocation algorithms that control the levels of interference, together with congestion control and routing policies. More specifically:

- In Chapter 2, the expression of the goodput in (1.6) is presented as a direct result of renewal theory. Alternative measures for goodput up to a finite number r of ACKs are introduced under the general description of *short-term measures*. When $r \to \infty$ these short-term measures converge to the renewal theory derived goodput expression. The success probability is considered constant and a function of power and rate without CSI $q(\rho, \mu)$. The optimal transmission rate as a function of power is derived from the maximization $\mu^{\max}(\rho) = \arg\max_\mu g(\rho, \mu)$. Further information $\mathcal{I}$ from higher layers is not taken into account. Observe that the optimization problems presented for goodput maximization do not even require the ACK/NACK feedback from the transmitter in the long-term case, while in short-term, feedback is required only for the transmitter to be informed when the cycle of r successful transmissions has been completed. The results in this chapter have been published in [5].

- Chapter 3 investigates the conditions under which a non-zero goodput can be guaranteed in ARQ communications. The ARQ protocols considered do not adapt to the channel conditions. The success probabilities are fixed and dependent only on the current retransmission effort of the process. The higher layer information available is namely $\mathcal{I} = \{Z_t\}$ and we write $q(Z_t)$ to show the dependence. The notion of a *reliable* ARQ protocol is introduced. Simply stated this is a protocol for which the instantaneous goodput after an ACK is fed back drops under a fixed positive goodput value only finitely many times, as the retransmission process evolves to infinity. A theorem proves that ergodicity of the ARQ chain introduced is necessary and sufficient for reliability. Based on well known criteria for the stability of Markov Chains, sufficient conditions for the reliability and non-reliability of protocols are derived. These are further applied to a fading channel where the success probability is a function of power, expressed as outage. We can then write $q(\rho(Z_t))$ to express the dependence of power allocation and consequently the success probability on the current retransmission effort. The conditions result in asymptotic power allocations that lead to ergodic (reliable) and non-ergodic (unreliable) protocols. The results can be found in [4].

- The more practical and realistic assumption of a finite ARQ chain is adopted in Chapter 4. Due to delay restrictions in communications the transmission of a packet cannot be prolonged over some bounds, since this shall result in violation of the required Quality-of-Service user demand. The chapter investigates the optimal number of retransmission efforts for a single packet to be transmitted under delay and dropping costs, the latter incurred in case the maximum retransmission number is reached before acceptance. To this aim the theory of Optimal Stopping is adopted in order to analyze the ARQ markovian model presented in the previous chapter. The results are finally applied to specific cases of ARQ protocols where the tradeoffs between delay, dropping and gain due to packet transmission are illustrated. The related publication can be found in [8].

1.5. Outline

- Queuing aspects are incorporated in Chapter 5 where a single queue with an ARQ markovian protocol is investigated. The aim here is to find the control policy which brings the optimal tradeoff between queue length and packet dropping average. Whether to drop a packet or not is put as action that a controller can decide on, depending on the current queue length, the retransmission effort as well as the success or failure of the previously transmitted packet. Hence the goodput expression in (1.11) is defined here per time-slot by the availability of information $\mathcal{I} = \{u, X, Z\}$ and we write

$$g(\vec{u}_t, X_t, Z_t) = \mu \cdot q(\vec{u}_t, X_t, Z_t) \tag{1.12}$$

  since power and rate allocation are not considered and CSI is not available. The aim is to optimize the long term average system performance. The results include extraction of structural properties of the optimal policy, e.g. related to monotonicity, as well as bounds for the maximum queue length under the optimal strategy. The results have been published in [2].

- The investigation on ARQ protocols within queuing multiuser systems starts at Chapter 6 where a downlink communications scenario is introduced. The main question to be answered is which is the stability region of such a system, taking interference into account. The stability region defines the maximal amount of data that can be transmitted through the downlink communications link error-free. In the current model, transmission rate per user is considered fixed and only power control is available. A power allocation policy is derived that is able to achieve transmission rates described by the stability region. The policy depends on the per slot user queue length, which is considered to be available from higher layers and the expression for goodput is now

$$g(\vec{u}_t) = \mu \cdot q(\rho(\vec{u}_t)) \tag{1.13}$$

  The policy comes as a solution of a non-convex weighted sum optimization problem with sum power constraints. The closed form solution is difficult to be extracted due to the non-convexity of the objective function and two heuristic algorithms are applied and compared that bring almost optimal results, but are rather useful in describing the way the optimal policy works. In short, users with longer queues and lower transmission rates in each slot are given higher priority in scheduling. For a publication see [7].

- The final part of the Thesis, Chapter 7, approaches the ARQ control problem from a network perspective where data can enter the system from different source nodes and should flow through the wireless network to some destination. Power and rate control algorithms are derived that achieve the maximum stability region. The optimal scheduling policy for the amount of data transmitted per hop is the well known backpressure policy for goodput. The requirement here however is that the decision of each node considering power allocation should be made in a decentralized manner, since no central controller is available. The nodes can then exchange information over the queue lengths and slow fading channel coefficients and further explore measurements over their received interference level, in order to decide on an appropriate power allocation based on game theory algorithms. The results are published in [3] and [1].

Part I

Single User Systems with ARQ

Chapter 2

Measures of Goodput

The typical measure of goodput in communication systems is given in (1.6) and simply equals the information transmission rate times the probability of success. This is a result which originates from renewal-theory and equals the time- as well as the ensemble- average reward in rate that the system can obtain in the presence of errors. Its derivation is based on the fact that the channel statistics remain unchanged during the entire process up to infinity. This assumption, however, is not any more valid when scheduling decisions on rate and power change over time or when errors appear in an irregular fashion e.g. in bursts. Alternative measures can, in such cases, be suggested which describe the expected goodput in the short term, when the error statistics are considered constant only for finite time intervals. Application of different measures of goodput to channels with outages leads to different optimal power and transmission rate allocations and emphasizes the crucial role that use of the appropriate measure plays in the optimization of system performance.

2.1 Some Results from Renewal Theory

Based on renewal-reward theory retransmissions can be understood as a renewal process. In this case a renewal event occurs when an ACK is fed back after a certain non-negative number of consecutive NACKs due to erroneous packet transmission. The inter-renewal interval is a random variable denoted by N_{ACK}, with uncountable discrete state-space $\mathbb{N}_+ = \{1, 2, \ldots\}$ the number of efforts until correct packet reception. The time at which a renewal occurs is further a discrete process (arrival process) given as the sum of the inter-renewal intervals up to the current renewal epoch. $S_k = N_{ACK,1} + \ldots + N_{ACK,k}$ is the time of occurence for the k-th renewal. With the above described renewal processes a *reward function* $R(t)$ is further introduced that models a rate at which the renewal process accumulates a reward. The value of $R(t)$ depends on the *age* of the process t and the *duration* of the inter-renewal interval containing time t. Here the reward may be viewed as a rate gain each time a message is correctly received. For a general example, if the transmission rate of the system at the k-th renewal epoch equals $R_k = \mu_k$ and $N_{ACK,k} = n$ is the inter-renewal interval for $S_{k-1} < t \leq S_k$, the rate gain between the $k-1$-th and k-th ACK equals $\frac{\mu_k}{n}$. This is the instantaneous goodput of the system for the k-th renewal, which here refers to the transmission of the k-th packet or codeword up to success. The following two theorems [Gal96], [Ros96, pp.133-134] can provide the long-term system goodput of a communications system using ARQ protocols. The first one focuses on limiting behaviors of time averages while the second one on ensemble averages. Variables t and τ take values on the non-negative discrete time axis since the communications systems are usually considered time-slotted.

Theorem 1. Let $R(t)$ be a renewal-reward function providing the accumulated rate gain of the ARQ system up to time t, with expected inter-renewal time $\mathbb{E}[N_{ACK}]$. If $\mathbb{E}[N_{ACK}] < \infty$ or $\mathbb{E}[R_k] < \infty$, then with probability one

$$\lim_{t \to \infty} \frac{1}{t} \sum_{\tau=0}^{t} R(\tau) = \frac{\mathbb{E}[R_k]}{\mathbb{E}[N_{ACK}]} \qquad (2.1)$$

where for constant rate rewards $R := \mu$

$$R_k = (S_k - S_{k-1}) \cdot \frac{\mu}{n} = n \cdot \frac{\mu}{n} = \mu \quad \& \quad N_{ACK,k} = n$$

Then the long-term ARQ goodput equals

$$\lim_{t \to \infty} \frac{1}{t} \sum_{\tau=0}^{t} R(\tau) = \frac{\mu}{\mathbb{E}[N_{ACK}]} \qquad (2.2)$$

Theorem 2. Let $R(k)$ be a renewal-reward function providing the accumulated rate gain of the ARQ system up to renewal time k, with expected inter-renewal time $\mathbb{E}[N_{ACK}]$. If renewals occur only at integer time instants ($t \in \mathbb{N}$) then with probability one

$$\lim_{t \to \infty} \mathbb{E}[R(t)] = \frac{\mathbb{E}[R_k]}{\mathbb{E}[N_{ACK}]} \qquad (2.3)$$

2.2. Alternative Goodput Measures

where for constant rate rewards $R := \mu$ the long-term goodput equals

$$\lim_{t \to \infty} \mathbb{E}\left[R(t)\right] = \frac{\mu}{\mathbb{E}\left[N_{ACK}\right]} \quad (2.4)$$

Observe here the *equality of the limiting behavior for the time and ensemble average of the renewal process*. The value of the above average depends solely on the distribution of the inter-arrival times and assumes that inter-arrival random variables are independent identically distributed (i.i.d.) throughout the renewal process.

If the success probability per retransmission is assumed constant and equal to $\mathbb{P}[X=1] = q$, the inter-renewal time between consecutive ACKs is geometrically distributed and the expectation $\mathbb{E}[N_{ACK}] = \frac{1}{q}$.

Corollary 1. *The long-term goodput g_{l-t} of the ARQ system, with fixed transmission rate μ and success probability per retransmission q is given by the renewal-reward Theorems 1, 2 and equals*

$$g_{l-t} = \lim_{t \to \infty} \frac{1}{t} \sum_{\tau=0}^{t} R(\tau) = \lim_{t \to \infty} \mathbb{E}[R(t)] = \mu \cdot q \quad (2.5)$$

The above corollary explains the expression for goodput presented in (1.6). The two theorems above have been vastly used in the ARQ literature for deriving closed form expressions for the system goodput [ZR97], [AB03], and find good application especially in more general cases where the rewards are dependent on the inter-renewal intervals [CT01] or on channel conditions and adaptive modulation schemes [ZV05].

2.2 Alternative Goodput Measures

Consider now a scenario where multiple access terminals within a cell communicate with a base station. For each user a generalized SR-ARQ protocol is implemented for correction of possible erroneous transmissions, with success probability per trial, which depends on the chosen rate and power allocation without CSI knowledge, equal to $q(\rho, \mu)$ (see 1.7). In multiuser systems a fundamental problem is the optimal scheduling of resource allocation among the users with the aim to maximize goodput and minimize delay. Scheduling decisions regarding the pair of power and rate allocation variables can take into account possible information $\mathcal{I}$ from higher layers $(\rho(\mathcal{I}), \mu(\mathcal{I}))$, as shown in (1.11). These can be put into action after each message retransmission circle has successfully (or unsuccessfully in the case of truncated ARQ protocols) been finalized and will affect the next packet waiting in the buffer. In such scenarios the channel's probability of error is bound to change each time a new scheduling decision is made. Other possible cases for a change of the fading statistics with time is when the acknowledgement history is used to optimize decisions over future retransmissions, as suggested in [Mod99], [ZW00], or when bursty errors occur often in an unpredicted fashion.

In the cases mentioned above estimation of the goodput in the long-run based on the renewal-reward theorem is not any more applicable. This is due to the simple fact that the inter-arrival times between consecutive ACKs are not identically distributed. In such scenarios the assumption that the renewal process probabilistically starts anew after each packet reception [Gal96] does not hold.

An alternative goodput measure can be suggested for such cases where the renewal-reward theorem cannot be applied. This measure is the expected value up to some predefined *finite* number of acknowledgements (ACKs), say r, for which the error probability of the channel is expected to remain constant and afterwards probably changes due to scheduling or variation of the fading statistics. In a way this is a *short-term goodput measure* since the expectation is taken over a finite pre-defined number of renewal events.

Given a scenario where change of q takes place after each ACK, the *short-term goodput* measure can be derived as the ensemble average of the reward up to next ACK, namely $\mathbb{E}\left[\frac{\mu}{N_{ACK}}\right]$. In what follows geometrically distributed inter-arrival times between renewal epochs are considered, however the analysis can as well be applied when more complicated distributions are considered. $N_{ACK}^{(r)}$ resembles the random variable for the inter-arrival period between r consecutive ACKs and has in the current text a *negative binomial* distribution. As the number of r is allowed to increase, tending to infinity, the convergence to the long-term goodput in (2.5) is guaranteed.

Theorem 3. For an ARQ protocol with probability of success equal to q and constant, the expected value of goodput up to first ACK equals

$$g_{s-t} = \mathbb{E}\left[\frac{\mu}{N_{ACK}}\right] = \mu \frac{q}{1-q} \log\left(\frac{1}{q}\right) \qquad (2.6)$$

The above expression is the *short-term system goodput*.

2.2. Alternative Goodput Measures

The expected value until r successful message receptions equals

$$g_{s-t}^{(r)} = \mu \cdot \mathbb{E}\left[\frac{r}{N_{ACK}^{(r)}}\right] = \mu \cdot \left[\sum_{j=1}^{r-1} \frac{-r}{r-j}\left(\frac{-q}{1-q}\right)^j + \left(\frac{-q}{1-q}\right)^r r \log(q)\right] \quad (2.7)$$

As the number of accepted messages approaches infinity the expected value of goodput has the following limit

$$\lim_{r \to \infty} g_{s-t}^{(r)} = \mu \cdot q = \frac{\mu}{\mathbb{E}[N_{ACK}]} = g_{l-t} \quad (2.8)$$

This is the *long-term system goodput* equal to that using the renewal-reward theorem.

Proof. The random variable N_{ACK} is used for the waiting time until first ACK and suppose that the number of retransmissions required for the correct transmission of a single message is $N_{ACK} = n$. The goodput of the system for this single successful transmission equals $g(n) = \frac{\mu}{n}$ and this is given as reward due to the occurence of a renewal at the n-th trial. The p.d.f. of the number of efforts up to first ACK is geometrically distributed and given by $f(n) = p^{n-1}q$. The expected value of the rewards in a single renewal period (short-term) is

$$\begin{aligned} g_{s-t} &= \mathbb{E}\left[\frac{\mu}{N_{ACK}}\right] = \mu \cdot \mathbb{E}\left[\frac{1}{N_{ACK}}\right] = \mu \sum_{n=1}^{\infty} g(n) \cdot f(n) \\ &= \sum_{n=1}^{\infty} \frac{\mu}{n} \cdot p^{n-1} q = \frac{\mu \cdot q}{p} \sum_{n=0}^{\infty} \frac{p^{n+1}}{n+1} \end{aligned} \quad (2.9)$$

The series $\sum_{n=0}^{\infty} x^n$ converges uniformly for $|x| \le 1 - \epsilon$ where $0 < \epsilon \le 1$ [CJ89]. The circle of convergence is denoted as $C = [0, 1 - \epsilon]$. Given a sequence of decreasing ϵ_k, namely $\epsilon_k = \epsilon \cdot k^{-1}$ we have that the series converges uniformly for the circle $\bigcup_{k=1}^{\infty} C_k \Leftrightarrow |x| < 1$. Since the integral of the term x^n equals $\frac{x^{n+1}}{n+1}$, from [CJ89, p.537] the series at the right handside of (2.9) also converges uniformly and we can write $\int_0^p \sum_{n=0}^{\infty} x^n dx = \int_0^p \frac{1}{1-x} dx = -\log(q)$. Then

$$g_{s-t} = -\mu \frac{q}{1-q} \log(q)$$

For r successful transmissions (r times ACK) the waiting time until the $r - th$ success is a random variable $N_{ACK}^{(r)}$ with probability $\mathbb{P}\{N_{ACK}^{(r)} < r\} = 0$. $N_{ACK}^{(r)}$ follows a negative binomial distribution [Fel68]

$$\mathbb{P}\{N_{ACK}^{(r)} = n\} = \binom{n-1}{r-1} q^r p^{n-r} = f^{(r)}(n)$$

The reward for r acknowledgements equals $g^{(r)}(n) = \frac{r\mu}{n}$ and the expected value of the reward over the distribution of waiting time is

$$\begin{aligned} g_{s-t}^{(r)} &= \mathbb{E}\left[\frac{r \cdot \mu}{n}\right] = \sum_{n=r}^{\infty} g^{(r)}(n) \cdot f^{(r)}(n) \\ &= \mu \sum_{n=r}^{\infty} \frac{r}{n} \cdot \binom{n-1}{r-1} q^r p^{n-r} \\ &= \mu \left(\frac{q}{p}\right)^r \sum_{n=r}^{\infty} \frac{r}{n} \cdot \binom{b-1}{r-1} p^b = \mu \left(\frac{q}{p}\right)^r w(p) \end{aligned}$$

Taking the first derivative of the function $w(p)$

$$\begin{aligned} \frac{dw(p)}{dp} &= r \sum_{n=r}^{\infty} \binom{n-1}{r-1} p^{n-1} \stackrel{n-r=v}{=} \\ &= rp^{r-1} \sum_{v=0}^{\infty} \binom{v+r-1}{v} p^v = \\ &\stackrel{(a)}{=} \sum_{v=0}^{\infty} rp^{r-1} \binom{-r}{v}(-p)^v \stackrel{(b)}{=} r(1-p)^{-r} p^{r-1} \end{aligned}$$

where equality (a) comes from the fact that $\binom{v+r-1}{v} = (-1)^v \binom{-r}{v}$ and equality (b) from Newton's binomial formula [CJ89]. Then

$$g_{s-t}^{(r)} = \mu \left(\frac{q}{p}\right)^r \cdot \int_0^p r(1-x)^{-r} x^{r-1} dx$$

The integral can be evaluated by repeated integrations. For $r = 2$ we have

2.2. Alternative Goodput Measures

$$\begin{aligned} g_{s-t}^{(2)} &= \mu \left(\frac{q}{p}\right)^2 \cdot \int_0^p 2(1-x)^{-2} x\, dx \\ &= \mu \left(\frac{q}{p}\right)^2 \cdot \int_0^p 2x\, d\left((1-x)^{-1}\right) \\ &= \mu \left(\frac{q}{p}\right)^2 \cdot \left[2x(1-x)^{-1}\big|_0^p - \int_0^p 2(1-x)^{-1} dx\right] \\ &= 2\mu \frac{q}{p} + 2R\left(\frac{q}{p}\right)^2 \log(1-p) \end{aligned}$$

Generally for any r

$$\begin{aligned} g_{s-t}^{(r)} &= \mu \cdot \mathbb{E}\left[\frac{r}{N_{ACK}^{(r)}}\right] \\ &= \mu \sum_{j=1}^{r-1} (-1)^{j-1} \frac{r}{r-j} \left(\frac{1-p}{p}\right)^j + \mu \left(\frac{p-1}{p}\right)^r r \log(1-p) \end{aligned} \qquad (2.10)$$

For $r \to \infty$ we can rewrite (2.10) as follows

$$\frac{g_{s-t}^{(r)}}{\mu} = r\left(\frac{-q}{1-q}\right)^r \left[\sum_{j=1}^{r-1} \frac{1}{j-r} \left(\frac{-q}{1-q}\right)^{j-r} + \log(q)\right]$$

Then for $r+1$ we get the following recursive form

$$\frac{g_{s-t}^{(r+1)}}{\mu} = \frac{r+1}{r} \cdot \frac{-q}{1-q} \left[\frac{g_{s-t}^{(r)}}{\mu} - 1\right] \qquad (2.11)$$

Taking limits for both sides of (2.11) for $r \to \infty$ we obtain the value for $g_{s-t}^\infty := \lim_{r \to \infty} g_{s-t}^{(r)}$

$$\frac{g_{s-t}^{(\infty)}}{\mu} = \frac{-q}{1-q} \left[\frac{g_{s-t}^{(\infty)}}{\mu} - 1\right] \Rightarrow g_{s-t}^{(\infty)} = \mu \cdot q = g_{l-t}$$

$\square$

Corollary 2. *The short-term goodput with $r = 1$ has a greater value compared to the long-term one.*

$$g_{s-t} \geq g_{l-t} \Leftrightarrow \mathbb{E}\left[\frac{\mu}{N_{ACK}}\right] \geq \frac{\mu}{\mathbb{E}[N_{ACK}]} \qquad (2.12)$$

Proof. This comes directly from Jensen's inequality since

$$\mathbb{E}[g(x)] \geq g(\mathbb{E}[x])$$

for $g(x)$ convex function of x. In our case $g(x) = \mu/x$ (convex) and (2.12) holds.

□

The conclusion that the actual expected average per stage until first ACK (or up to $r < \infty$ ACKs in general) $\mathbb{E}\left[\frac{\mu}{N_{ACK}}\right]$ has a greater value compared to the result from the renewal-reward theory $\frac{\mu}{\mathbb{E}[N_{ACK}]}$ may at a first glance seem a bit unexpected and possibly paradoxal. In an effort to provide some intuition and explain the results, we notice that the gains in short-term actually are a result of *stopping* the observation of the renewal process at a desired moment, namely when exactly r ACKs have been received. In such cases the probability of occurence of very long NACK runs is very small. As the process may be allowed to continue forever, extremely long runs are expected to happen. It can actually be found in Feller [Fel68] that using the law of iterated logarithm, the length of the longest appearing run after t efforts $N_t^{longest}$ in a sequence of Bernoulli trials behaves with probability 1 as follows

$$\limsup \frac{N_t^{longest}}{\log_{1/p} t} = 1 \qquad (2.13)$$

The distribution of the longst run for a process generated by fair coin tossing is known as the Erdös-Rényi law. Relevant investigations over the distribution of the longest run in a sequence of Bernoulli trials can be found in the literature [ER75], [GO80], [GSW86]. The length of the longest run of NACKs then asymptotically tends to infinity as the number of trials $t \to \infty$. Occurence of such rare extrema has an averaging out effect for the strong law of large numbers to hold. By stopping the process after a certain finite number r such extrema are not probable to happen.

2.3 Maximization of Goodput Measures for Channels with Outage

When practical systems are under study, there is great interest in estimating which is the maximum achievable goodput and aim to adapt the systems' operation in order to optimize

2.3. Maximization of Goodput Measures for Channels with Outage

performance and stay always near the maximum value. The adaptation takes place in terms of optimal transmission rate and power allocation, which results in goodput maximization. Rather interestingly use of different measures provides different results. This actually implies that the use of appropriate goodput measures in different communication scenarios can be rather critical in terms of performance optimization.

Transmission errors can be described as outages [OSW94]. An outage occurs when CSI at the transmitter is either not known or imperfect and the chosen rate exceeds the capacity limit given by the Shannon's formula. This probability is denoted by $\mathcal{P}_{out}(\rho,\mu)$, which is a function of transmission power ρ and supported rate μ.

$$\mathcal{P}_{out}(\rho,\mu) = \mathbb{P}_h[\log(1 + h \cdot \rho) \leq \mu] \qquad (2.14)$$

For a simple example, related to channels with channel gain p.d.f. given by the Rayleigh distribution, the outage probability gets the following closed form expression

$$\mathcal{P}_{out}(\rho,\mu) \stackrel{Rayleigh}{=} 1 - \exp\left(-\rho^{-1}\left(e^{\mu} - 1\right)\right) \qquad (2.15)$$

The success probability function equals simply

$$q(\rho,\mu) = 1 - \mathcal{P}_{out}(\rho,\mu) \qquad (2.16)$$

Keeping rate and power fixed, thus q constant, the retransmissions resemble Bernoulli trials and the long-term goodput from (2.5) merely equals $g_{l-t} = \mu \cdot (1 - \mathcal{P}_{out})$. In this case N_{ACK} is geometrically distributed. Based on this approach, where communication errors are regarded as outages, the authors in [CT01] have derived explicit expressions for the long-term goodput of different Hybrid-ARQ protocols operating in channels with Gaussian noise and interference, whereas in [AB03] and assuming equal success probabilities per trial the authors have introduced a new metric, namely the *Maximum Zero-outage Throughput* (MZT) which equals the maximum achievable goodput in fading channels with errors. For the Rayleigh fading case an explicit solution has been derived [BS00]

$$MZT(\rho) = \sup_{\mu} \mu \cdot (1 - \mathcal{P}_{out}(\rho,\mu)) \qquad (2.17)$$

$$\stackrel{Rayleigh}{=} \sup_{\mu} \mu \cdot \exp\left(-\rho^{-1}\left(e^{\mu} - 1\right)\right) \qquad (2.18)$$

The argument that maximizes expression (2.18) equals

$$\mu_{l-t}^{\max}(\rho) = W(\rho) \qquad (2.19)$$

where $W(z)$ solves the equation $W(z) \cdot e^{W(z)} = z$ and is called the Lambert W function [CGH⁺96]. Using now the short-term goodput measure presented in the previous section 2.2 the *Maximum Zero-outage short-term Throughput* (MZT_{s-t}) can be adequately defined

$$MZT_{s-t}(\rho) := g_{s-t}^{\max}(\rho) = \sup_{\mu} \mu \frac{q(\rho,\mu)}{1-q(\rho,\mu)} \log\left(\frac{1}{q(\rho,\mu)}\right) \qquad (2.20)$$

Assumption of Rayleigh fading statistics simplifies analysis and can provide analytic results which are easier to compare. The rate $\mu_{s-t}^{\max}$ achieving MZT_{s-t} is given in (2.21).

Theorem 4. The rate $\mu_{s-t}^{\max}(\rho) = \arg\max_{\mu} g_{s-t}(\rho,\mu)$ maximizing the short-term goodput, for the case of Rayleigh fading channels and for small values of $\frac{1-e^{\mu}}{\rho}$ equals

$$\mu_{s-t}^{\max}(\rho) \approx W((2\rho+1) \cdot e) - 1 \qquad (2.21)$$

Proof. For Rayleigh fading, equation (2.6) yields

$$g_{s-t}(\rho,\mu) = \mu \cdot \left(1 - \frac{1}{1 - e^{\frac{1-e^{\mu}}{\rho}}}\right) \cdot \frac{1-e^{\mu}}{\rho}$$

The first derivative of g_{s-t} w.r.t. μ is taken. Replace $\gamma = \frac{1-e^{\mu}}{\rho}$ to make the form easier to handle

$$\frac{dg_{s-t}(\rho,\mu)}{d\mu} = \left(1 - \frac{1}{1-e^{\gamma}}\right)\gamma + \mu\left(1 - \frac{1}{1-e^{\gamma}}\right)\left(\gamma - \frac{1}{\rho}\right) - \mu\gamma\frac{\left(\gamma - \frac{1}{\rho}\right)e^{\gamma}}{(1-e^{\gamma})^2}$$

Set the derivative equal to zero

$$\frac{-e^{\gamma}(1-e^{\gamma})\gamma - \mu\left(\gamma - \frac{1}{\rho}\right)e^{\gamma}(1-e^{\gamma})}{(1-e^{\gamma})^2} - \frac{\mu\gamma e^{\gamma}\left(\gamma - \frac{1}{\rho}\right)}{(1-e^{\gamma})^2} = 0 \Rightarrow$$

$$(1-e^{\gamma})\left[-\gamma - \mu\left(\gamma - \frac{1}{\rho}\right)\right] - \mu\gamma\left(\gamma - \frac{1}{\rho}\right) = 0 \ \& \ \mu \neq 0$$

2.3. Maximization of Goodput Measures for Channels with Outage

Approximate the exponential term by its Taylor expansion until the 2nd power

$$e^\gamma \approx 1 + \frac{\gamma}{1!} + \frac{\gamma^2}{2!}$$

$$\left(\gamma + \frac{\gamma^2}{2}\right) \cdot \left[\gamma + \mu\left(\gamma - \frac{1}{\rho}\right)\right] = \mu\gamma\left(\gamma - \frac{1}{\rho}\right) \Rightarrow$$

$$\gamma^2 \cdot \left[1 + \frac{1}{2}\left(\gamma + \mu(\gamma - \frac{1}{\rho})\right)\right] = 0 \quad \overset{\mu \neq 0,\ replace\ \gamma}{\Rightarrow}$$

$$2\rho + 1 - e^\mu - \mu e^\mu = 0 \Rightarrow$$

$$e^\mu (\mu + 1) = 2\rho + 1 \Rightarrow$$

$$e^{\mu+1}(\mu + 1) = (2\rho + 1) \cdot e$$

concluding in (2.21).

□

Theorem 5. For the case of Rayleigh fading channels the transmission rate maximizing the short-term goodput is greater than the argument maximizing the long-term one, for each choice of transmission power ρ.

$$\mu_{s-t}^{\max}(\rho) \geq \mu_{l-t}^{\max}(\rho) \qquad (2.22)$$

Proof. From Theorem 4 and the solution for the MZT_{l-t} problem in (2.19), the following two arguments maximize goodput in the short and long term respectively, given fixed ρ

$$\mu_{l-t}^{\max}(\rho) = \mathcal{W}(\rho) := \mu_1$$
$$\mu_{s-t}^{\max}(\rho) = \mathcal{W}((2\rho + 1) \cdot e) - 1 := \mu_2$$

in the following the inequality $\mu_2 \geq \mu_1$ is proved by contradiction.

$$\left.\begin{array}{r}(\mu_2 + 1)e^{\mu_2+1} = (2\rho+1) \cdot e \\ \mu_1 e^{\mu_1} = \rho\end{array}\right\} \Rightarrow \left.\begin{array}{r}\mu_2 + \log(\mu_2 + 1) = \log(2\rho+1) \\ \mu_1 + \log(\mu_1) = \log(\rho)\end{array}\right\} \overset{(-)}{\Rightarrow}$$

$$\mu_2 - \mu_1 + \log\left(\frac{\mu_2 + 1}{\mu_1}\right) = \log\left(2 + \frac{1}{\rho}\right) \Rightarrow e^{\mu_2-\mu_1}\frac{\mu_2 + 1}{\mu_1} = 2 + \frac{1}{\rho}$$

Suppose that $\mu_2 < \mu_1$. Then

$$2 + \frac{1}{\rho} = e^{\mu_2 - \mu_1}\frac{\mu_2 + 1}{\mu_1} < 1 + \frac{1}{\mu_1} \Rightarrow \mu_1 < \frac{\rho}{1+\rho} \Rightarrow e^{W(\rho)} < e^{\frac{\rho}{1+\rho}} \Rightarrow$$

$$W(\rho) \cdot e^{W(\rho)} < \frac{\rho}{1+\rho} \cdot e^{\frac{\rho}{1+\rho}} \Rightarrow \rho < \frac{\rho}{1+\rho} \cdot e^{\frac{\rho}{1+\rho}} \Rightarrow$$

$$\log(1+\rho) - \frac{\rho}{1+\rho} = v(\rho) < 0$$

But $v(0) = 0$ and is monotone non-decreasing w.r.t $\rho \geq 0$, since $\frac{dv(\rho)}{d\rho} = \frac{\rho}{(1+\rho)^2} > 0$. Then $v(\rho) \geq v(0) = 0$ and we have proved by contradiction that $\mu_2 \geq \mu_1$. □

Given specific power $\rho = 10^3$ and assuming Rayleigh fading, the expected goodput vs rate plots are illustrated in Fig.2.1. The doted horizontal and vertical lines denote the value of ergodic capacity. Of course expected goodput cannot exceed this limit, however the plots support also the conclusions in [AB03] and [AKB04] that in systems with retransmissions, the transmission rate may actually be allowed to exceed the ergodic limit and probable errors will be corrected with the use of retransmissions. In such cases there is a non-zero probability that transmitted bits at an instantaneous rate higher than the ergodic may be correctly decoded. If an error occurs, retransmissions take place resulting in a lower effective rate. In average however goodput is always definitely less than the ergodic capacity. The figure illustrates that the rate achieving MZT_{s-t} is higher than the one that brings MZT. The actual maximum goodput values for short-term and long-term measures exhibit the same behavior. The change of the maximum rate and goodput values as power increases is shown in Fig.2.2, where the relative gains make short-term measures more appropriate in scenarios where the error probability is considered to change after each correct packet reception.

2.3. Maximization of Goodput Measures for Channels with Outage

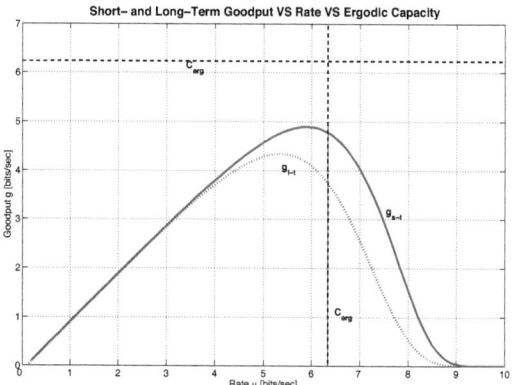

Figure 2.1: Goodput vs transmission rate curves. Comparison with ergodic capacity

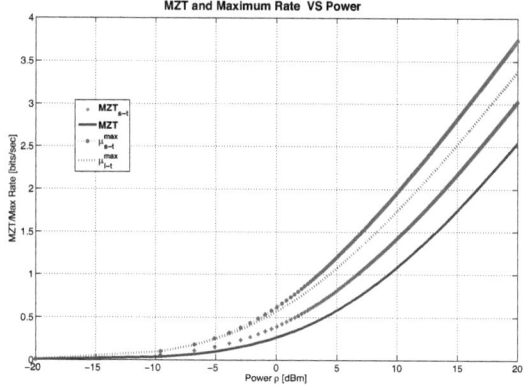

Figure 2.2: Short-term and long-term MZT and optimal rate vs power

Chapter 3

Protocol Stability and Reliability in ARQ Communications

When the success probability is assumed to take a different but fixed value per retransmission, denoted by $q(Z_t)$, where Z_t is the current retransmission effort at slot t, the ARQ process is described as a success run. ARQ protocols - hybrid or not - that do not adapt to the channel conditions but rather apply a fixed *a priori* strategy to optimize performance by minimizing e.g. delay or power, can be described by such Markov Chains. What is rather important, however, is that the protocol can always guarantee a non-zero goodput. This is related to the *reliability* of an ARQ protocol. A rigorous definition of a *reliable* ARQ protocol is provided in this chapter, whereas it is proven that reliability is equivalent to *ergodicity* of the success run. Conditions for ergodicity, recurrence and transience are derived. These are based on Foster's [Fos53] and Pakes' [Pak69] criteria for ergodicity using the drift function, as well as Kaplan's [Kap79] sufficient conditions for the non-ergodicity of Markov chains (see also [MT93] for a thorough treatment). These conditions are further applied to the case of channels with outages due to Rayleigh fading, in order to derive asymptotic expressions for power allocation leading to reliable and unreliable ARQ protocols.

3.1 Protocols under Study

The current chapter deals with a specific type of discrete time Markov Chains which arise in packetized communications when Automatic Repeat ReQuest (ARQ) protocols are used. This chain is a variation of random walk in one-dimension better known as a *success run*

[Fel68], [Bre99]. Success runs are sufficient to describe ARQ protocols when the transmitter has no knowledge of - and hence does not adapt to - the instantaneous fading conditions of the communications channel other than the fading statistics (type of distribution e.g. Rayleigh, X^2 etc.). In this setting we consider a fixed infinite sequence of per effort success probabilities, denoted by $\{q_k\}$, whose values depend on the type of modulation [YK05], coding [BLZ08], [TVPH03], [VTH], power allocation and type of protocol used which may exploit or not previously erroneous efforts.

The model can be especially useful for SR-ARQ as well SW-ARQ protocols. On the other hand if the acknowledgement round-trip delay goes to zero the same model is sufficient to describe the generalized ARQ protocol with instantaneous feedback, described in section 1.3. Considering the way packets are processed at the receiver, the three protocols investigated in [CT01] and [Tun07] can also be included in the model: 1) ALO, where like in slotted Aloha protocols the same packet is transmitted until correct reception and the receiver examines only the most recent packet version. 2) RTD, where the same codeword is always transmitted during retransmission efforts but erroneous packets are held at the receiver, which performs maximum ratio combining (Repetition Time Diversity). 3) INR (Incremental Redundancy) where after the first transmission, only redundand information is sent and optimally combined with previous erroneous efforts of the packet at the receiver. The last two schemes are considered as Hybrid-ARQ (H-ARQ) schemes.

In what follows, possible choices of the sequences $\{q_k\}$ are investigated, which can lead to a definitely positive goodput and exclude all cases for which this will be zero. This is strongly related to the *liveness* and hence *correctness* of ARQ protocols [BG92]. It is proven in section 3.3 that ergodicity of the Markov chain describing the success run is a necessary and sufficient condition for strictly positive goodput. Despite common sense which suggests that repeating retransmissions will definitely lead to a correct packet reception sooner or later, several non-trivial situations are presented in the current chapter, where this does not actually happen.

3.2 ARQ as a Success Run

Define the process $\{Z_t\}$ with countably infinite state space $\{1, 2, \ldots\}$, $Z_1 = 1$, where the random variable Z_t is the number of retransmission effort at the t-th time slot. Suppose that at time slot t the system is at the k-th trial of some message, in other words $Z_t =$

3.2. ARQ as a Success Run

k. There are two possibilities for the states of variable Z_{t+1}, either to move on to stage $Z_{t+1} = k + 1$ if a negative acknowledgement comes or to return to stage $Z_{t+1} = 1$ for the first transmission of the next message in case of ACK. The feedback from the receiver is considered instantaneous and define the binary feedback ACK/NACK process $\{X_t\}$ with state space $\{0, 1\}$, where 0 denotes NACK and 1 an ACK. The realization of Z_t is given by z_t and of X_t by x_t. In the current chapter the probability of a successful transmission X_t is assumed to depend only on the current retransmission effort. In other words the probability of success is fixed per effort and varies with $k \in \mathbb{N}_+$.

$$\mathbb{P}\{X_t = 0 | Z_t = k\} = \mathbb{P}\{Z_{t+1} = k + 1 | Z_t = k\} = p_k \tag{3.1}$$

$$\mathbb{P}\{X_t = 1 | Z_t = k\} = \mathbb{P}\{Z_{t+1} = 1 | Z_t = k\} = q_k \tag{3.2}$$

Since the events $\{X_t = 0 | Z_t = k\}$ and $\{X_t = 1 | Z_t = k\}$ (respectively $\{Z_{t+1} = k + 1 | Z_t = k\}$ and $\{Z_{t+1} = 1 | Z_t = k\}$) are mutually exclusive and exhaustive

$$p_k + q_k = 1, \ \forall k = 1, 2, \ldots \tag{3.3}$$

For this reason the notation $q(Z_t)$ can also be introduced, in order to emphasize the explicit dependence of the success probability on the information $\mathcal{I} = \{Z_t\}$ for the retransmission state in t. The Markovian property of the discrete stochastic process $\{Z_t\}$ obviously holds.

$$\mathbb{P}\{Z_{t+1} = z_{t+1} | Z_t = z_t, \ldots, Z_1 = z_1\} = \mathbb{P}\{Z_{t+1} = z_{t+1} | Z_t = z_t\} \tag{3.4}$$

The one step transition probability matrix, which describes a *success run* is

$$\mathbf{P}_{\{Z_t\}} = \begin{pmatrix} q_1 & p_1 & 0 & 0 & 0 & \cdots \\ q_2 & 0 & p_2 & 0 & 0 & \cdots \\ q_3 & 0 & 0 & p_3 & 0 & \cdots \\ \vdots & \vdots & \vdots & \vdots & \ddots & \vdots \end{pmatrix} \tag{3.5}$$

Such matrices have already appeared in the ARQ literature as a general description of the protocol state evolution [Sin77], [LWZ04]. Each time an ACK is received after some (or none) failures, the process returns to the state 1. The probability that the first return to origin (first ACK) occurs at step k is

$$f_{1,1}^{(k)} = p_1 \cdot p_2 \cdot \ldots \cdot p_{k-1} \cdot q_k = q_k \cdot \prod_{j=1}^{k-1} p_j \qquad (3.6)$$

which reduces to the well known geometric distribution in the case that $p_k = p < 1, \forall k$. The chain in (3.5) is irreducible if $q_k < 1, \forall k$ and aperiodic if no $\mathcal{L}$ states exist s.t. $p_1 = p_2 = \ldots = p_{\mathcal{L}-1} = 1$ and $p_{\mathcal{L}} = 0, \forall \mathcal{L} \geq 1$. Then the restriction $q_k < 1$ ($p_k > 0$), $\forall k$ is made, for irreducible aperiodic Markov chains with countably infinite states, of the form (3.5). If the chain is also positive recurrent it is called *ergodic*.

The entries of the matrix in (3.5) can be given using the outage definition [OSW94] for the protocols ALO, RTD and INR described in section 3.1 (see [CT01] and [Tun07]). Then the probability $\mathbb{P}(Z_t = k|Z_{t-k+1} = 1) = p_1 \cdot \ldots \cdot p_{k-1}$, an event which occurs after $k-1$ consecutive errors, assumes the following form

$$\mathbb{P}(Z_t = k|Z_{t-k+1} = 1) = \begin{cases} \mathbb{P}\left(\sum_{j=1}^{k-1} \log\left(1 + \rho_j h_j\right) < \mu\right) & \text{INR} \\ \mathbb{P}\left(\log\left(1 + \sum_{j=1}^{k-1} \rho_j h_j\right) < \mu\right) & \text{RTD} \\ \prod_{j=1}^{k-1} \mathbb{P}\left(\log\left(1 + \rho_j h_j\right) < \mu\right) & \text{ALO} \end{cases} \qquad (3.7)$$

The transmission rate is considered fixed to $\mu > 0$ [bits/sec], the power allocated at the j-th step is ρ_j watt and h_j is the fading gain during j-th retransmission.

By the Markovian property and applying Bayes' rule $p_k = \mathbb{P}(Z_{t+1} = k+1|Z_t = k, Z_{t-k+1} = 1) = \frac{\mathbb{P}(Z_{t+1}=k+1|Z_{t-k+1}=1)}{\mathbb{P}(Z_t=k|Z_{t-k+1}=1)}$ and from the above expressions

$$p_k = \begin{cases} \frac{\mathbb{P}\left(\sum_{j=1}^{k} \log(1+\rho_j h_j) < \mu\right)}{\mathbb{P}\left(\sum_{j=1}^{k-1} \log(1+\rho_j h_j) < \mu\right)} & \text{INR} \\ \frac{\mathbb{P}\left(\log(1+\sum_{j=1}^{k} \rho_j h_j) < \mu\right)}{\mathbb{P}\left(\log(1+\sum_{j=1}^{k-1} \rho_j h_j) < \mu\right)} & \text{RTD} \\ \mathbb{P}\left(\log(1 + \rho_k h_k) < \mu\right) & \text{ALO} \end{cases} \qquad (3.8)$$

In the expressions in (3.8) varying the power allocation per retransmission ρ_j leads to different values of the error probabilities. Observe that although $\mathbb{P}(Z_t = k|Z_{t-k+1} = 1)$ definitely decreases with the number of efforts k this does not necessarily hold for the conditional values p_k. This depends on the choice of power per retransmission effort ρ_j. Using the chain in (3.5) the expected delay up to first ACK, in other words the expectation of the inter-renewal

3.2. ARQ as a Success Run

interval N_{ACK} equals the average time of return of the success run to state 1

$$\begin{aligned} \mathbb{E}[N_{ACK}] &= \sum_{k=1}^{\infty} k \cdot f_{1,1}^{(k)} = \sum_{k=1}^{\infty} k \cdot q_k \cdot \prod_{j=1}^{k-1} p_j \\ &= q_1 + 2 p_1 q_2 + 3 p_1 p_2 q_3 + \ldots \\ &= 1 + \sum_{k=1}^{\infty} p_1 p_2 \ldots p_k \end{aligned} \quad (3.9)$$

and the long term system goodput is a direct consequence of the renewal-reward theorem (2.2), (2.4)

$$g_{l-t} = \frac{\mu}{\mathbb{E}[N_{ACK}]} \quad (3.10)$$
$$\stackrel{geometric}{=} \mu \cdot q$$

Observe that the expression for goodput acquires its form (2.5) in the case of $q(Z_t) = q := const$. Since the process $\{Z_t\}$ has an infinite state space and no packet dropping is considered, the goodput expression in (3.10) with $\mathbb{E}[N_{ACK}]$ given in (3.9) represents the expected amount of bits per second that can be received over the wireless link error-free. Hence, it is a measure of the rate with which packets can be *reliably* transmitted. When the delay goes to infinity the above expression is zero and hence reliability is impossible even when sofisticated protocols implementing packet combining are used.

Remark 1. The importance of the kind of measure used for goodput - as discussed in chapter 2 - for communications reliability using ARQ, is highlighted by the following observation. The short-term goodput of the ARQ system, given in (2.6) takes in the case of a success run the following form

$$g_{s-t} = \mathbb{E}\left[\frac{\mu}{N_{ACK}}\right] \stackrel{success\ run}{=} \sum_{k=1}^{\infty} \frac{\mu}{k} \cdot q_k \prod_{j=1}^{k-1} p_j \quad (3.11)$$

The strict positivity of the expected short-term goodput is trivially guaranteed when $\mu > 0$ and $q_k > 0$ for at least one $k \in \mathbb{N}_+$. In such a case the system remains always reliable by transmission of some positive rate with a positive power in a certain effort, while this is not generally true for the long-term system goodput as shown in Theorems 10 and 14 that follow.

3.3 Reliability in ARQ Communications

As discussed in the previous paragraph reliable communications are guaranteed when the long-term goodput (3.10) achieved by the ARQ protocol is strictly positive. Since however different measures of goodput lead to conflicting results the following definition of *reliability* in communications with ARQ protocols is provided, which is based on instantaneous values of goodput rather than expectations.

Definition 1. In an ARQ system where the transmission rate μ is constant throughout the retransmission process, the instantaneous system goodput after an ACK is fed back equals

$$g_{inst} := \frac{\mu}{n} \qquad (3.12)$$

where $N_{ACK} = n$ is the waiting time up to successful packet transmission, the so called inter-renewal interval. The waiting time N_{ACK} is a random variable distributed as $f_{1,1}^{(n)}$ in (3.6). The ARQ protocol is called *reliable* and error-free communications is possible if and only if there exists a strictly positive goodput $\tilde{g} > 0$, such that

$$\mathbb{P}\{g_{inst} \leq \tilde{g}\} = 0 \qquad (3.13)$$

Based on the above definition, communications with ARQ protocols are reliable, if and only if the instantaneous goodput can drop lower than a strictly positive value $\tilde{g}$ only finitely many times, while it is higher than $\tilde{g}$ infinitely often. In other words

$$ARQ \text{ is reliable} \quad \Leftrightarrow \quad g_{inst} > \tilde{g} > 0 \quad (a.s.) \qquad (3.14)$$

The following Theorem 6 relates *reliability* in communications with the *ergodicity* of the chain in (3.5).

Theorem 6. An ARQ protocol is *reliable* based on Definition 1 if and only if the chain $\{Z_t\}$ is ergodic.

Proof. • *Necessity:* Let $\mathcal{A}_n$ be the event that for a successful transmission of a packet

3.3. Reliability in ARQ Communications

$N_{ACK} = n$ and $g_{inst} = \frac{\mu}{n} \leq \tilde{g}$, where $\tilde{g}$ is some upper bound. The possibility that $\tilde{g} = 0$ is not excluded.

$$\frac{\mu}{n} \leq \tilde{g} \Rightarrow n \geq \frac{\mu}{\tilde{g}}$$

Suppose that number $\tilde{N}_{\tilde{g}}$ is the minimum positive integer greater than or equal to $\frac{\mu}{\tilde{g}}$ and $\tilde{N}_{\tilde{g}} = \infty$ for $\tilde{g} = 0$. This is written as

$$\tilde{N}_{\tilde{g}} = \begin{cases} \left\lceil \frac{\mu}{\tilde{g}} \right\rceil & \text{if } \tilde{g} > 0 \\ \infty & \text{if } \tilde{g} = 0 \end{cases}$$

Using the above

$$\begin{aligned} \mathbb{P}\left[\mathcal{A}_n\right] = \mathbb{P}\left[n \geq \frac{\mu}{\tilde{g}}\right] &= \mathbb{P}\left[n \geq \tilde{N}_{\tilde{g}}\right] \\ &= \begin{cases} \prod_{j=1}^{\tilde{N}_{\tilde{g}}-1} p_j & \text{if } \tilde{g} > 0 \\ \lim_{n \to \infty} \prod_{j=1}^{n} p_j & \text{if } \tilde{g} = 0 \end{cases} \end{aligned} \quad (3.15)$$

If the chain is ergodic then by application of Foster's criterion [Fos53] (see also proof of Theorem 8), the infinite product for the case $\tilde{g} = 0$ is zero (3.18), while the series $\sum_{\tilde{N}_{\tilde{g}}=1}^{\infty} \prod_{j=1}^{\tilde{N}_{\tilde{g}}} p_j = \sum_{n=1}^{\infty} \mathbb{P}\left[\mathcal{A}_n\right]$ converges as shown in (3.19).

- For the case $\tilde{g} = 0$, the probability $\mathbb{P}\left[n = \infty\right] = \lim_{n \to \infty} \prod_{j=1}^{n} p_j = 0$. Hence we conclude that $\mathbb{P}\left[g_{inst} \leq 0\right] = 0$.

- For the case of $\tilde{g} > 0$, applying the first Borel-Cantelli Lemma [Fel68, p.201], since the above series converges when the chain $\{Z_t\}$ is ergodic, only finitely many of the events $\mathcal{A}_n$ can occur. That means that also in this case $\mathbb{P}\left[g_{inst} < \tilde{g}\right] = 0$ and the result is proven.

- *Sufficiency:* If a strictly positive $\tilde{g} > 0$ exists, such that $\mathbb{P}\left[\frac{\mu}{n} \leq \tilde{g}\right] = 0$, then it holds that $\mathbb{P}\left[n \geq N_{\tilde{g}}^*\right] = p_1 \cdot \ldots \cdot p_{N_{\tilde{g}}^*-1} = 0$, where

$$N_{\tilde{g}}^* = \left\lceil \frac{\mu}{\tilde{g}} \right\rceil < \infty$$

From the above probability one can easily conclude that

$$\begin{cases} \lim_{k\to\infty} \prod_{j=1}^{k} p_j = 0 \\ 1 + \sum_{k=1}^{\infty} \prod_{j=1}^{k} p_j = 1 + \sum_{k=1}^{N_g^*-1} \prod_{j=1}^{k} p_j < \infty \end{cases}$$

and hence the chain is ergodic (see (3.18) and (3.19)) from direct application of Foster's criterion [Fos53], [Fel68].

□

In the following the descriptions *ergodic protocol*, *stable protocol* and *reliable protocol* will be interchangeably used to refer to an ARQ protocol that forms an ergodic Markov Chain and can hence guarantee reliable communications in the sense of Definition 1.

3.4 Conditions for Recurrence and Ergodicity

The analysis that follows investigates conditions for the recurrence and ergodicity of the ARQ protocols described by (3.5). These are also conditions for the reliability of the protocols, as shown in Theorem 6. It should be noted here that recurrence is simply a weaker notion of stability. Theorem 7 can be found in [Bre99, pp.106-107] and its proof is based on the definition of recurrence and the conditions for convergence of an infinite product [Bre99, p.422], which are restated in the Lemmata that follow.

Lemma 1. Assume $p_k \in (0, 1]$, $\forall k$. The infinite product $\lim_{n\to\infty} \prod_{k=1}^{n} p_k = c > 0$ if and only if $\sum_{k=1}^{\infty} \log(p_k)$ converges.

Lemma 2. Assume $q_k \in [0, 1)$, $\forall k$. Then $\sum_{k=1}^{\infty} \log(1 - q_k)$ converges absolutely, if and only if $\sum_{k=1}^{\infty} q_k$ converges.

Theorem 7. A Markov chain with one-step transition probability matrix given in (3.5), $p_k \in (0, 1]$, $\forall k$, is **recurrent** if and only if the series $\sum_{k=1}^{\infty} q_k$ diverges (alternatively if and only if $\lim_{n\to\infty} \prod_{k=1}^{n} p_k = 0$).

To get a better notion of the result presented above let us denote with $\mathcal{E}_k$ the event that an ACK is received at step k when all previous feedback signals are NACK's. Then $\mathbb{P}\{\mathcal{E}_k\} = \mathbb{P}\{Z_{k+1} = 1 | Z_k = k\} = q_k$. The events $\mathcal{E}_k$ are independent and since $\sum_{k=1}^{\infty} \mathbb{P}\{\mathcal{E}_k\} = \sum_{k=1}^{\infty} q_k$ diverges, infinitely many of the events $\mathcal{E}_k$ should occur with probability 1, as a direct result of the second Borel-Cantelli Lemma [Fel68, pp.201-202].

3.4. Conditions for Recurrence and Ergodicity

Theorem 8. If $\limsup_{k \to \infty} p_k < 1$ the chain in (3.5) is **ergodic**.

Proof. From Foster's necessary and sufficient condition for ergodicity [Fos53], restated in Feller [Fel68], in the case of irreducible and aperiodic chains, the system is ergodic if and only if there exist numbers $\pi_k > 0$, $k = 1, 2, \ldots$ such that

$$\sum_{k=1}^{\infty} \pi_k = 1 \quad \& \quad \pi_k = \sum_{i=1}^{\infty} \pi_i p_{i,k} \tag{3.16}$$

The second equation can be written in a vector form

$$\vec{\pi} = \vec{\pi} \mathbf{P}_{\{Z_t\}} \Rightarrow \begin{cases} \pi_k = \pi_{k-1} p_{k-1} & k \geq 2 \\ \pi_1 = q_1 \pi_1 + \ldots + q_k \pi_k + \ldots & \text{state } 1 \end{cases} \tag{3.17}$$

and replacing the values of π_k in the expression for π_1

$$\begin{aligned}
\pi_1 &= \pi_1 q_1 + \pi_1 p_1 q_2 + \pi_1 p_1 p_2 q_3 + \ldots \\
&= \pi_1 (q_1 + p_1 q_2 + p_1 p_2 q_3 + \ldots) \\
&= \pi_1 \left(1 - \lim_{n \to \infty} \prod_{k=1}^{n} p_k \right)
\end{aligned}$$

Then a solution to (3.16.b) exists if

$$\lim_{n \to \infty} \prod_{k=1}^{n} p_k = 0 \tag{3.18}$$

Furthermore, from (3.16.a) and replacing (from 3.17) the values π_k, $\forall k \geq 2$

$$\sum_{k=1}^{\infty} \pi_k = 1 \Rightarrow \pi_1 \left(1 + \sum_{k=1}^{\infty} p_1 \ldots p_k \right) = 1$$

Requiring that all states are persistent non-null, means $\pi_k \neq 0$, $\forall k$, hence an equivalent to condition (3.16) for our problem is

$$\sum_{k=1}^{\infty} p_1 \ldots p_k < \infty \tag{3.19}$$

Altogether, the system is ergodic if and only if the infinite product in (3.18) converges to zero and the infinite series in (3.19) converges. However $\limsup_{k\to\infty} p_k < 1$ means by definition [Sok39] that there exists a $c > 0$, such that $p_k \leq 1 - c, \forall k \geq N^*$, $N^* = N^*(c)$. Using these inequalities, the infinite series $\sum q_k = \sum_{k=1}^{N^*} q_k + \sum_{k=N^*+1}^{\infty} q_k \geq \sum_{k=1}^{N^*} q_k + \sum_{k=N^*+1}^{\infty} c$ always diverges. This implies that $\lim_{n\to\infty} \prod_{k=1}^{n} p_k = 0$ and the system is always recurrent, by application of Theorem 7. Furthermore, from the Ratio Test [Sok39] $\limsup_{k\to\infty} \frac{p_1 \cdots p_k}{p_1 \cdots p_{k-1}} = \limsup_{k\to\infty} p_k < 1$, implying that the series in (3.19) always converges under the Theorem's condition. □

The proof of the above theorem up to form (3.19) can be found in [Bre99, p.107]. Upper-bounding the asymptotic probability of the tail events $\mathcal{A}_n$ in (3.15), a further sufficient condition for ergodicity is provided.

Theorem 9. If $\mathbb{P}\{k > n\} = p_1 \cdot \ldots \cdot p_n = O\left(\frac{1}{n^\beta}\right), \beta > 1$ then the chain in (3.5) is ergodic.

Proof. If $p_1 \cdot \ldots \cdot p_n = O\left(\frac{1}{n^\beta}\right)$, there exist constants $C, N^* > 0$ s.t. $p_1 \cdot \ldots \cdot p_n \leq C \cdot \frac{1}{n^\beta}$ holds $\forall n \geq N^*$ [Aig99]. Using the Cauchy criterion for series convergence [Sok39] and assuming $\beta > 1$, we can see that $\sum_{k=n}^{m} p_1 \cdot \ldots \cdot p_k \leq \sum_{k=n}^{m} C \cdot \frac{1}{k^\beta} = \epsilon < \infty, \forall m, n \geq N^*(\epsilon)$. Then the series in (3.19) converges and hence the chain is ergodic. □

Theorem 10. The following two sufficient conditions hold:

- If $\lim_{k\to\infty} \sup (1 - q_k \cdot k) < 0$ then (3.5) is **ergodic**.

- If $\lim_{k\to\infty} \inf (1 - q_k \cdot k) > 0$ then (3.5) is **non-ergodic**.

Proof. The first condition of the above theorem derives directly from the Foster-Lyapunov stability criterion [MT93] which extends Pakes' [Pak69] sufficient conditions for ergodicity. The second from Kaplan's [Kap79] sufficient conditions for non-ergodicty.

Suppose that the Lyapunov function used is $V(x) = x : \mathbb{N}_+ \to \mathbb{N}_+$ and C is a finite subset of $\mathbb{N}_+$. A Markov chain is positive recurrent if $\epsilon > 0$ and b is a constant such that the drift function satisfies $\gamma_k = \mathbb{E}\{V(Z_{t+1})|V(Z_t = k)\} - V(Z_t = k) \stackrel{V(x)=x}{=} \sum_{j=1}^{\infty} (j-k) P_{k,j} \leq -\epsilon + b \cdot \mathbf{1}_C$, where $\mathbf{1}_C$ is the indicator function $\mathbf{1}_{\{k \in C\}} = 1$. The element of $\mathbf{P}_{\{Z_t\}}$ at the k-th row and l-th column is denoted by $P_{k,j}$. Using the chain in (3.5) the inequality is written as $\gamma_k = 1 - k \cdot q_k, k \in \mathbb{N}_+$ and $1 - k \cdot q_k < 1$. Choose $b = 1$. If $k \notin C$ then $1 - k \cdot q_k \leq -\epsilon$ for infinitely many k's and does not hold only for a finite subset C. From the definition of $\limsup$ [Sok39] the condition can be written as $\lim_{k\to\infty} \sup (1 - q_k \cdot k) < 0$.

3.4. Conditions for Recurrence and Ergodicity

Using now Kaplan's conditions, a Markov chain is non-ergodic if for some integer $N \geq 1$ and constants $B \geq 0$, $c \in [0, 1]$ the following two conditions hold

$$\sum_{j=1}^{\infty} (j - k) P_{k,j} > 0 \qquad \forall k \geq N$$

$$z^k - \sum_{j=1}^{\infty} P_{k,j} z^j \geq -B(1 - z) \qquad \forall k \geq N, \ \forall z \in [c, 1]$$

The conditions are reduced to

$$(1 - k) q_k + p_k = 1 - k \cdot q_k > 0 \qquad \forall k \geq N$$

$$z^k - q_k \cdot z - p_k \cdot z^{k+1} \geq -B(1 - z) \qquad \forall k \geq N, \ \forall z \in [c, 1]$$

The second inequality is satisfied for $c = 1$, $B = 0$. From the first condition it is required that infinitely many k's satisfy the inequality $1 - k \cdot q_k > 0$ and only a finite subset of $\mathbb{N}_+$ should be left out. From the lim inf definition [Sok39] it reduces to $\lim_{k \to \infty} \inf (1 - q_k \cdot k) > 0$. □

The strength of the aforementioned results will be shown in the following examples

Example 1. Assume that the ARQ success probabilities are of the form $q_k = \frac{1+D}{k+C}$. Since $0 \leq q_k < 1$ then the constants have the following restrictions: $D \geq -1$ and $D < C$. Using Theorem 10 the ergodic property holds for $\lim_{k \to \infty} \sup \left(1 - \frac{1+D}{k+C} \cdot k\right) = \lim_{k \to \infty} \sup \left(\frac{-D+C/k}{C/k+1}\right) = -D < 0$. This results in the condition $C > D > 0$. The policies with $-1 \leq D < 0$, $C > D$ are non-ergodic.

Theorem 10 cannot give an answer for the case $C > D = 0$, where $q_k = \frac{1}{k+C}$ and $p_k = \frac{k+C-1}{k+C}$. Then $1 + p_1 + p_1 \cdot p_2 + p_1 \cdot p_2 \cdot p_3 + \ldots = 1 + \frac{C}{1+C} + \frac{C}{2+C} + \frac{C}{3+C} + \ldots$ which diverges. From Theorem 7 however $\sum q_k$ also diverges hence this case is recurrent null.

Then as numerical example $D = 1$, $C = 2 > D = 1$ lead to $1 + p_1 + p_1 \cdot p_2 + p_1 \cdot p_2 \cdot p_3 + \ldots = 1 + \frac{1}{3} + \frac{1 \cdot 2}{3 \cdot 4} + \frac{1 \cdot 2}{4 \cdot 5} + \ldots = 1 + 2 \sum_{n=1}^{\infty} \frac{1}{(n+1)(n+2)} = 1 + 2 \sum_{n=1}^{\infty} \frac{1}{(n+1)} - \frac{1}{(n+2)} = 2 < \infty$.

For $D = -0.5$, $C = 0 > -0.5$ we have $1 + p_1 + p_1 \cdot p_2 + p_1 \cdot p_2 \cdot p_3 + \ldots = 1 + \frac{1}{2} + \frac{1 \cdot 3}{2 \cdot 4} + \frac{1 \cdot 3 \cdot 5}{2 \cdot 4 \cdot 6} + \ldots = \lim_{x \to 1} \frac{1}{\sqrt{1-x}} = \infty$.

Example 2. Assume policies of the form $q_k = \frac{1+D}{(k+C)^\beta}$, $C > D > -1$, $\beta > 0$. Then $\lim_{k \to \infty} \sup \left(1 - \frac{1+D}{(k+C)^\beta} \cdot k\right) = \lim_{k \to \infty} \sup \left(1 - \frac{(1+D)k^{1-\beta}}{(1+C/k)^\beta}\right)$. The limit is negative (ergodic) if $\beta < 1$, equals $-D$ if $\beta = 1$ and is positive (non-ergodic) if $\beta > 1$. For $\beta = 1$ the problem reduces to Example 1.

Example 3. For the policies $\{q_k\} = \{\frac{1}{k \cdot (\log(k))^\beta}\}$, for $\beta > 0$ we get $\lim_{k\to\infty} \sup\left(1 - \frac{1}{(\log(k))^\beta}\right) = 1 > 0$ hence they are always non-ergodic. For $\beta \leq 1$ the series in Theorem 7 diverges hence the chain is recurrent null, whereas for $\beta > 1$ the series converges hence the chain is transient.

Example 4. If for the sequence $\{q_k\}$, $q_k < 1$ increase with k then $\lim_{k\to\infty} \sup(1 - q_k \cdot k) = -\infty < 0$, hence the chain for increasing conditional success probabilities is always ergodic.

Notice here that $1 - q_k \cdot k \leq 1 - q_k, \forall k \Rightarrow \lim_{k\to\infty} \sup(1 - q_k \cdot k) < \lim_{k\to\infty} \sup(1 - q_k)$ hence Theorem 7 is a special case of Theorem 10. Furthermore, it is very important that Theorem 10 holds in general for $\limsup_{k\to\infty} p_k \leq 1$. The case $\limsup_{k\to\infty} p_k = 1$ is not trivial since it represents a great variety of possible ARQ strategies. For example in a time sharing policy e.g. round-robin, the transmitter is not provided with resources for every time slot, hence p_k can periodically equal 1. Another case is for example if one decides to use a great portion of the available resources during the first transmissions in an effort to achieve very low error probabilities and hence reduced latency, but unfortunately the message is not correctly received and the resources are reduced in later steps so that p_k in (3.8) tends to 1 as $k \to \infty$.

3.5 Recurrence for Rayleigh Fading Channels

In the current paragraph a point-to-point wireless link free of interference is considered, where channel fading is Rayleigh distributed and changes block-wise. The retransmission codewords span a single block. Using this channel as example, Theorems 7-10 of the previous section can be applied to describe how power per retransmission should be asymptotically allocated so that the protocol be recurrent or ergodic. The measure to be used in the following analysis is again the information outage probability, which depends only on the channel statistics and its value can be controlled by rate and power allocation decisions. No code combining at the receiver is considered in the current example (see ALO in section 3.1 as well as (3.8)) although an extension of the following analysis to more complicated scenarios is possible due to the generality of the derived theorems. In this example, keeping the transmission rate $\mu > 0$ [bits/sec] fixed, the outage probability provides a 1-1 mapping of the power allocation per retransmission $\{\rho_k\}$ into the values $\{p_k\}$ (or $\{q_k\}$). Defined in [OSW94], the outage probability of the Rayleigh fading channel during the k-th retransmission is de-

3.5. Recurrence for Rayleigh Fading Channels

pendent on the power allocation at the k-th step ρ_k and equals (see also (2.15) and (2.16))

$$p_k := p(\rho_k, \mu) = \mathbb{P}\left(\log(1 + \rho_k \cdot h_k) < \mu\right) = 1 - \exp\left(\frac{1 - e^\mu}{\rho_k}\right) \quad (3.20)$$

where h_k is the channel fading gain for Rayleigh distribution during the k-th retransmission. A sufficient condition (upper bound) for non-recurrence as well as a necessary (lower bound) condition for recurrence related to the power allocation per retransmission $\{\rho_k\}$ is derived in Theorems 11 and 12 respectively. Theorems 13 and 14 further provide important sufficient conditions for ergodicity and thus communication reliability.

Theorem 11. If $\rho_k = O(1/k)$ the ARQ chain is non-recurrent.

Proof. Combining Theorem 7 with the Root Test for series convergence [Sok39], the series $\sum q_k$ converges and the chain is non-recurrent, if $\limsup_{k\to\infty} \sqrt[k]{1 - p_k} < 1$. Substituting the outage probability (3.20) $\limsup_{k\to\infty} \exp\left(\frac{1-e^\mu}{k\cdot\rho_k}\right) < 1 \Leftrightarrow \limsup_{k\to\infty} \frac{1-e^\mu}{k\cdot\rho_k} < 0$ from the continuity of the logarithmic function. Since $\mu > 0$ the latter is equivalent to $\limsup_{k\to\infty} \frac{1}{k\cdot\rho_k} > 0$, meaning $\exists \bar{c} < \infty$ and N^* s.t. $\forall k \geq N^*$, $\frac{\rho_k}{1/k} \leq \bar{c}$ which is written $\rho_k = O(1/k)$ [Aig99]. □

Theorem 12. If $\{\rho_k\}$ leads to a recurrent ARQ chain then it holds $\rho_k^{-1} = o(k)$.

Proof. Using the previous method one can find that since $\rho_k \geq 0$, no power allocation satisfies $\limsup_{k\to\infty} \sqrt[k]{1 - p_k} > 1$. Then recurrent events may occur only when the limit equals $\limsup_{k\to\infty} \sqrt[k]{1 - p_k} = 1$. Since the test fails to decide on the convergence or not of $\sum q_k$, this is a necessary condition, written [Aig99] as $\rho_k^{-1} = o(k)$. □

Theorem 13. If ρ_k is lower bounded $\forall k$, meaning $\rho_k \geq \underline{\rho} > 0$ the ARQ chain is ergodic.

Proof. Rewritting Theorem 7 as $\liminf_{k\to\infty} q_k > 0$, $\exists \epsilon \in (0, 1)$ and $N^*(\epsilon)$ s.t. $\forall k > N^*$, it holds $q_k \geq \epsilon \Leftrightarrow \rho_k \geq \frac{e^\mu - 1}{|\log \epsilon|} = \underline{\rho} > 0$. □

Theorem 14. Suppose ρ_k is upper bounded $\forall k$, meaning $\rho_k \leq \bar{\rho} < \infty$. Then, if $\rho_k = \Omega(1/\log k)$, the chain is ergodic. If $\rho_k = O(1/\log k)$ the chain is non-ergodic.

Proof. We rewrite the sufficient ergodicity condition from Theorem 10 as $\liminf_{k\to\infty} k \cdot q_k > 1 \Leftrightarrow \liminf_{k\to\infty} \frac{\rho_k \cdot \log(k) + 1 - e^\mu}{\rho_k} > 0 \overset{0<\rho_k\leq\bar\rho}{\Leftrightarrow} \liminf_{k\to\infty} \frac{\rho_k}{1/\log k} > e^\mu - 1 > 0$. Then $\exists N^*(\mu)$: $\forall k > N^*, \rho_k > (e^\mu - 1) \cdot \frac{1}{\log k}$ and from [Aig99] this is equivalent to $\rho_k = \Omega(1/\log k)$. Using the inequality $\limsup_{k\to\infty} k \cdot q_k < 1$ we find that a sufficient condition for non-ergodicity is $\rho_k = O(1/\log k)$. □

Notice that in this special case of Rayleigh fading statistics, comparing a given power allocation with the sequences $1/k$ and $1/\log k$ asymptotically, one can tell whether the ARQ chain is non-recurrent (if $\rho_k = O(1/k)$), recurrent-null (if $\rho_k = O(1/\log k)$ and $\rho_k^{-1} = o(k)$) or positive recurrent (if $\rho_k = \Omega(1/\log k)$).

The expected power up to correct packet reception equals

$$\begin{aligned} \mathbb{E}[\rho] &= q_1\rho_1 + p_1q_2 \cdot (\rho_1 + \rho_2) + p_1p_2q_3 \cdot (\rho_1 + \rho_2 + \rho_3) + \dots \\ &= \rho_1 + p_1 \cdot \rho_2 + p_1p_2 \cdot \rho_3 + \dots \end{aligned} \quad (3.21)$$

If this series converges, the average power for a single correct packet transmission is finite. This happens if $\limsup_{k \to \infty} p_{k-1}\rho_k < 1$ (using the Ratio Test [Sok39]). The latter inequality is always satisfied when $\rho_k \to 0$, since $p_k \leq 1$. The theorems derived in this section, for which the power allocation tends asymptotically to 0 with the number of retransmissions, suggest that reliable communications is possible with finite power per packet transmission, however not guaranteed. This depends on the ergodicity of the protocol under study.

Chapter 4

Truncating ARQ Protocols using Optimal Stopping

Occasionally - even with H-ARQ - a large number of retransmissions may be required resulting in an unacceptable delay, which can be reduced by limiting the maximum allowable retransmission number. This leads to ARQ truncation techniques [ML00], which optimize goodput at the expense of packet loss when the truncation number is exceeded. A cross-layer combination of adaptive modulation and coding with truncated ARQ has been investigated in [LZG04]. In most current approaches in the literature, the truncated version of ARQ is accepted as realistic and optimal in terms of delay-throughput tradeoff. However the maximum number of retransmissions is considered as a predefined constant.

In the current chapter, using the model for ARQ protocols suggested in chapter 3, we make use of the conceptual framework of sequential analysis and optimal stopping [Shi78] to determine the optimal number of retransmissions in an ARQ chain, given a sequence of rewards and costs per retransmission and a terminal cost, for the case that the packet fails to be correctly received before the truncation number is exceeded. The costs per trial as well as final cost are related to the desired QoS.

The stochastic process sequentially observed is the binary feedback after each packet (re-)transmission $\{X_n\}$. A reward-cost process $\{Y_n^C\}$ (payoff) is constructed as a function of the observed sequence up to time n. The reward sequence $\{R_n\}$ can be related to some rate gain for successful transmission, whereas the costs can be interpreted as a power/delay cost per retransmission $\{D_n\}$ as well as a final cost in case of dropping at step n, equal to $\{\delta_n\}$. After each observation of X_n one can decide either to stop and receive the related instantaneous payoff Y_n^C or allow for a new retransmission. We are looking for a stopping rule T to maximize the expected payoff providing the optimal truncation time.

4.1 On Optimal Stopping Rules

Consider a filtered space $(\Omega, \mathcal{F}, \{\mathcal{F}_n\}, \mathbb{P})$ where $(\Omega, \mathcal{F}, \mathbb{P})$ is a probability triple. $\{\mathcal{F}_n : n \in \mathbb{N}\}$ is a filtration, that is an increasing family of sub-σ-algebras of $\mathcal{F}$: $\mathcal{F}_0 \subseteq \mathcal{F}_1 \subseteq \ldots \subseteq \mathcal{F}$. Each $\mathcal{F}_n$ contains all the null sets of $\mathcal{F}$. Consider further a stochastic process $\{X_n\} = (X_n : n \geq 0)$ defined on this probability space each random variable X_n having state space $\mathbb{R}$, measurable with respect to the Borel σ-algebra $\mathcal{B}(\mathbb{R})$. The process is called *adapted* to the filtration $\{\mathcal{F}_n\}$, meaning that for each n, X_n is $\mathcal{F}_n$-measurable. To simplify consider the case of the natural filtration where $\mathcal{F}_n = \sigma(X_0, X_1, \ldots, X_n)$. Since the process is adapted the value $X_n(\omega)$, $\omega \in \Omega$ is known at time n.

The random variable $\tau = \tau(\omega) : \Omega \to \{1, 2, \ldots, \infty\}$ defined in $(\Omega, \mathcal{F}, \mathbb{P})$ is said to be a *Markov Time* [Shi78] with respect to the filtration $\{\mathcal{F}_n\}$, if for each $n \in \mathbb{N} \cup \{\infty\}$

$$\{\omega : \tau(\omega) \leq n\} \in \mathcal{F}_n \qquad (4.1)$$

where $\mathcal{F}_\infty := \sigma(\bigcup_n \mathcal{F}_n) \subseteq \mathcal{F}$. This is actually the *non-anticipativity* requirement [DK94], i.e. the linear equality constraint $\mathbb{P}(\tau \leq n | \mathcal{F}_n) = \mathbf{1}_{\{\tau \leq n\}}$. If it further holds that the Markov time is finite with probability one

$$\mathbb{P}\{\tau(\omega) < \infty\} = 1 \qquad (4.2)$$

then it is called a *Stopping Time*. The stopping time is a time when we decide to stop our process based solely on the already available samples that are observed up to and including time n $\{X_1(\omega), \ldots, X_n(\omega)\}$ and this is exactly what (4.1) implies. The problem of optimal stopping can be described as follows. The sequence of random variables $\{X_1, \ldots, X_n, \ldots\}$ is observed until we decide at some step n to stop and receive a payoff $Y_n(\omega) = f_n(X_1(\omega), \ldots, X_n(\omega))$, which is an $\mathcal{F}_n$ measurable function $f_n : \Omega \to \mathbb{R}$, $f_n^{-1} : \mathcal{B}(\mathbb{R}) \to \mathcal{F}_n$. We are looking for a stopping rule $\tau = T$ with the attributes (4.1) and (4.2) that maximizes the expected payoff $\mathbb{E}[Y_\tau]$ in the class of all stopping times C for which the expectation exists. Since the expectation is a Lebesgue integral and one can write $Y = Y^+ - Y^-$,

4.1. On Optimal Stopping Rules

where $Y^+ = \max\{0, Y\}$ and $Y^- = \max\{-Y, 0\}$, the expectation is defined if one of the two terms is finite [Rud64]. Furthermore $Y_\tau \leq \sup_n Y_n$. Hence under the condition that

$$\mathbb{E}\left[\sup_n Y_n^+\right] < \infty \qquad (4.3)$$

the expectation is always good defined, possibly infinite and it holds in particular $-\infty \leq \mathbb{E}[Y_\tau] \leq \mathbb{E}[\sup_n Y_n^+] < \infty$. The maximum expected reward equals

$$V := \sup_{\tau \in C, 1 \leq \tau < \infty} \mathbb{E}[Y_\tau] \qquad (4.4)$$

and we are looking for the rule $T \in C$ (if it exists) such that

$$\mathbb{E}[Y_T] = V \qquad (4.5)$$

Under assumption (4.3) and if $\mathbb{P}(T < \infty) = 1$, such an optimal stopping rule can be shown to exist (see Theorem 1 in [CR63] and [Fer00]). The rule that maximizes the expected return is then given by the *principle of optimality* [Ber03], [Fer00]. Having already observed the first n realizations of the process, the maximum expected reward for the remaining stages equals

$$V_n = \operatorname*{ess\,sup}_{n \leq \tau < \infty} \mathbb{E}[Y_\tau | \mathcal{F}_n], \ n \in \mathbb{N}_+ \qquad (4.6)$$

where the *ess* sup is taken over all stopping rules $n \leq \tau < \infty$. V_n is the Snell envelope of the process $\{Y_n\}$, it is uniformly integrable in view of condition (4.3) and satisfies the recursion

$$V_n = \max(Y_n, \mathbb{E}[V_{n+1} | \mathcal{F}_n]) \qquad (4.7)$$

By the principle of optimality the stopping rule

$$T := \min\{n : Y_n = V_n, \ n \in \mathbb{N}_+\} \qquad (4.8)$$

provides the optimal stopping time, namely the minimum time among all which maximize the expectation of the reward function (4.5). The above results can be analytically found in [DK94], [Shi78], [CR63]. In simple words, the optimality principle suggests that one ought to continue the observations as long as the future expected payoff is greater than the present reward and stop immediately otherwise. The solution to the optimal stopping problem can be simplified if it can be shown that the problem is *monotone*. If the sequence of rewards $\{Y_1, Y_2, \ldots\}$ is such that for every $n = 1, 2, \ldots$

$$\mathbb{E}(Y_{n+1}|\mathcal{F}_n) \leq Y_n \Rightarrow \mathbb{E}(Y_{n+2}|\mathcal{F}_{n+1}) \leq Y_{n+1} \quad (4.9)$$

we say we are in the monotone case and the optimal stopping rule is the *one-step look-ahead (myopic) rule* [CR63], [Ber03], [Fer00].

$$T_{myopic} := \min\{n : Y_n \geq \mathbb{E}[Y_{n+1}|\mathcal{F}_n], n \in \mathbb{N}_+\} \quad (4.10)$$

Generally the one-step look-ahead rule is optimal for finite monotone stopping problems, with horizon N. In the infinite horizon case $N \to \infty$ the same holds under (4.3), (4.2) and $V^{(N)} \stackrel{N \to \infty}{\to} V$, where $V^{(N)}$ is the maximum expected reward for finite horizon N. Conditions for the later to hold can be found in [Fer00] and are generally satisfied in the problem treated in the current analysis.

4.2 ARQ as an Optimal Stopping Problem

In the case of ARQ the evolving process is the feedback to the transmitter which contains the information whether a message has been correctly or erroneously received. The observed discrete-time random process with finite state space is described as follows

$$X_n = \begin{cases} 1 & \text{if NACK} \\ 0 & \text{if ACK} \end{cases} \quad (4.11)$$

Note here that in the entire analysis up to now, value 0 represents a successful reception instead of unsuccessful, however this convention is introduced in the current chapter to simplify notation in what follows and that is why it is adopted.

The random variables X_n are generally not independent since their distribution depends on the previous history of the process (see also (3.1) and (3.2)). That is, if the last ACK was received at time $\tilde{n}$, $X_{\tilde{n}} = 0$, then $\mathbb{P}(X_n = 0|X_{\tilde{n}} = 0, X_{\tilde{n} < n' \leq n-1} = 1) = q_{n-\tilde{n}}$ and $\mathbb{P}(X_n = 1|X_{\tilde{n}} = 0, X_{\tilde{n} < n' \leq n-1} = 1) = p_{n-\tilde{n}}$. That is, the current value of success probability depends on the number of consecutive unsuccessful retransmissions up to this point

4.2. ARQ as an Optimal Stopping Problem

and this information is contained within the observed sequence $\{X_j(\omega), j \leq n-1\}$. The expected values $\mathbb{E}[X_n] = 0 \cdot q_k + 1 \cdot p_k \leq 1$, $k \leq n$.

Define further a *reward process* $\{Y_n\} = f^n(X_0, \ldots, X_n)$ where $f^n : \underbrace{\{0,1\} \times \ldots \times \{0,1\}}_{n-times} \to \mathbb{R}$ is an $\mathcal{F}_n$-measurable function. Let us construct in the following the reward processes of interest.

The random variable defined as $M_n := X_1 \cdot \ldots \cdot X_n$, $M_0 = 1$ is non-negative and can take values from the state space $\{0, 1\}$. If at some point $\tilde{n}$, $X_{\tilde{n}} = 0$ (ACK), then $M_{n \geq \tilde{n}} = 0$ that means that the process may only stay constant or decrease. Then the process forms a *super-martingale* [Wil91]

$$\begin{aligned}
\mathbb{E}[M_n|\mathcal{F}_{n-1}] &= X_1 \cdot \ldots \cdot X_{n-1} \cdot \mathbb{E}[X_n|\mathcal{F}_{n-1}] \\
&\leq X_1 \cdot \ldots \cdot X_{n-1} \\
&= M_{n-1}
\end{aligned} \qquad (4.12)$$

The process $\{-M_n\}$ eventually forms a non-positive *sub-martingale*.

Suppose now that before any observation X_n a bet (reward) R_n is placed, the value of which is chosen considering only the known observations $\{X_1(\omega) = x_1, X_2(\omega) = x_2, \ldots, X_{n-1}(\omega) = x_{n-1}\}$. Then since $\{R_n\}$ is $\mathcal{F}_{n-1}$ measurable and independent of X_n it forms a *previsible* process. Some interesting choices of the previsible process for the ARQ analysis could be some sequence of rates e.g. $R_n = \mu$, $R_n = \frac{\mu}{n}$ or $R_n = \beta^n \mu$, $0 < \beta \leq 1$.

The reward to be received for observing the random variable X_n equals $R_n \cdot (M_{n-1} - M_n)$. Then if $M_{n-1} = 1$ meaning that an ACK is not yet received up to step $n-1$ the n-th step reward can either equal R_n if $X_n = 0$ (ACK at step n) or 0 if the n-th retransmission is again unsuccessful. If $M_{n-1} = 0$ then definitely $M_n = 0$ and the n-th step reward is 0. The total reward up to n equals

$$\begin{aligned}
Y_n &= \sum_{k=1}^{n} R_k \cdot (M_{k-1} - M_k) & (4.13) \\
&= \sum_{k=1}^{n} R_k \cdot X_1 \cdot \ldots \cdot X_{k-1} \cdot (1 - X_k) & (4.14)
\end{aligned}$$

and the n-th step reward is just the difference $Y_n - Y_{n-1} = R_n \cdot (M_{n-1} - M_n)$. Observe that the way the reward function (4.13) was created, implies that if no ACK is received until n and given that $M_0 = 1$ we have a total reward equal to $Y_n = 0$. If an ACK is received for the first time at some step $k \leq n$, then $Y_n = R_k$ and remains constant for all $n' \geq n$.

Optimal stopping problems usually include a cost per observation as well as a terminal cost. For the case of ARQ it is reasonable to consider as cost the delay added to the system or the lost power due to an unsuccessful transmission. The costs per observation sum up and are deterministic, that is they do not depend on the values of the observed process directly. Their sum depends only on the number of observations. Furthermore the terminal cost is related to some penalty in case one stops before a specific goal is achieved - that is in our case a penalty for stopping before an ACK is received. Such a penalty is reasonable since the unsuccessful packet will be dropped and this will affect the user's quality of service. In the following a general expression of the *reward-cost* process is provided

$$Y_n^C = \sum_{k=1}^{n} R_k \cdot (M_{k-1} - M_k) - \sum_{k=1}^{n} D_k - M_n \cdot \delta_n \qquad (4.15)$$

where D_k are the non-negative costs per retransmission, δ_k are the terminal costs for stopping at stage k, before an ACK is received. Different values of the costs and penalty can reflect a different quality of service. That is a high value of D_k's can correspond to a service with high delay sensitivity as for example the VoIP, while high values of δ_k's correspond to services sensitive with respect to dropped packets.

The above problem can be understood as a variation of the problem of selling an asset [CR63], [Fer00]. Here a salesman is familiar with the whole sequence of offers that come at each stage $\{R_n\}$. He decides on whether or not he will accept the offer by a rather peculiar way. Each time an offer comes, he tosses an unfair coin which has probability of 'heads' q_n at the n-th effort. If the result is 'heads' he accepts the offer. For each offer to come he has to wait a known time $\{D_n\}$ which resembles the cost. Finally if he waits too long and no 'heads' comes up he may consider to stop receiving offers, but then there will be a penalty since the asset will finally not be sold.

We are generally looking for a stopping rule $\tau : \{\tau \leq n\} \in \mathcal{F}_n$, $\forall n \leq \infty$ that decides when it is 'worth' stopping the process of retransmissions. Stopping at time n brings a payoff (reward) equal to Y_n^C. We are looking for a rule to maximize the expected value of this payoff. The basic theory of optimal stopping considering existence and computation of optimal stopping rules can be found in [Shi78], [CRS71]. Rather noteworthy is furthermore the work in [TR99] where convergent approximate solutions for optimaly stopping a Markov process are suggested.

4.3 The ARQ Stopping Problem without Cost

In this section conditions to optimally stop the countably infinite ARQ process with reward function $\{Y_n\}$ given by (4.14) are investigated. This special case does not include any supplementary cost per retransmission or final cost. A first Lemma is initially provided before continuing further to the computation of optimal stopping rules

Lemma 3. The reward process $\{Y_n\}$ is a sub-martingale under the condition that $\{R_n\}$ is a non-negative, bounded and previsible process.

Proof. It has already been shown in (4.12) that $-M_n$ is a sub-martingale. Then, conditioned that $\{R_n\}$ is a non-negative, bounded, previsible process (see [Wil91, Theorem 10.7]) it can directly be deduced that

$$\mathbb{E}\left[Y_n - Y_{n-1} | \mathcal{F}_{n-1}\right] = R_n \cdot \mathbb{E}\left[-M_n + M_{n-1} | \mathcal{F}_{n-1}\right] \geq 0$$

$\square$

Proof. (*Alternative*) The following analysis which shows a bit more in detail what was easily proved in the previous lemma, will provide the Doob decomposition of the total reward. This will be used in what follows. Doob's decomposition [Wil91] is required to decompose $-M_n$ into a sum of a martingale N_n and a non-decreasing previsible process A_n. Both are null at $n = 0$.

$$-M_n = -X_1 \cdot \ldots \cdot X_n = N_n + A_n - M_0 \quad (4.16)$$

where $-M_0$ is the value of the sub-martingale at step 0 equal to $-M_0 = -1$. The previsible process is constructed as follows

$$\begin{aligned}
A_n &= \sum_{k=1}^{n} \mathbb{E}\left[-M_k + M_{k-1} | \mathcal{F}_{k-1}\right] \\
&= \sum_{k=1}^{n} \mathbb{E}\left[X_1 \cdot \ldots \cdot X_{k-1}(1 - X_k) | \mathcal{F}_{k-1}\right] \\
&= \sum_{k=1}^{n} X_1 \cdot \ldots \cdot X_{k-1} \mathbb{E}\left[1 - X_k | \mathcal{F}_{k-1}\right] \quad (4.17)
\end{aligned}$$

Since $q_k \geq 0$, $\forall k$ we can easily find that

$$\mathbb{P}(A_n - A_{n-1} \geq 0) = \mathbb{P}(X_1 \cdot \ldots \cdot X_{n-1} \cdot \mathbb{E}[1 - X_n | \mathcal{F}_{n-1}] \geq 0) = 1 \quad (4.18)$$

We conclude that the previsible part of the decomposition is a.s. non-decreasing.

We find in the next step the martingale part N_n:

$$\begin{aligned} N_n - M_0 &= -M_n - A_n \\ &= -X_1 \cdot \ldots \cdot X_n - \sum_{k=1}^{n} X_1 \cdot \ldots \cdot X_{k-1} \mathbb{E}[1 - X_k | \mathcal{F}_{k-1}] \end{aligned} \quad (4.19)$$

Then N_n is indeed a martingale since

$$\begin{aligned} \mathbb{E}[N_n - N_{n-1} | \mathcal{F}_{n-1}] &= \mathbb{E}[X_1 \cdot \ldots \cdot X_{n-1}(1 - X_n) - X_1 \cdot \ldots \cdot X_{n-1} \cdot \mathbb{E}[1 - X_n | \mathcal{F}_{n-1}] | \mathcal{F}_{n-1}] \\ &= \mathbb{E}[X_1 \cdot \ldots \cdot X_{n-1}(\mathbb{E}[X_n | \mathcal{F}_{n-1}] - X_n) | \mathcal{F}_{n-1}] \\ &= 0 \end{aligned} \quad (4.20)$$

Furthermore since $N_0 = 0$ we have:

$$\begin{aligned} N_n &= \sum_{k=1}^{n} N_k - N_{k-1} \\ &= \sum_{k=1}^{n} X_1 \cdot \ldots \cdot X_{k-1}(\mathbb{E}[X_k | \mathcal{F}_k] - X_k) \end{aligned} \quad (4.21)$$

The total reward can be rewritten as:

$$\begin{aligned} Y_n &= \underbrace{\sum_{k=1}^{n} R_k \cdot (N_k - N_{k-1})}_{Y_{n,A}} + \underbrace{\sum_{k=1}^{n} R_k \cdot (A_k - A_{k-1})}_{Y_{n,B}} \quad (4.22) \\ &= \sum_{k=1}^{n} R_k \cdot X_1 \cdot \ldots \cdot X_{k-1}(\mathbb{E}[X_k | \mathcal{F}_{k-1}] - X_k) \\ &+ \sum_{k=1}^{n} R_k \cdot X_1 \cdot \ldots \cdot X_{k-1} \cdot (1 - \mathbb{E}[X_k | \mathcal{F}_{k-1}]) \end{aligned} \quad (4.23)$$

where $Y_{n,A}$ is a martingale (null at $n = 0$) if $\{R_n\}$ is a bounded non-negative previsible process and $Y_{n,B}$ is a non-dereasing previsible process null at 0. Then we can conclude that $\{Y_n\}$ is a sub-martingale null at 0. □

4.3. The ARQ Stopping Problem without Cost

The above result implies that the expected value of the next step conditioned on the knowledge we have about the process up to this point $\mathbb{E}[Y_{n+1}|\mathcal{F}_n]$ is always greater or equal to (at least as good as) the present gain Y_n.

The use of the optimality equation (recursion) (4.7) and the principle of optimality (4.8) presented in section 4.1 under the condition (4.3) provide the optimal stopping rule T. If furthermore the stopping time is a.s. finite (4.2) we say that an optimal stopping rule exists. We investigate in the following whether and when the above conditions hold true in the case of $\{Y_n\}$.

Lemma 4. If the sequence $\{R_n\}$ is non-negative and upper-bounded by some value $K > 0$ then $\mathbb{E}\left[\sup_n Y_n^+\right] < \infty$.

Proof. Observe how the process $\{Y_n\}$ is constructed. It equals null as long as $X_1 = \ldots = X_n = 1$ (no ACK received) and takes the value R_k if $X_k = 0$ and $X_{n<k} = 1$, in other words when the first ACK occurs in step k. Furthermore for $n' > k$ it remains constant and equal to R_k. Then the supremum of the process equals R_k with probability $\mathbb{P}(\sup_n Y_n^+ = R_k) = q_k \cdot \prod_{j=1}^{k-1} p_j$. Furthermore it holds $R_k \leq K$, $\forall k \in \mathbb{N}_+$.

$$\begin{aligned}
\mathbb{E}\left[\sup_n Y_n^+\right] &= \sum_{k=1}^{\infty} R_k \cdot \mathbb{P}\left(\sup_n Y_n^+ = R_k\right) \\
&= \sum_{k=1}^{\infty} R_k \cdot q_k \cdot \prod_{j=1}^{k-1} p_j \\
&\leq K \cdot \sum_{k=1}^{\infty} q_k \cdot \prod_{j=1}^{k-1} p_j \\
&= K \cdot \left(1 - \prod_{k=1}^{\infty} p_k\right) \leq K < \infty
\end{aligned} \quad (4.24)$$

□

Lemma 5. For $\{R_n\}$ non-negative and upper-bounded by some $K > 0$ and given that $\mathbb{P}(\tau < \infty) = 1$ the maximum expected reward equals

$$V := \sup_\tau \mathbb{E}[Y_\tau] = \sum_{k=1}^{\infty} \left(R_k \cdot q_k \prod_{j=1}^{k-1} p_j\right) \leq K \quad (4.25)$$

Proof. The stopped process is written as $\{Y_{\tau \wedge n}\}$ where $a \wedge b$ is the inf operator. We have seen in Lemma 3 that the process $\{Y_n\}$ under the conditions of Lemma 5 is a submartingale. Furtermore from [Wil91], every stopped submartinagle is a submartingale. In (4.23) the reward was decomposed into a martingale $\{Y_{n,A}\}$ null at zero ($Y_{0,A} = 0$) and a non-decreasing previsible process $\{Y_{n,B}\}$, namely $Y_n = Y_{n,A} + Y_{n,B}$. Using Doob's Optional-Stopping Theorem [Wil91] under the condition $\mathbb{P}(\tau < \infty) = 1$ we have for the martingale part that $\mathbb{E}[Y_{\tau \wedge n,A}] = 0$.

$$\begin{aligned} \mathbb{E}[Y_{\tau \wedge n}] &= \mathbb{E}[Y_{\tau \wedge n,A}] + \mathbb{E}[Y_{\tau \wedge n,B}] \\ &= 0 + \mathbb{E}[Y_{\tau \wedge n,B}] \end{aligned} \qquad (4.26)$$

But $\{Y_{n,B}\}$ is a non-decreasing process meaning that $\mathbb{P}(Y_{n,B} - Y_{n-1,B} \geq 0) = 1$. Then $Y_{n,B} \uparrow Y_B = \lim_{n \to \infty} Y_{n,B}$ and from the monotone convergence theorem $\mathbb{E}[Y_{n,B}] \uparrow \mathbb{E}[Y_B]$. Furthermore $\mathbb{E}[Y_{\tau \wedge n,B}] \leq \mathbb{E}[Y_{n,B}] \leq \mathbb{E}[Y_B]$, for all $n \in \mathbb{N}_+$. We conclude that $\forall \tau \in C$ it holds

$$\begin{aligned} \sup_\tau \mathbb{E}[Y_\tau] &= \mathbb{E}[Y_B] \\ &= \mathbb{E}\left[\sum_{k=1}^\infty R_k \cdot X_1 \cdot \ldots \cdot X_{k-1} \cdot (1 - \mathbb{E}[X_k|\mathcal{F}_{k-1}])\right] \\ &= \sum_{k=1}^\infty R_k \cdot (1 \cdot \mathbb{P}(X_{m<k} = 1) \cdot (1 - \mathbb{E}[X_k|X_{m<k} = 1])) \\ &= \sum_{k=1}^\infty R_k \cdot q_k \left(\prod_{j=1}^{k-1} p_j\right) = \mathbb{E}\left[\sup_n Y_n^+\right] \leq K \qquad (4.27) \end{aligned}$$

□

We have further seen in section 4.1 that in the case of monotone problems the optimal stopping rule can be simplified by the use of the one-stage look-ahead rule (4.10). We prove in the following the monotone character of the ARQ stopping problem without cost.

Lemma 6. The ARQ problem without cost having reward $\{Y_n\}$ is a monotone stopping problem as defined in (4.9), under the following two conditions

  i. The process $\{R_n\}$ is a positive, bounded by some $K > 0$, previsible process

  ii. The stepwise success probabilities q_n given in (3.5) are all positive - probably up to a

4.3. The ARQ Stopping Problem without Cost

step k for which it holds $q_{m \geq k} = 0$.

Then the one-stage look-ahead rule is the optimal stopping rule.

Proof. Suppose that for some n it holds $\mathbb{E}[Y_n|\mathcal{F}_{n-1}] \leq Y_{n-1}$. Then for the next step we have

$$\begin{aligned}
\mathbb{E}[Y_{n+1}|\mathcal{F}_n] &= \mathbb{E}[Y_n + (Y_{n+1} - Y_n)|\mathcal{F}_n] \\
&= Y_n + \mathbb{E}[Y_{n+1} - Y_n|\mathcal{F}_n] \\
&= Y_n + \mathbb{E}[R_{n+1}(M_n - M_{n+1})|\mathcal{F}_n] \\
&= Y_n + \mathbb{E}[R_{n+1} \cdot X_1 \cdot \ldots \cdot X_n \cdot (1 - X_{n+1})|\mathcal{F}_n] \\
&= Y_n + R_{n+1} \cdot X_1 \cdot \ldots \cdot X_n \cdot \mathbb{E}[1 - X_{n+1}|\mathcal{F}_n]
\end{aligned} \quad (4.28)$$

- If for some $k \leq n$ it occurs $X_k = 0$ then from the right hand side of (4.28) $\mathbb{E}[Y_{n+1}|\mathcal{F}_n] = Y_n + 0 \leq Y_n$ and the monotone behaviour holds.

- If it holds $X_1 = \ldots = X_n = 1$ then $\mathbb{E}[Y_{n+1}|\mathcal{F}_n] = Y_n + R_{n+1} \cdot q_{n+1}$. But then - using the inequality for $n-1$: $\mathbb{E}[Y_n|\mathcal{F}_{n-1}] = Y_{n-1} + R_n \cdot q_n \leq Y_{n-1} \Rightarrow R_n \cdot q_n = 0$. Then if $\{R_n\}$ is positive then it should hold $q_n = 0$. Furthermore $Y_{n-1} = 0$. The monotone behaviour can then hold if $q_{n+1} = 0$.

□

In the cases that conditions (i) and (ii) of Lemma 6 do not hold, for example if there exists a $q_k = 0$ but $q_{k+1} \neq 0$, the one-stage look-ahead rule is not optimal. In [Fer00] it is suggested that a better solution is the following: Use the 1-stage look-ahead rule until it tells you to stop and then use the 2-stage look-ahead rule. This can be generalized for k-stage look-ahead rules, generally defined as

$$T_k = \min\left\{n \in \mathbb{N}_+ : Y_n \geq \mathbb{E}\left[V_{n+1}^{(n+k)}|\mathcal{F}_n\right]\right\} \quad (4.29)$$

Problem 1. For the ARQ problem without cost, having transition probability matrix given in (3.5), where $0 < q_n \leq 1$, and reward function $Y_n = \sum_{k=1}^n R_k \cdot (M_{k-1} - M_k)$, where $\{R_k\}$ is a positive previsible process, bounded by some $K > 0$, find an optimal stopping rule that brings a maximum expected reward equal to $V := \sup_\tau \mathbb{E}[Y_\tau] = \sum_{k=1}^\infty \left(R_k \cdot q_k \prod_{j=1}^{k-1} p_j\right)$.

Theorem 15. The optimal stopping rule T for problem 1 is to continue retransmissions until an ACK is received and then immediately stop. If the chain is ergodic $\mathbb{P}(T < \infty) = 1$.

Proof. Using the optimality of the one-stage look-ahead rule under the conditions of problem 1, we have from (4.28) that the condition to stop is as follows

$$\begin{aligned} \mathbb{E}[Y_{n+1}|\mathcal{F}_n] &= Y_n + R_{n+1} \cdot X_1 \cdot \ldots \cdot X_n \cdot \mathbb{E}[1 - X_{n+1}|\mathcal{F}_n] \leq Y_n \\ &\Rightarrow R_{n+1} \cdot X_1 \cdot \ldots \cdot X_n \cdot \mathbb{E}[1 - X_{n+1}|\mathcal{F}_n] \leq 0 \end{aligned} \qquad (4.30)$$

- If for some $k \leq n$ it holds $X_k = 0$ (ACK is received) the left hand side in (4.30) equals 0 and the rule is satisfied.

- If $X_1 = \ldots = X_n = 1$ (no ACK received up to n) the left hand side is given by $R_{n+1} \cdot \mathbb{E}[1 - X_{n+1}|X_1 = \ldots = X_n = 1] = R_{n+1}q_{n+1} \leq 0$ impossible under the conditions in problem 1.

Then we reach the conclusion that we have to continue until the first ACK is received and immediately stop. We will have to wait for finite steps a.s. if the chain is ergodic. This is guaranteed under the conditions given in Theorems 8 - 10. Observe that in Problem 1, the constraint $q_n > 0$, $\forall n$ suffices to guarantee ergodicity by Theorem 8. □

Remark 2. The above result could be directly deduced from Lemma 3 and the one-stage look-ahead rule, since the reward Y_n has been shown to be a submartingale. The current analysis will prove much more helpful however in more complicated situations when the costs and penalties are taken into account in the next section.

Remark 3. It was shown in (4.25) that waiting until the first ACK provides a maximum expected reward equal to $V = \sum_{k=1}^{\infty} \left(R_k \cdot q_k \prod_{j=1}^{k-1} p_j \right)$. This is equal to the short-term system goodput for $R_n = \frac{\mu}{n}$ given in (3.11). In the case that all success probabilities are constant and equal to $0 < q < 1$, V takes the form as in (2.6)

$$\begin{aligned} V &= \sum_{k=1}^{\infty} \left(\frac{R}{k} \cdot q \cdot p^{k-1} \right) \\ &= R \frac{p-1}{p} \log(1-p) \end{aligned} \qquad (4.31)$$

4.4 The ARQ Stopping Problem with Cost

This is a result that was more or less expected, since V equals the maximal reward obtained up to first ACK and is not related to the long-term goodput where the process is allowed to evolve for $t \to \infty$.

4.4 The ARQ Stopping Problem with Cost

The investigation is further continued to derive a solution of the ARQ stopping problem with cost, where the reward-cost function is given by

$$Y_n^C = \sum_{k=1}^{n} R_k \cdot (M_{k-1} - M_k) - \sum_{k=1}^{n} D_k - M_n \cdot \delta_n \qquad (4.32)$$

as described in section 4.2.

Lemma 7. If the sequence $\{R_n\}$ is non-negative and upper-bounded by some value $K > 0$ and $\{\delta_n\}$, $\{D_n\}$ are non-negative sequences, then

$$\mathbb{E}\left[\sup_n \left(Y_n^C\right)^+\right] < \infty \qquad (4.33)$$

Proof. Since $\left(Y_n^C\right)^+ \leq Y_n$ a.s. under the conditions of Lemma 4 for the sequences $\{R_n\}$, $\{\delta_n\}$ and $\{D_n\}$, it obviously holds $\sup_n \left(Y_n^C\right)^+ \leq \sup_n Y_n^+ \Rightarrow \mathbb{E}\left[\sup_n \left(Y_n^C\right)^+\right] \leq \mathbb{E}\left[\sup_n Y_n\right] < \infty$. □

Theorem 16. The maximum expected reward for the ARQ problem with cost equals

$$\begin{aligned} V^C : &= \sup_\tau \mathbb{E}\left[Y_\tau^C\right] \\ &= \sum_{k=1}^{n^*} q_k \prod_{j=1}^{k-1} p_j \cdot \left(R_k - \sum_{j=1}^{k} D_j\right) - \delta_{n^*} \cdot \prod_{k=1}^{n^*} p_k \end{aligned} \qquad (4.34)$$

where

$$n^* = \min\left\{n : q_n \leq \frac{D_n - \delta_{n-1} + \delta_n}{R_n + \delta_n}\right\} - 1 \qquad (4.35)$$

under the condition that the sequences $\{R_n\}$, $\{D_n\}$, $\{\delta_n\}$ and $\{q_n\}$ should have a behaviour such that for each $n \in \mathbb{N}_+$

$$q_n \leq \frac{D_n - \delta_{n-1} + \delta_n}{R_n + \delta_n} \quad \Rightarrow \quad q_{n+1} \leq \frac{D_{n+1} - \delta_n + \delta_{n+1}}{R_{n+1} + \delta_{n+1}} \qquad (4.36)$$

Chapter 4. Truncating ARQ Protocols using Optimal Stopping

Proof. We follow the analysis as in the proof of Lemma 5. Furthermore we make use of the decomposition of Y_n given in (4.16) and of $-M_n$ in (4.22), (4.23).

$$\begin{aligned} Y_n^C &= Y_n - \sum_{k=1}^n D_k - M_n \cdot \delta_n \\ &= Y_{n,A} + Y_{n,B} - \sum_{k=1}^n D_k + \delta_n \left(N_n + A_n - M_0 \right) \\ &= \left(Y_{n,A} + \delta_n \cdot N_n \right) + \left(Y_{n,B} + \delta_n \cdot A_n \right) - \left(\sum_{k=1}^n D_k + \delta_n \cdot M_0 \right) \end{aligned}$$

where the term in the first parenthesis is a martingale, in the second one a non-negative non-decreasing previsible process whereas in the third a non-negative non-decreasing sequence. Note $M_0 = 1$. Applying expectation, we get for any stopping time $\tau \in C$

$$\begin{aligned} \mathbb{E}\left[Y_{\tau \wedge n}^C \right] &= 0 + \mathbb{E}_\tau \left[Y_{\tau \wedge n, B} + \delta_{\tau \wedge n} \cdot A_{\tau \wedge n} \right] - \mathbb{E}_\tau \left[\sum_{k=1}^{\tau \wedge n} D_k + \delta_{\tau \wedge n} M_0 \right] \\ &= \mathbb{E}_\tau \left[\sum_{k=1}^{\tau \wedge n} (R_k + \delta_{\tau \wedge n}) \cdot X_1 \cdot \ldots \cdot X_{k-1} \left(1 - \mathbb{E}\left[X_k | \mathcal{F}_{k-1} \right] \right) \right] \\ &\quad - \mathbb{E}_\tau \left[\sum_{k=1}^{\tau \wedge n} D_k + \delta_{\tau \wedge n} \right] \end{aligned} \quad (4.37)$$

The expected value is the difference of two non-decreasing terms w.r.t. n. For the first term, given a stopping rule τ the following inequality holds true $\mathbb{E}_\tau \left[Y_{\tau \wedge n, B} + \delta_{\tau \wedge n} \cdot A_{\tau \wedge n} \right] \leq \mathbb{E}\left[Y_{n,B} + \delta_n \cdot A_n \right] \uparrow \lim_{n \to \infty} \mathbb{E}\left[Y_{n,B} + \delta_n \cdot A_n \right]$. Since the same behaviour holds also for the second term, there definitely exists some point $n = n^*$ for which $\mathbb{E}\left[Y_{\tau \wedge n}^C \right]$ is maximized, for each τ.

Let us try two examples of stopping rules. The first is $\tau_1 := \min\{n \in \mathbb{N}_+ : X_n = 0\}$ which implies that the process is stopped as in the case with no cost in the previous section, after the first ACK. This gives us the following expectation in the above expression, for $n \to \infty$

4.4. The ARQ Stopping Problem with Cost

$$\begin{aligned}
\mathbb{E}\left[Y_{\tau_1}^C\right] &= \sum_{\tau=1}^{\infty} \mathbb{P}\left[\tau_1 = \tau\right] \cdot \left[-\delta_{\tau_1} + \sum_{k=1}^{\tau_1}(R_k + \delta_{\tau_1}) \cdot X_1 \cdot \ldots \cdot X_{k-1}(1 - \mathbb{E}\left[X_k | \mathcal{F}_{k-1}\right]) - D_k\right] \\
&= \sum_{\tau=1}^{\infty} \mathbb{P}\left[X_1 = \ldots = X_{\tau-1} = 1, X_\tau = 0\right] \cdot \left(-\delta_\tau + (R_\tau + \delta_\tau) - \sum_{k=1}^{\tau} D_k\right) \\
&= \sum_{\tau=1}^{\infty}\left(q_\tau \prod_{j=1}^{\tau-1} p_j \cdot R_\tau\right) - \sum_{\tau=1}^{\infty}\left(q_\tau \prod_{j=1}^{\tau-1} p_j \cdot \sum_{k=1}^{\tau} D_k\right)
\end{aligned}$$

The second rule is deterministic $\tau_2 := \{n \in \mathbb{N}_+ : n = n^*\}$.

$$\mathbb{E}\left[Y_{\tau_2}^C\right] = \sum_{k=1}^{n^*}\left(q_k \prod_{j=1}^{k-1} p_j \cdot R_k\right) - \sum_{k=1}^{n^*} D_k - \delta_{n^*} \prod_{k=1}^{n^*} p_k$$

It is obvious that for the rule τ_1 the "reward" part is greater in expectation, since $n \to \infty$. On the other hand, using rule τ_2 the "loss" due to the terms D_k, $k = 1, \ldots, n^*$ and δ_{n^*} can be lower than in τ_1 by appropriate choice of n^*. One can expect then that the optimal rule should be some combination of rules τ_1 and τ_2.

Furthermore, the expectation of the payoff in (4.37) without considering stopping times, has the monotone behaviour as explained in (4.9) under the condition that the sequences $\{R_n\}, \{D_n\}$ and $\{\delta_n\}$ are such that

$$q_n \leq \frac{D_n - \delta_{n-1} + \delta_n}{R_n + \delta_n} \Rightarrow q_{n+1} \leq \frac{D_{n+1} - \delta_n + \delta_{n+1}}{R_{n+1} + \delta_{n+1}} \qquad (4.38)$$

To see this

$$\begin{aligned}
\mathbb{E}\left[Y_n^C | \mathcal{F}_{n-1}\right] &= \mathbb{E}\left[Y_{n-1}^C + \left(Y_n^C - Y_{n-1}^C\right) | \mathcal{F}_{n-1}\right] \leq Y_{n-1}^C \Rightarrow \\
Y_{n-1}^C &\overset{(4.32)}{\geq} Y_{n-1}^C - D_n + R_n \mathbb{E}\left[M_{n-1} - M_n | \mathcal{F}_{n-1}\right] + \mathbb{E}\left[M_{n-1}\delta_{n-1} - M_n\delta_n | \mathcal{F}_{n-1}\right] \Rightarrow \\
D_n &\geq R_n \cdot X_1 \ldots X_{n-1}(1 - \mathbb{E}\left[X_n | \mathcal{F}_{n-1}\right]) + X_1 \ldots X_{n-1}\mathbb{E}\left[\delta_{n-1} - X_n\delta_n | \mathcal{F}_{n-1}\right]
\end{aligned}$$

This last inequality holds true if

i. For some $k \leq n - 1$ we have $X_k = 0$ (ACK received)

ii. For all $X_k = 1$, $k \leq n - 1$ (no ACK received). Then the condition is simplified to

$$R_n \cdot q_n + \delta_{n-1} - p_n \cdot \delta_n \leq D_n \Rightarrow q_n \leq \frac{D_n - \delta_{n-1} + \delta_n}{R_n + \delta_n}$$

The "monotonicity" of the stopping rule actually means that given a stopping rule τ there is a gain in expectation by increasing n, as long as

$$q_n > \frac{D_n - \delta_{n-1} + \delta_n}{R_n + \delta_n}$$

For $n' > n^* = \min\left(n : q_n \leq \frac{D_n - \delta_{n-1} + \delta_n}{R_n + \delta_n}\right) - 1$, the expectation either stays constant or decreases.

From the above the maximum expected reward equals the expression given in (4.34), under the condition (4.38). □

Problem 2. For the ARQ problem with cost, where the ARQ process forms an ergodic chain having transition probabilty matrix given in (3.5) and the reward-cost function is given by Y_n^C in (4.32), $\{R_n\}$ being a positive previsible process, bounded by some $K > 0$ and $\{\delta_n\}$, $\{D_n\}$, $\{q_n\}$ that satisfy (4.36), find an optimal stopping rule that brings a maximum expected reward.

Corollary 3. The optimal stopping rule for Problem 2 is to continue retransmissions until the first ACK is received or the inequality $q_n \leq \frac{D_n - \delta_{n-1} + \delta_n}{R_n + \delta_n}$ is satisfied for the first time. In other words

$$T = \min\left\{n \in \mathbb{N}_+ : X_n = 0 \text{ or } q_n \leq \frac{D_n - \delta_{n-1} + \delta_n}{R_n + \delta_n}\right\} \tag{4.39}$$

Furthermore, the maximum expected reward equals V^C given in (4.34).

Remark 4. The average short-term goodput for the optimally truncated ARQ protocol is obviously less than or equal to the case for non-truncated protocols, given in (3.11)

$$g_{s-t}^{tr} = \mathbb{E}_{tr}\left[\frac{\mu}{n}\right] = \sum_{k=1}^{n^*}\left(\frac{\mu}{k} \cdot q_k \cdot \prod_{j=1}^{k-1} p_j\right) \tag{4.40}$$

This however does not hold for the long-term case. To see this, from the expression (3.9)

4.5. Special Truncation Cases

$$g_{l-t}^{tr} = \frac{\mu}{1 + \sum_{k=1}^{n^*} \prod_{j=1}^{k} p_j} \geq \frac{\mu}{1 + \sum_{k=1}^{\infty} \prod_{j=1}^{k} p_j} = g_{l-t} \qquad (4.41)$$

This implies that truncating ARQ protocols can be very beneficial for the long-term system goodput, as well as the packet delay, at the cost of a percentage of *dropped* packets.

Remark 5. The expected time up to first *dropping* $\mathbb{E}\left[N_{1^{st} \, drop}\right]$ is a rather important measure for the performace of the truncated protocol. This can be derived using a variation of the so called *generalized geometric distribution* [PGP83], [PM86] with success probabilities q_k, instead of q constant. This is the distribution of the number of transmissions and retransmissions until n^* consequtive NACKs occur.

$$\mathbb{E}\left[N_{1^{st} \, drop}\right] = \frac{1 + p_1 + \ldots + p_1 \ldots p_{n^*-1}}{p_1 \ldots p_{n^*}} \qquad (4.42)$$

The expectation is obviously increasing with n^*.

4.5 Special Truncation Cases

In the current section the main result for the optimal stopping time is used, as expressed in (4.39) to investigate some special cases of truncation. We note here that the stopping time T as expressed in (4.39), truncates the infinite chain to a finite length n^* equal to (4.35).

1. No retransmissions allowed - the Case $T = 1$

    This case occurs when stopping takes place after the first transmission and the retransmission process is not activated. This is optimal when

    $$q_1 \leq \frac{D_1 - \delta_0 + \delta_1}{R_1 + \delta_1} \stackrel{\delta_0 := 0}{=} \frac{D_1 + \delta_1}{R_1 + \delta_1} \qquad (4.43)$$

    The expected reward equals

    $$V_1^C := (R_1 + \delta_1) \cdot q_1 - \delta_1 - q_1 \cdot D_1 \qquad (4.44)$$

2. No communications allowed - the Case $T = 0$

Observe that if the value of V_1^C in (4.44) above is negative not even the first transmission should take place since a cost is more probable that a reward in case of packet transmission.

$$0 > (R_1 + \delta_1) \cdot q_1 - \delta_1 - q_1 \cdot D_1 \Rightarrow q_1 < \frac{\delta_1}{R_1 + \delta_1 - D_1} \quad (4.45)$$

For $D_1 > R_1$ (and $D_1 < R_1 + \delta_1$) we get - from (4.45) - the condition $q_1 \leq 1$. Hence regardless the value of success probability for the first transmission no communications should take place.

3. Infinite truncation time - Equivalence of the ARQ problems with and without cost

   The case where no truncation should take place occurs when the inequality

$$q_n > \frac{D_n - \delta_{n-1} + \delta_n}{R_n + \delta_n} \quad (4.46)$$

holds true $\forall n \in \mathbb{N}_+$. As an example, given $\delta_n = \delta$ and $D_n = D$ constant costs, and furthermore $q_n = q$, the condition reduces to $q > \frac{D}{R_n + \delta}, \forall R_n$. Hence, if $q > \frac{D}{\delta}$ then no finite truncation time exists.

4.6 Applications

In the following, the optimal stopping criterion given in (4.39) will be applied in specific protocols wirh success probabilities $\{q_n\}$ and reward sequences $\{R_n\}$. The section will also provide a better understanding of the impact of choice for the costs $\{D_n\}$ and $\{\delta_n\}$.

4.6.1 Constant success probabilities $q_n = q$

In the case of ARQ retransmissions a message is sent at each time slot/trial with a rate μ bits/sec/Hz. The effective coding rate or instantaneous goodput (3.12) for the current message equals $\frac{\mu}{n}$. The rewards for the process in this case are simply $R_n = \frac{\mu}{n}$. The probability of success per retransmission is considered constant as in chapter 2. This is true e.g. when no CSI, rather only the channel statistics, are available to the receiver and the supported rate μ and consumed power ρ remain constant until an ACK is received. The error probability

4.6. Applications

$p = 1 - q$ can then be expressed as the outage probability of the channel. Furthermore assume constant costs $D_n = D$ and $\delta_n = \delta$.

The aim is to find the optimal stopping rule in order to support a predefined rate μ [b/sec/Hz]. The optimality of the one-step look-ahead rule should initially be shown. The criterion in (4.39) clearly holds true for the specific choice of R_n, D_n, δ_n and q_n of interest

$$q \leq \frac{D}{\frac{\mu}{n} + \delta} \Rightarrow q \leq \frac{D}{\frac{\mu}{n+1} + \delta}$$

The solution of (4.35) is rewritten as

$$n^* = \left\lceil \frac{\mu}{\frac{D}{q} - \delta} \right\rceil - 1 \qquad (4.47)$$

where $\lceil \ldots \rceil$ is the ceiling function, under the condition that $\frac{D}{q} - \delta > 0$. Furthermore the stopping rule can be $T > 0$ - in other words transmissions are allowed - if as shown in (4.45) - $q \geq \frac{\delta}{\mu+\delta-D}$. The above two conditions on D and μ, given R and q provide the range of D given μ

$$\delta \cdot q < D \leq \mu \cdot q - \delta \cdot p \qquad (4.48)$$

Since the left hand side is increasing with δ and the right hand side decreasing, we have that δ cannot exceed an upper value given by the equality $\delta q = \mu q - \delta p$. The solution provides the range of values for δ

$$0 \leq \delta \leq \mu \cdot q \qquad (4.49)$$

The solution in (4.47) implies that given δ and D costs that lie within the accepted range (4.48) and (4.49) the optimal number of retransmissions increases when the supported rate and/or the success probability increases. On the other hand given a desired rate to support as well as a success probability, the optimal number of retransmissions decreases as the cost per trial D increases or the terminal cost δ decreases. This is reasonable since a higher cost per trial discourages a high truncation number while a higher dropping cost urges for more attempts until the message is eventually correctly received.

The above remarks can be illustrated in the following two plots. In the first figure $\delta = 0.5$ is kept fixed while the optimal number of retransmissions as a function of D is shown to vary for different supported rates $\mu = \{1\ 2\ 4\ 6\}$. The constant success probability equals $q = 0.9$. Given that the delay cost is fixed to $D = 1.5$ the optimal length of the protocol equals $n^*_{\mu=2} = 1$, $n^*_{\mu=4} = 3$, $n^*_{\mu=6} = 5$. In the second figure the same scenario is repeated with $\delta = 0$, where the packet dropping is cost free. The optimal length of the protocol is in all cases reduced, in particular $n^*_{\mu=2} = 1$, $n^*_{\mu=4} = 2$, $n^*_{\mu=6} = 3$.

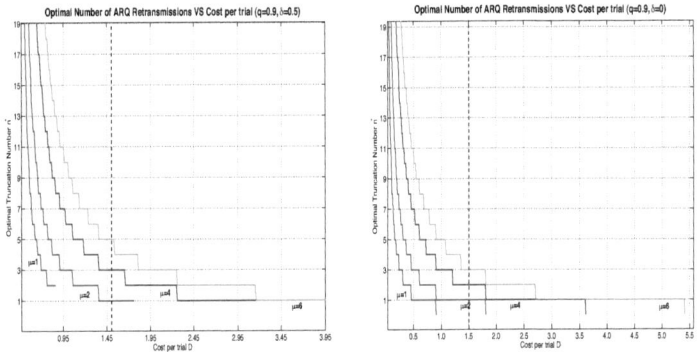

Figure 4.1: Optimal truncation for $q_n = q$ vs delay cost for (a) positive, (b) zero penalty

4.6.2 Exponentially increasing success probabilities $q_n = 1 - e^{-\gamma n}$

The error probability, given that finite length codewords are transmitted, can be shown to be upper-bounded by an exponential function. The error exponent indicates how fast the error vanishes as the length of the code tends to infinity. It is shown in [GNG] that in the case of incremental redundancy H-ARQ the error exponent of the upper bound, keeping the code length fixed and finite increases proportional to the number of retransmissions. Then $p_n \leq e^{-\gamma \cdot n}$, $\gamma > 0$. Generally γ depends on the supported rate μ. In the following we assume that the error probability equals this upper bound. Furthermore we consider a sequence of discounted gains $\mu \cdot e^{-\beta \cdot n}$ where the gain μ which is the transmission rate per trial, is stepwise discounted by a factor $e^{-\beta} < 1$. Consider $\delta = 0$ and constant $D_n = D$ in what follows.

The function $q(x) \cdot R(x) := (1 - e^{-\gamma x}) \cdot \mu e^{-\beta x}$ is monotone decreasing for $\gamma, \beta > 0$ that

4.6. Applications

satisfy the following relation

$$\frac{1}{\mu}\frac{dq(x)R(x)}{dx} = -\beta e^{-\beta x}\left(1 - e^{-\gamma x}\right) + e^{-\beta x}\gamma e^{-\gamma x} < 0 \;\Rightarrow\; \beta > (\beta + \gamma)e^{-\gamma x} \quad (4.50)$$

The above relation should hold $\forall x \in \mathbb{N}_+$, $x = 1, 2, \ldots$ hence it just has to hold for $x = 1$. Then the $\gamma, \beta > 0$ should satisfy

$$\beta + \gamma < \beta \cdot e^{\gamma} \quad (4.51)$$

so that the 1-stage look-ahead rule to be optimal. Then stopping occurs for the minimum n that satisfies the following inequality

$$n^* = \min\left\{n \in \mathbb{N}_+ : 1 \leq \frac{D}{\mu}e^{\beta n} + e^{-\gamma n}\right\} - 1 \quad (4.52)$$

Given that transmissions occur if the expected gain at the first step is non-negative,

$$0 \leq D \leq \mu \cdot e^{-\beta}\left(1 - e^{-\gamma}\right) \quad (4.53)$$

is the range for D. In the following keeping $\gamma, \beta > 0$ fixed so that they satisfy (4.51) (specifically $\beta = 0.8, \gamma = 0.5$) the optimal truncation lengths are plotted for different supported rates $\mu = \{1\ 2\ 4\ 6\}$ and zero dropping penalty, as a function of cost D. The cost varies within (4.53). Given that $D = 0.2$ we get $n^*_{\mu=2} = 2$, $n^*_{\mu=4} = 3$, $n^*_{\mu=6} = 4$.

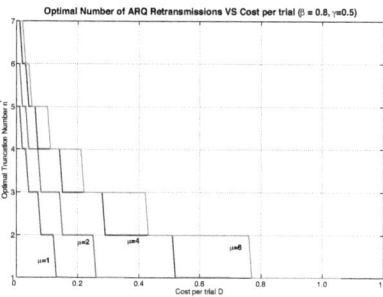

Figure 4.2: Optimal truncation for $q_n = 1 - e^{-\gamma n}$ vs delay cost for zero penalty

Observe that although $q_1 = 1 - e^{-1} = 0.632 < 0.9 = q$ in the previous application, here the optimal maximum number of retransmissions is reduced even for low cost per trial D due to the exponentially decreasing behaviour of the error probability.

Chapter 5

Dynamic Truncation of ARQ Protocols in a Single Queue

Queuing aspects of the ARQ problem are introduced in the current chapter. As was shown in Chapter 4 the delay and dropping cost directly influences the optimal truncation time of the protocols. In a single queue incorporating retransmissions the delay issue becomes very important since this affects the average packet waiting time as well as the maximum incoming supported data rate in the buffer. On the other hand a certain number of retransmissions should be allowed so that each packet can have certain chance to be received successfully. In other words there is a trade-off between delay, packet dropping average and reliability.

In the current chapter, we use again the well known ARQ model of the previous two chapters where the per effort sequence of success probabilities $\{q_k\}$ in each ARQ round, up to correct packet reception, is a priori defined. The protocol is considered to evolve at the server of a single queue where packet transmission is repeated each time an error occurs, with an effort-dependent predefined probability. A Markov Decision Problem (MDP) is formulated [Put05] where at each state a controller has to choose between *continuing* retransmitting the erroneous packet and *dropping* it to proceed to the first transmission of the next packet waiting. The investigation here seeks optimal policies that provide the best possible tradeoff between average delay and percentage of dropped packets. These are two conflicting performance mesures both of great importance concerning QoS guarantees.

The current work is a small contribution to numerous efforts of optimizing ARQ protocols, in the sense of reducing necessary retransmission efforts with economy in resources at the same time. The current literature contains a large amount of publications related to this matter. Power control per retransmission to maximize the throughput of ARQ protocols has been investigated in [Tun07]. In [VTH] the optimal sequence of redundancy per effort is found based on a dynamic programming formulation. The work in [AB02] investigates the optimal power and rate allocation among SW-ARQ retransmissions, that guarantees average delay or throughput constraints, based on some CSI at the receiver. A trade-off between throughput and energy consumption when the CSI is partially observable is given in [ZW02] through a Markov Decision Process formulation, while delay- and overflow-aware joint rate and power adaptation for type-I and power adaptation for type-II HARQ protocols is provided in [DKB07] and [KDB06b], respectively. Rather noteworthy is also the work in [BS06], where the average delay of a single user wireless communication system, which includes a buffer and incorporates SW-ARQ retransmissions in cases of outage, is optimized by combined power and rate control.

5.1 A Discrete Time Markov Decision Problem

Consider a single-server communications system, where data packets arriving from some information source are stored in a buffer while waiting for service. The time axis is considered time-slotted, all slots having equal length T. During each slot an arrival of a new packet may occur (or not) with probability $0 < \lambda \leq 1$ (respectively $1 - \lambda$), i.e. the arrival process is Bernoulli. The service rate is considered constant $\mu = 1$ [$packet/slot$] and a transmission of a packet is *attempted* at the end of each time slot under the condition that the queue is not empty. For error correction an SW-ARQ protocol with transition matrix as described in chapters 3 and 4 is used in the DLC layer, which retransmits erroneous detected packets. The success probabilities depend on the current retransmission effort Z_n on slot n and are denoted by $q(Z_n)$ (or $p(Z_n)$ for the error probabilities respectively). The transition probability matrix is given in (3.5).

For the single queue system under study, in case an ACK is fed back, $X_n = 0$, the packet is removed from the buffer and the first transmission of the next packet waiting in queue takes place during the next time slot (a nonpreemptive First Come First Serve service principle is assumed). On the other hand in case a NACK is fed back, $X_n = 1$, two possibilities are available. Either the transmission of the erroneous packet is repeated at the next slot or the packet is discarded (we say that *dropping* occurs) and the next waiting packet is served during the $n + 1$-th slot. The two possibilities may be considered as *actions*

5.1. A Discrete Time Markov Decision Problem

that a controller may choose in order to optimize the system performance. For each slot we introduce further the pair of random variables (u_n, Z_n) which describe the state of the system at each slot. The first one provides the current queue length whereas the second one the current retransmission number at slot n. The pair takes values within the set $\mathbb{N} \times \mathbb{N}_+$.

Consider a Markov Decison Process [Put05] $\{\mathcal{T}, \mathcal{S}, \mathcal{A}, \mathbb{P}(\bullet|S, A), c(S, A)\}$, with set of decision epochs $\mathcal{T} = \{0, 1, \ldots\}$ and state space $\mathcal{S} = \mathbb{N} \times \mathbb{N}_+$ the state in our problem being the pair of random variables $S_n = (u_n, Z_n)$ at n, as explained previously. The action set is binary $\mathcal{A} = \{0, 1\}$, $\mathbb{P}(\bullet|S, A)$ is the transition probability distribution of the system which is conditioned on the current state and action, whereas c is the system cost per time slot as a function of state S_n and action A_n, $c : \mathbb{N} \times \mathbb{N}_+ \times \{0, 1\} \to \mathbb{R}_+$.

At the beginning of slot n the state information $S_n = (u_n, Z_n)$ is available at the controller. Using possibly some further knowledge over the entire history $h_n = \{S_1, A_1, \ldots, A_{n-1}\}$ of previous states and actions taken the controller may choose between two actions, which will affect the packet transmission at the *next slot* $n + 1$. Either choose action $A_n = 0$ and continue the retransmission cycle in the next slot in case a NACK is fed back ($X_n = 0$), or choose $A_n = 1$ and break the retransmission cycle irrespective of the result of decoding of the transmitted packet in n and begin in $n + 1$ a new transmission round. It is important to note that choosing action $A_n = 1$ does not necessarily result in a dropped packet. The packet will be actually dropped only in the case of $X_n = 0$, with probability $p(Z_n)$.

$$A_n = \begin{cases} 0 & \text{retransmit at } n + 1 \text{ if } X_n = 0 \\ 1 & \text{start a new ARQ round at } n + 1, \forall X_n \end{cases} \quad (5.1)$$

During slot n an arrival of a new packet $\alpha_n \in \{0, 1\}$ may occur with probability λ, which will be taken into account for the value of the queue length at the next state, together with the result of the current packet transmission X_n. Then for the state evolution $S_{n+1} = (u_{n+1}, Z_{n+1})$

$$u_{n+1} = \begin{cases} [u_n - X_n]^+ + \alpha_n & \text{if } A_n = 0 \\ [u_n - 1]^+ + \alpha_n & \text{if } A_n = 1 \end{cases} \quad (5.2)$$

$$Z_{n+1} = \begin{cases} 1 + Z_n(1 - X_n) & \text{if } A_n = 0 \\ 1 & \text{if } A_n = 1 \end{cases} \quad (5.3)$$

The state transition probabilities are given in table 5.1.

Table 5.1: Transition probabilities $\mathbb{P}(\bullet|S_n, A)$ of the MDP under study

	$\alpha_n = 0$	$\alpha_n = 1$
$A_n = 0$, $u_n > 0$		
ACK	$\mathbb{P}((u_n - 1, 1)|S_n, 0) = q(Z_n)(1 - \lambda)$	$\mathbb{P}((u_n, 1)|S_n, 0) = q(Z_n)\lambda$
NACK	$\mathbb{P}((u_n, Z_n + 1)|S_n, 0) = p(Z_n)(1 - \lambda)$	$\mathbb{P}((u_n + 1, Z_n + 1)|S_n, 0) = p(Z_n)\lambda$
$A_n = 1$, $u_n > 0$	$\mathbb{P}((u_n - 1, 1)|S_n, 1) = 1 - \lambda$	$\mathbb{P}((u_n, 1)|S_n, 1) = \lambda$
$A_n = \{0, 1\}$, $u_n = 0$	$\mathbb{P}((u_n, Z_n)|S_n, A_n) = 1 - \lambda$	$\mathbb{P}((u_n + 1, 1)|S_n, A_n) = \lambda$

In the scenario described above two measures are rather important for the performance of the single queue system. The first one is the average *queue length* $\bar{u}$, related by Little's Law $\bar{u}/\lambda = W$ [Kle75] to the average packet delay (average waiting time per packet in the buffer) W. The second is the average number of dropped packets $\bar{\Delta}$ in case the ARQ cycle is interrupted by the controller prior to correct packet reception. A cost per time slot is introduced which equals the actual queue length while dropping is incorporated as a penalty, weighted by $\delta > 0$. As mentioned earlier, dropping occurs if action $A_n = 1$ is chosen at slot n *and* the packet is not correctly received ($X_n = 0$), i.e. the dropping cost term equals $\delta A_n (1 - X_n)$. Since the result of decoding is known at the end of each slot and the cost per slot depends on the random variable X_n, we use an expected cost, the expectation taken over the random disturbance X_n (see [Put05, p. 20]). In this way the cost can be written as a function of the state and action taken

$$c_\delta((u_n, Z_n), A_n) = \mathbb{E}_{X_n}[u_n + \delta A_n(1 - X_n)]$$
$$= u_n + \delta A_n p(Z_n) \quad (5.4)$$

For the case where $u_n = 0$ we have $c_\delta((0, Z_n), A_n) = 0$. In this work we aim to find a *deterministic stationary policy*, which is optimal among all history dependent randomized policies $\pi \in \Pi^{HR}$, in terms of minimizing the average expected cost, for a certain value of the weight $\delta > 0$ and initial state S_o

$$J_\pi(\delta, S_o) := \limsup_{N \to \infty} \frac{1}{N} \mathbb{E}^{\pi, S_o}\left[\sum_{n=1}^{N} c_\delta(S_n, A_n)\right] \quad (5.5)$$

The optimal strategy $\pi^* \in \Pi^{HR}$ is defined as the one that satisfies $J_{\pi^*}(\delta, S_o) = J^*(\delta, S_o) \leq$

5.1. A Discrete Time Markov Decision Problem

$J_\pi(\delta, S_o)$, $\forall \pi \in \Pi^{HR}$. Since the model can be easily verified to be *unichain* [Put05, pp. 348-354] (the transition matrix of each stationary deterministic policy has a single positive recurrence class) the optimal average cost (if it exists) is equal for all initial states S_o.

Remark 6. Observe that the transition probabilities and instantaneous cost are both stationary. The latter is unbounded since there may exist (possibly finitely many) sample paths $\{S_n\}$ for which the queue length can increase beyond any bound. For stable queues such paths occur with probability 0.

Remark 7. We use the lim sup definition of the average cost instead of lim, in case the optimal policy of the minimization problem is not stationary [Put05, pp.332-334]. The lim sup average cost may not be finite $\forall \pi \in \Pi^{HR}$. This situation occurs in two cases:

- The chain in (3.5) is non-ergodic (see part b. of Theorem 10 for conditions of non-ergodicity) and hence there exists a non-zero probability for the ARQ chain never to return to state $Z_n = 1$

- The arrival rate is greater than the minimum average service rate, where the latter equals the long-term system goodput without truncation (3.9) and (3.10). In this case $\lambda > \mu_{\min} := \left(1 + \sum_{k=1}^{\infty} p_1 \ldots p_k\right)^{-1}$.

In such cases the queue is unstable and all queue states are recurrent-null or transient. However there definitely exist policies for which the average cost remains finite. Two such families important for the investigation are provided in the following.

Definition 2. A stationary policy truncating the ARQ protocol up to the K-th retransmission number for all states of the queue length so that $A_n = 1$ if $Z_n \geq K$ is called a **K-retransmitting policy**.

Definition 3. A policy which does not allow retransmissions after a certain queue length L, in other words $A_n = 1$, if $u_n \geq L$ is called an **L-truncating policy**.

These two families definitely stabilize the single queue system. To see this:

- By appropriate choice of K in the first case we can have an increase of the system goodput due to truncation (4.41) in which case $g_{l-t}^{tr} := \hat{\mu} = \left(1 + \sum_{k=1}^{K-1} p_1 \ldots p_k\right)^{-1} \geq \lambda > \mu_{\min}$.

- For the second case, since the arrival process is Bernoulli, the queue length remains upper bounded by L (see (5.2) for $A_n = 1$ and $u_n = L$) for all n.

Generally speaking, the control problem at hand provides δ-dependent control policies which optimally drop packets after a certain retransmission number, taking into account the current queue state, to keep the queue a.s. finite and provide the optimal trade-off between average queue length and average number of packets discarded. In other words the solution of the problem provides the optimal success probability choice $q(S_n)$, given information $\mathcal{I} = \{u, Z\}$ from the MAC and DLC layers respectively.

The minimization problem in (5.5) can be further understood as a Lagrangian methodology [MMS86] to solve the following constrained minimization problem

$$\begin{aligned}\min \quad & \bar{u}^\pi := \limsup \tfrac{1}{N}\mathbb{E}^\pi \sum_{n=1}^{N} u_n \\ \text{s.t.} \quad & \bar{\Delta}^\pi := \liminf \tfrac{1}{N}\mathbb{E}^\pi \sum_{n=1}^{N} A_n p(Z_n) \le \Delta\end{aligned} \quad (5.6)$$

where Δ is an upper bound constraint on the average number of dropped packets whereas the objective function is the average queue length. The minimization takes place over the set of admissible policies $\Pi_\Delta^{HR} := \{\pi \in \Pi^{HR} : \bar{\Delta}^\pi \le \Delta\}$. In (5.5) δ is simply the non-negative Lagrange multiplier which is related to the actual value of Δ. This approach has already been used in [BG02] and [GKS03]. We provide the following theorem which explains in which way the Lagrangian problem in (5.5) solves the constrained problem in (5.6). For a proof the reader is referred to [MMS86].

Theorem 17. *Any policy $\pi^* \in \Pi^{HR}$ which (a) yields the expressions $\bar{u}^{\pi^*}$ and $\bar{\Delta}^{\pi^*}$ as limits, (b) meets the constraint with equality $\bar{\Delta}^{\pi^*} = \Delta$, and (c) solves the unconstrained problem in (5.5) for some $\delta > 0$ necessarily solves the problem in (5.6).*

5.1.1 Vanishing Discount Approach

The solution of Markov Decision Problems with an average expected cost criterion is often studied in the literature [Put05], [Sch93], [ABFG 93] as the limit behavior of β-discounted models when the discount factor $0 < \beta < 1$ tends to 1. The *discounted expected cost* related to (5.5) is given by

5.1. A Discrete Time Markov Decision Problem

$$J_{\pi,\beta}(\delta, S_o) := \lim_{N \to \infty} \mathbb{E}^{\pi, S_o} \left[\sum_{n=1}^{N} \beta^{n-1} c_\delta(S_n, A_n) \right] \tag{5.7}$$

$J_\beta^*(\delta, S_o) \leq J_{\pi,\beta}(\delta, S_o), \forall \pi \in \Pi^{HR}$ is the solution of the discounted minimization problem. We will from now on neglect the dependence on δ in notation. From [Put05, Th.8.10.7 and 8.10.9] we have that under mild assumptions which can be verified for the problem at hand

$$J^* = \lim_{\beta \to 1} (1 - \beta) J_\beta^*(S_o) \tag{5.8}$$

for all $S_o \in S$. Furthermore, from [Sch93, Th.3.8] the optimal policy π^* is also *limiting discount optimal* in the sense that there exists a sequence $\beta_m \to 1$ and $S_m \to S$ such that $\pi^*(S) = \lim_{m \to \infty} \pi_{\beta_m}(S_m), \forall S \in S$. We may thus focus on discounted cost optimality and get the solution to the average cost problem passing to the limit $\beta \to 1$ in (5.8). See also the works [LK84] and [ZW02] for a similar approach.

For the discounted expected cost problem we provide the Bellman optimality equations of the problem at hand, for each state $S := (u, Z) = (l, k) \in S$. These are written as $J_\beta^*(l, k) = T J_\beta^*(l, k)$ [Put05, pp. 146-148], where for $l \geq 1$

$$\begin{aligned} T J_\beta^*(l, k) = \min\{ \quad & l + \beta \cdot \left[q_k (1 - \lambda) J_\beta^*(l-1, 1) + q_k \lambda J_\beta^*(l, 1) + \right. \\ & \left. + p_k (1 - \lambda) J_\beta^*(l, k+1) + p_k \lambda J_\beta^*(l+1, k+1) \right], \\ & l + \delta p_k + \beta \left[\lambda J_\beta^*(l, 1) + (1 - \lambda) J_\beta^*(l-1, 1) \right] \quad \} \end{aligned} \tag{5.9}$$

and for $l = 0$ respectively

$$T J_\beta^*(0, k) = \beta \left[\lambda J_\beta^*(1, k) + (1 - \lambda) J_\beta^*(0, k) \right] \tag{5.10}$$

5.1.2 Existence of Stationary Optimal Policies

The existence of an optimal solution to the above equations is guaranteed by the Banach fixed-point theorem [Put05, Th.6.2.3] conditioned that the Dynamic Programming operator $T : \mathcal{B}_w(S) \to \mathcal{B}_w(S)$ is a contraction mapping. $\mathcal{B}_w(S)$ is a Banach space

Chapter 5. Dynamic Truncation of ARQ Protocols in a Single Queue

with the weighted supremum norm $\|J\|_w = \sup_{S \in \mathcal{S}} w(S)^{-1} |J(S)|$, w is a positive lower bounded real-valued function on $\mathcal{S}$ and TJ_β^* is given in (5.9), (5.10). Problems arise when the costs are unbounded as in our case where the cost is a linear function of the queue length which may increase to infinity. In such cases, a unique solution to the equation $J_\beta^*(l,k) = TJ_\beta^*(l,k)$, $\forall (l,k)$ definitely exists [Put05, Th.6.10.4, Prop.6.10.5] under the following two conditions. $\forall A \in \mathcal{A}, S \in \mathcal{S}$

Cond.1: $\exists v < \infty$: $\sup_{A \in \mathcal{A}} |c(S,A)| \leq vw(S)$

Cond.2: $\exists Q > 0$: $\sum_{j \in \mathcal{S}} \mathbb{P}(j|S,A) w(j) \leq w(S) + Q$

These suggest that the maximum cost per stage grows no faster than $w(S)$ and that the upward expected change of the system state is bounded. *For our problem these may be easily verified, using the function $w(S) = u + \delta$.* Furthermore, using [Put05, Th.6.2.10.(a)], since $\mathcal{S}$ is discrete and $\mathcal{A}$ is finite we can prove that

Theorem 18. *There exists a stationary deterministic average cost optimal policy $\pi^* : \mathcal{S} \to \mathcal{A}$ as well as a constant lim sup-optimal cost J^*, for the minimization problem in (5.5), which can be derived by the solution of the related expected β-discounted cost problem in (5.7), passing to the limit $\beta \to 1$.*

Considering, from the previous, that the optimal policy of the average cost problem is limiting discount optimal the same holds for the average cost optimal policy as well.

5.1.3 Algorithmic Solution for Finite State Space: Value Iteration

Using value iteration algorithms [Put05, pp.160-161, pp. 364-365] we may find deterministic ϵ-optimal policies π_ϵ for both discounted and average cost problems. The algorithms may be implemented *only for finite state spaces*. We argue here that bounding the maximum queue length by $L_{\max} > 0$ and the maximum allowable retransmission number by $K_{\max} > 0$ provides an approximation to the optimal solution which is improving as $K_{\max}$ and $L_{\max}$ increase. In the following we provide two examples (see Table 5.2) of average cost optimal policies for two different sets of success probabilities $\{q_k\}, k = 1, \ldots, K$. The discount factor is $\beta = 0.99$ and the Bernoulli arrival rate is $\lambda = 0.4$ [packet/sec]. A maximum number of $K_{\max} = 6$ retransmissions is allowed, the queue length is restricted to a length of $L_{\max} = 10$ packets and the packets are *discarded* ($A = 1$) if either $K_{\max}$ or $L_{\max}$ is exceeded. In the first

5.2. Structural Properties of Optimal Policies

Table 5.2: Value Iteration for Finite State Space

	Example A							Example B					
L/K	1	2	3	4	5	6	L/K	1	2	3	4	5	6
0	0	0	0	0	0	0	0	0	0	0	0	0	0
1	0	0	1	1	1	1	1	0	0	0	0	0	1
2	0	1	1	1	1	1	2	1	1	0	0	0	1
3	1	1	1	1	1	1	3	1	1	1	1	1	1
4	1	1	1	1	1	1	4	1	1	1	1	1	1
5	1	1	1	1	1	1	5	1	1	1	1	1	1
6	1	1	1	1	1	1	6	1	1	1	1	1	1
7	1	1	1	1	1	1	7	1	1	1	1	1	1
8	1	1	1	1	1	1	8	1	1	1	1	1	1
9	1	1	1	1	1	1	9	1	1	1	1	1	1
10	1	1	1	1	1	1	10	1	1	1	1	1	1

example a *monotone decreasing* sequence of success probabilities is utilized, specifically having values $q_k = e^{-0.9k}$, $k = 1,\ldots,6$ and weight $\delta = 40$. In the second one the sequence of success probabilities is *monotone increasing*, $q_k = 1 - e^{-0.9k}$, $k = 1,\ldots,6$ and $\delta = 4$, an approach also found in section 4.6.2. The examples above suggest that the optimal policy for the actual problem behaves monotonically in both the *l*- (queue length-) and *k*- (number of efforts-) axis. Observe that the 1's in the last column which imply dropping and break the monotonicity in the second example are simply a result of the finite state-space and will not appear in the actual problem with countably infinite state space.

5.2 Structural Properties of Optimal Policies

As the examples in Table 5.2 indicate, for certain senarios, if it is optimal to drop at some specific queue length and number of retransmissions, it is as well optimal to drop for all greater queue states for the same k. The same result may be found for a fixed queue length and varying the retransmission number. The analysis that follows will be based on the assumption that the sequence of conditional success probabilities $\{q_k\}$ is either monotone non-increasing or non-decreasing w.r.t. k. This assumption is supported by results in [6] for the optimal choice of conditional success probabilities in the SW-ARQ case as well as by the fact that $\{q_k\}$ is definitely non-decreasing in the case of Type-II HARQ.

Remark 8. To get a feeling why the optimal sequence of success probabilities may be non-increasing, which may be intuitively not clear, consider an ARQ protocol which does not include packet combining (Simple SW-ARQ or Type-I HARQ). Then $q_1 \geq q_2 \geq \ldots$

describes policies where more resources are invested at initial efforts aiming to minimize the expected number of retransmissions, while resources are reduced for economy as the retransmission effort index increases, since time-diversity is utilized. To better understand this, the average retransmission number equals $\mathbb{E}[N_{ACK}] = 1 + \sum_{k=1}^{\infty} p_1 \ldots p_k$ where it is clear that the initial conditional error probabilities play a stronger role in determining the expectation. Furthermore, the probability of k erroneous retransmissions of a packet equals $\mathbb{P}(Z_{n+k} = k+1 | Z_n = 1) = p_1 \ldots p_k$ where the time diversity reduces the product with each effort.

The following notation is introduced as a means to reduce space. For value iteration we write $TJ^n(l,k) = \min\{C_1^{n+1}(l,k), C_2^{n+1}(l,k)\}$, while the index n is replaced by π_n for the policy iteration steps. The dependence of the values $J_\beta^n(l,k)$ in value iteration and $J_{\pi_n,\beta}$ in policy iteration on β is omitted.

$$C_1^{n+1}(l,k) = l + \beta[q_k(1-\lambda)J^n(l-1,1) + q_k\lambda J^n(l,1) +$$
$$+ p_k(1-\lambda)J^n(l,k+1) + p_k\lambda J^n(l+1,k+1)]$$
$$C_2^{n+1}(l,k) = l + \delta p_k + \beta[\lambda J^n(l,1) + (1-\lambda)J^n(l-1,1)]$$

Furthermore, rather useful for the analysis is the difference

$$\Delta J^{n+1}(l,k) = C_1^{n+1}(l,k) - C_2^{n+1}(l,k) =$$
$$-\delta p_k + \beta\{p_k(1-\lambda)[J^n(l,k+1) - J^n(l-1,1)]$$
$$+ p_k\lambda[J^n(l+1,k+1) - J^n(l,1)]\} \qquad (5.11)$$

For the proofs value and policy iteration methods [Put05] are used. Monotonicity properties of the value function are initially provided. We always choose $J^0(l,k) = 0, \forall (l,k)$.

Lemma 8. For all states $(l,k) \in S$, $m \in \mathbb{N}$ and iteration steps $n \in \{0, 1, \ldots\}$

$$J^n(l,k) \leq J^n(l+m,k) \qquad (5.12)$$

Proof. The inequality holds for $n = 0$. Suppose now that inequality (5.12) holds for iteration step n. We have to show that it also holds for $J^{n+1}(l,k) = TJ^n(l,k)$, the Dynamic

5.2. Structural Properties of Optimal Policies

Programming T operator given in (5.9), (5.10). We distinguish between two cases. (i) Suppose first that the 'continue' term $C_1^{n+1}(l+m,k)$ is the minimum. Then

$$TJ^n(l+m,k) \stackrel{(i)}{=} C_1^{n+1}(l+m,k) \stackrel{(5.12)}{\geq}$$
$$C_1^{n+1}(l,k) \geq \min\left\{C_1^{n+1}(l,k), C_2^{n+1}(l,k)\right\} = TJ^n(l,k)$$

(ii) In the same fashion, we may reach the above inequality when the 'drop' term is the minimum, by replacing $C_1^{n+1}(l+m,k)$ by $C_2^{n+1}(l+m,k)$. Thus we have proved that in both cases $J^{n+1}(l,k) \leq J^{n+1}(l+m,k)$. □

Lemma 9. For all states $(l,k) \in S$, $m \in \mathbb{N}$, iteration steps $n \in \{0,1,\ldots\}$ and monotone non-increasing conditional success probabilities $q_1 \geq q_2 \geq \ldots$, it holds

$$J^n(l,k) \leq J^n(l,k+m) \tag{5.13}$$

Proof. The inequality certainly holds for $n = 0$. Suppose hypothesis (5.13) holds for some n. We proceed as in the proof of Lemma 8 and distinguish here the cases where the minimum in $TJ^n(l,k+m)$ is (i) $C_1^{n+1}(l,k+m)$ and (ii) $C_2^{n+1}(l,k+m)$. Then

$$TJ^n(l,k) \leq C_1^n(l,k) \stackrel{(\alpha)}{\leq} C_1^n(l,k+m) \stackrel{(i)}{=} TJ^n(l,k+m)$$

(α) holds from hypothesis (5.13), $p_{k+m} \geq p_k$ and under the condition that $(1-\lambda)[J^n(l,k+1) - J^n(l-1,1)] + \lambda[J^n(l+1,k+1) - J^n(l,1)] \geq 0$, which is satisfied since $J^n(l,k+1) \stackrel{(5.12)}{\geq} J^n(l-1,k+1) \stackrel{(5.13)}{\geq} J^n(l-1,1)$. For the case (ii) the above inequality also holds replacing index 1 by 2 and (α) is simply due to (5.12) and the fact that $p_{k+m} \geq p_k$. Then we have proved that if $q_1 \geq q_2 \geq \ldots$ inequality (5.13) holds $\forall n$. □

Combining the above two Lemmata we obtain

Corollary 4. For all states $(l,k) \in S$, $n \in \{0,1,\ldots\}$ and non-increasing success probabilities

$$J^n(l,k) \stackrel{(5.12)}{\geq} J^n(l-1,k) \stackrel{(5.13)}{\geq} J^n(l-1,1) \tag{5.14}$$

We may now state the following Theorem.

Theorem 19. Suppose $q_1 \geq q_2 \geq \ldots$ Given a fixed queue state l and varying the retransmission number k, the optimal policy is of threshold type, i.e. there exists a critical state $(l, \hat{k}_l)$, possibly dependent on l, such that dropping is optimal for $k \geq \hat{k}_l$, while continue is optimal for $k < \hat{k}_l$.

Proof. Suppose continue is optimal for some state $(l, \hat{k})$. Then using (5.11), $\Delta J^{n+1}(l, \hat{k}) \leq 0$. We have to prove that $\Delta J^{n+1}(l, k) \leq 0$, $\forall k < \hat{k}$. From (5.11) we have

$$(1 - \lambda) J^n (l, \hat{k} + 1) + \lambda J^n (l + 1, \hat{k} + 1)$$
$$\leq \delta/\beta + (1 - \lambda) J^n (l - 1, 1) + \lambda J^n (l, 1)$$

Using Lemma 9 for the left handside we have $(1 - \lambda) J^n (l, k + 1) + \lambda J^n (l + 1, k + 1) \leq (1 - \lambda) J^n (l, \hat{k} + 1) + \lambda J^n (l + 1, \hat{k} + 1)$, $\forall k < \hat{k}$. Then there exists some maximum threshold value $\hat{k}_l \geq 1$ such that continue is optimal for $k < \hat{k}_l$ and drop for $k \geq \hat{k}_l$. The result holds $\forall n$ and consequently also for the optimal discounted and average reward policy as $n \to \infty$. □

Given now a fixed retransmission effort and varying the queue state, in all examples tested by the authors (see also the examples in the previous paragraph) the threshold form of the optimal policy also holds. In other words, given k there exists some threshold queue length $\hat{l}_k$ such that dropping is optimal $\forall l \geq \hat{l}_k$ and continuing retransmissions is optimal for $l < \hat{l}_k$. To show this the following inequality would suffice to hold $\forall k = 1, 2, \ldots$ and $l \geq 1$.

$$J^n (l, 1) + J^n (l, k + 1) \leq J^n (l + 1, k + 1) + J^n (l - 1, 1)$$

Unfortunately, a proof of this statement was not possible to be attained and is left as a *conjecture*. Instead we can prove the following important property, for β less but sufficiently close to 1. Remember from Theorem 18 that this is exactly the case of interest for the average cost problem in (5.5).

Theorem 20. For the optimal policy π^* there exists a threshold queue length $l_{\pi^*}^{th}$ such that $\forall l \geq l_{\pi^*}^{th}$, $\forall k$, it holds that $\pi^* (l, k) = 1$ and

$$J_{\pi^*} (l + 2, 1) - J_{\pi^*} (l + 1, 1) \geq J_{\pi^*} (l + 1, 1) - J_{\pi^*} (l, 1) \quad (5.15)$$

$$J_{\pi^*} (l + 1, 1) \geq J_{\pi^*} (l, 1) \quad (5.16)$$

5.2. Structural Properties of Optimal Policies

Furthermore, the threshold on the l-axis is always finite and more specifically

$$l_{\pi^*}^{th} \leq \delta \max_k q_{k+1} + (1 - \lambda) \tag{5.17}$$

Proof. Consider a sequence π_n, $n = 1, 2, \ldots$ of policies generated by the policy iteration algorithm which converge to π^* as $n \to \infty$. Suppose that for a certain n the policy π_n has the following two properties

- **P1**: π_n has a threshold value $l_{\pi_n}^{th}$ such that $\pi_n(l, k) = 1$, $\forall l \geq l_{\pi_n}^{th}$ & $\forall k$

- **P2**: The following inequalities hold $\forall l \geq l_{\pi_n}^{th}$

$$J_{\pi_n}(l+2, 1) - J_{\pi_n}(l+1, 1) \geq J_{\pi_n}(l+1, 1) - J_{\pi_n}(l, 1)$$
$$J_{\pi_n}(l+1, 1) \geq J_{\pi_n}(l, 1)$$

(P2) implies that the difference $J_{\pi_n}(l, 1) - J_{\pi_n}(l - 1, 1)$ is non-negative and monotone non-decreasing for the specified set of states.

We will prove that each policy π_n as defined above, generates a π_{n+1} with properties (P1) and (P2). Thus the optimal policy π^* exhibits the same behavior.

We have to first provide a π_0 that satisfies (P1) and (P2) and initialize the policy iteration for $n = 0$. Consider the policy π_0 for which $\pi_0 = 1$, $\forall (l, k)$. In this case only a single transmission is allowed irrespective of the queue and retransmission state. The policy obviously has threshold $l_{\pi_0}^{th} = 0$ and property (P1) is fulfilled. We have to show that property (P2) also holds. This we will prove by induction. We first show the following inequality is satisfied for $l = 0$

$$J_{\pi_0}(2, 1) - J_{\pi_0}(1, 1) \geq J_{\pi_0}(1, 1) - J_{\pi_0}(0, 1)$$

Since always dropping takes place, using the expressions for $C_2(2, 1), C_2(1, 1), C_2(0, 1)$

$$J_{\pi_0}(2,1) - J_{\pi_0}(1,1) = 1 + \beta\lambda(J_{\pi_0}(2,1) - J_{\pi_0}(1,1)) +$$
$$\beta(1-\lambda)(J_{\pi_0}(1,1) - J_{\pi_0}(0,1))$$
$$J_{\pi_0}(1,1) - J_{\pi_0}(0,1) = 1 + \delta p_1$$

Solving the first equation for $J_{\pi_0}(2,1) - J_{\pi_0}(1,1)$ and taking the difference of the above two

$$J_{\pi_0}(2,1) - 2J_{\pi_0}(1,1) + J_{\pi_0}(0,1) =$$
$$\frac{\beta(1-\lambda)(1+\delta p_1) + 1}{1-\beta\lambda} - 1 - \delta p_1$$

The above expression is positive if $\beta \geq 1 - \frac{1}{1+\delta p_1}$ hence the inequality holds for β sufficiently close to 1, as δ ranges from 0 to ∞. Given now that the inequality in (P2) holds for $l-1$ by induction we prove it also holds for l.

$$J_{\pi_0}(l+2,1) - J_{\pi_0}(l+1,1) \overset{(P1)}{=}$$
$$\frac{1}{1-\beta\lambda}[1 + \beta(1-\lambda)(J_{\pi_0}(l+1,1) - J_{\pi_0}(l,1))] \overset{l-1,(P2)}{\geq}$$
$$\frac{1}{1-\beta\lambda}[1 + \beta(1-\lambda)(J_{\pi_0}(l,1) - J_{\pi_0}(l-1,1))] \overset{(P1)}{=}$$
$$J_{\pi_n}(l+1,1) - J_{\pi_n}(l,1)$$

Furthermore, since $J_{\pi_0}(l+1,1) - J_{\pi_0}(l,1) \geq J_{\pi_0}(1,1) - J_{\pi_0}(0,1) \geq 0$, the second inequality of (P2) is also proved to be true. Thus, both properties hold for π_0 which we can use to initialize the policy iteration algorithm.

We further continue using induction. Choose $l \geq l_{\pi_n}^{th} + 1$. Since we assume that π_n satisfies (P1) and (P2), this implies that dropping occurs for the states $(l+1, k+1)$ as well as $(l, k+1)$.

5.2. Structural Properties of Optimal Policies

$$
\begin{aligned}
J_{\pi_n}(l, k+1) - J_{\pi_n}(l-1, 1) &= \\
C_2^{\pi_n}(l, k+1) - J_{\pi_n}(l-1, 1) &= \\
l + \delta p_{k+1} + \lambda \left[\beta J_{\pi_n}(l, 1) - J_{\pi_n}(l-1, 1) \right] &+ \\
(1-\lambda) \left[\beta J_{\pi_n}(l-1, 1) - J_{\pi_n}(l-1, 1) \right] &
\end{aligned}
\tag{5.18}
$$

Observe now that for $\beta \to 1$, the last term vanishes. Since the difference $J_{\pi_n}(l, 1) - J_{\pi_n}(l-1, 1)$ is by (P2) non-decreasing for $l \geq l_{\pi_n}^{th} + 1$ then so is $J_{\pi_n}(l, k+1) - J_{\pi_n}(l-1, 1)$. The same result holds for all queue states greater than l.

Let us now proceed to the policy improvement step of the policy iteration algorithm. Using the previous observation and the expression of $\Delta J_{\pi_{n+1}}(l, k)$ from (5.11)

$$
\begin{aligned}
\Delta J_{\pi_{n+1}}(l, k) &= \\
-\delta p_k + \beta p_k (1-\lambda) \left[J_{\pi_n}(l, k+1) - J_{\pi_n}(l-1, 1) \right] &+ \\
+ \beta p_k \lambda \left[J_{\pi_n}(l+1, k+1) - J_{\pi_n}(l, 1) \right] &
\end{aligned}
\tag{5.19}
$$

we conclude that $\Delta J_{\pi_{n+1}}(l, k)$ is non-decreasing w.r.t. l.

We cannot include the case $l = l_{\pi_n}^{th}$ in the above analysis since we do not know whether $J_{\pi_n}(l_{\pi_n}^{th}+1, 1) - J_{\pi_n}(l_{\pi_n}^{th}, 1) \geq J_{\pi_n}(l_{\pi_n}^{th}, 1) - J_{\pi_n}(l_{\pi_n}^{th}-1, 1)$. This we have first to prove. We know that for π_n dropping occurs for $l = l_{\pi_n}^{th}$ and $l = l_{\pi_n}^{th} + 1$. Then

$$
J_{\pi_n}\left(l_{\pi_n}^{th}+1, 1\right) - J_{\pi_n}\left(l_{\pi_n}^{th}, 1\right) \stackrel{(P1)}{=}
$$
$$
\frac{1}{1-\beta\lambda} \left[1 + \beta(1-\lambda)\left(J_{\pi_n}\left(l_{\pi_n}^{th}, 1\right) - J_{\pi_n}\left(l_{\pi_n}^{th}-1, 1\right) \right) \right] \stackrel{\beta \to 1}{\Rightarrow}
$$

$$
\stackrel{\beta \to 1}{\Rightarrow} J_{\pi_n}\left(l_{\pi_n}^{th}+1, 1\right) - J_{\pi_n}\left(l_{\pi_n}^{th}, 1\right) = J_{\pi_n}\left(l_{\pi_n}^{th}, 1\right) - J_{\pi_n}\left(l_{\pi_n}^{th}-1, 1\right) + \frac{1}{1-\lambda}
\tag{5.20}
$$

and we conclude $\Delta J_{\pi_{n+1}}\left(l_{\pi_n}^{th}+1, k\right) \geq \Delta J_{\pi_{n+1}}\left(l_{\pi_n}^{th}, k\right)$.

Then for each k there exists a threshold $l_{\pi_{n+1}}^{th}(k)$ such that $\pi_{n+1}(l, k) = 1$ for $l \geq l_{\pi_{n+1}}^{th}(k)$.

Since the expression in (5.18) is non-decreasing and unbounded, the threshold for π_{n+1} is always finite $\forall k$. We have $l^{th}_{\pi_{n+1}} = \max\left\{\max_k l^{th}_{\pi_{n+1}}(k), l^{th}_{\pi_n}\right\}$. The threshold defined in this way may either stay the same as in π_n or increase (by a finite number of queue states). This we will use to verify (P2) for π_{n+1}.

Since the threshold satisfies $l^{th}_{\pi_{n+1}} \geq l^{th}_{\pi_n}$ then for all (l,k) with $l \geq l^{th}_{\pi_{n+1}}$, dropping occurs according to policy π_n. Then $\forall l \geq l^{th}_{\pi_{n+1}}$ it holds

$$2 \cdot J_{\pi_{n+1}}(l+1,1) = 2 \cdot C_2^{\pi_{n+1}}(l+1,1) \overset{(P2)}{\leq} C_2^{\pi_{n+1}}(l+2,1) + C_2^{\pi_{n+1}}(l,1)$$
$$= J_{\pi_{n+1}}(l+2,1) + J_{\pi_{n+1}}(l,1)$$

and the inequality follows assuming that (P2) holds for π_n. For the second inequality we have for $l \geq l^{th}_{\pi_{n+1}}$, using the expression in (5.18) and $\beta \approx 1$

$$J_{\pi_{n+1}}(l+1,1) - J_{\pi_{n+1}}(l,1) \overset{(P1)}{=}$$
$$C_2^{\pi_{n+1}}(l+1,1) - C_2^{\pi_{n+1}}(l,1) \overset{(5.18)}{=}$$
$$1 + [\lambda J_{\pi_n}(l+1,1) + (1-\lambda)J_{\pi_n}(l,1)] -$$
$$[\lambda J_{\pi_n}(l,1) + (1-\lambda)J_{\pi_n}(l-1,1)] \overset{(5.20)}{=}$$
$$J_{\pi_n}(l+1,1) - J_{\pi_n}(l,1) \overset{(P2)}{\geq} 0$$

Hence policy π_{n+1} shares the same properties as π_n and the proof of the first part of the proposition is complete. For the second part using (5.19) together with (5.18) and $\beta \approx 1$ we can write after some manipulations

$$\Delta J_{\pi_{n+1}}\left(l^{th}_{\pi_n}, k\right) = -\delta p_k + p_k\left(l^{th}_{\pi_n} + \delta p_{k+1}\right)$$
$$+ p_k\lambda\left[J_{\pi_n}\left(l^{th}_{\pi_n}+1,1\right) - J_{\pi_n}\left(l^{th}_{\pi_n},1\right)\right] - p_k(1-\lambda)$$

If $\Delta J_{\pi_{n+1}}\left(l^{th}_{\pi_n}, k\right) \geq 0$ then the threshold will stay the same for π_{n+1}. This reduces to

$$l^{th}_{\pi_n} + \lambda\left[J_{\pi_n}\left(l^{th}_{\pi_n}+1,1\right) - J_{\pi_n}\left(l^{th}_{\pi_n},1\right)\right] \geq \delta q_{k+1} + (1-\lambda)$$

5.2. Structural Properties of Optimal Policies

The left handside is an expression that depends only on $l_{\pi_n}^{th}$, whereas the right handside is a constant that depends on system parameters. The inequality will definitely be satisfied $\forall k$ for $l_{\pi_n}^{th} \geq \delta \max_k q_{k+1} + (1 - \lambda)$, since by the second inequality of (P2) the difference in brackets is non-negative. Then using the policy iteration algorithm the aforementioned threshold cannot be exceeded and the threshold is always finite.

□

Theorem 21. It is always optimal to drop - in other words $l_{\pi^*}^{th} = 0$, if

$$\delta \leq \frac{1 + \lambda/(1 - \lambda) + \lambda}{1 + (1 - \lambda)p_1 - \min_{k \neq 1} p_k} \quad (5.21)$$

The bound is non-decreasing with λ and tends to ∞ for $\lambda \to 1$.

Proof. Assume that the policy iteration algorithm is initialized by π_0 as described in the proof of the previous theorem. The optimal policy will be $\pi^* = \pi_0$ if the threshold $l_{\pi_n}^{th} = 0$, $\forall n$. Asssume that $\pi_n = \pi_0$. Let us first bound the difference $\Delta J_{\pi_{n+1}}(l, k)$. Since $J_{\pi_n}(l+1, 1) - J_{\pi_n}(l, 1)$ is increasing in l, $\forall l \geq 0$, then

$$\Delta J_{\pi_{n+1}}(l, k) \geq -\delta p_k + \beta p_k \lambda [J_n(2, k+1) - J_n(1, 1)]$$
$$+ \beta p_k (1 - \lambda) [J_n(1, k+1) - J_n(0, 1)]$$

Omitting the details of the calculations, the following bound can be derived

$$\Delta J_{\pi_{n+1}}(l, k) \geq -\delta p_k + \beta p_k [1 + \delta(p_{k+1} - p_1)]$$
$$+ \beta p_k \frac{\beta \lambda}{1 - \beta \lambda} [1 + \beta(1 - \lambda)(1 + \delta p_1)]$$

Then, if the right handside is $\geq 0 \Rightarrow \Delta J_{\pi_{n+1}}(l, k) \geq 0$, $\forall (l, k)$. By simple calculations we get the expression in (5.21). The bound can be further written as

$$\frac{1}{(1 - \lambda)[1 + (1 - \lambda)p_1 - \min_{k \neq 1} p_k]} + \frac{\lambda}{1 + (1 - \lambda)p_1 - \min_{k \neq 1} p_k}$$

clearly non-decreasing w.r.t λ and tending to ∞ for $\lambda \to 1$. □

The results for the existence of a threshold on the l-axis in Theorem 20 and the optimality of the *always-drop* policy in Theorem 21 hold irrespective of the choice of success probabilities. For the case of monotone non-decreasing success probabilities we can prove by induction using policy iteration equivalently to Theorem 19 that dropping is optimal for $k < \hat{k}_l$ and continue for $k \geq \hat{k}_l$, where the k-axis threshold is l-dependent.

Theorem 22. Consider the case of monotone non-decreasing success probabilities $q_1 \leq q_2 \leq \ldots$, with $q_k \to 1$, as $k \to \infty$. For all states $(l, k) \in S$, $m \in \mathbb{N}_+$ the following two inequalities hold for the optimal policy π^*

$$J_{\pi^*}(l, k) \geq J_{\pi^*}(l-1, 1) \tag{5.22}$$

$$J_{\pi^*}(l, k) \geq J_{\pi^*}(l, k+m) \tag{5.23}$$

Furthermore, given a fixed queue state l and varying the retransmission number k, the optimal policy is of threshold type, i.e. there exists a critical state $(l, \hat{k}_l)$, possibly dependent on l, such that dropping is optimal for $k < \hat{k}_l$, while continue is optimal for $k \geq \hat{k}_l$.

Proof. Let us show first that the two inequalities hold for policy π_0, where only dropping is chosen as action for all states. Inequality (5.23) is easy to verify since $J_{\pi_0}(l, k) = C_2(l, k) = l + \delta p_k + \beta \lambda J_{\pi_0}(l, 1) + \beta(1-\lambda) J_{\pi_0}(l-1, 1) \geq J_{\pi_0}(l, k+m)$, since $p_k \geq p_{k+m}$, $\forall k \in \mathbb{N}_+$. For the inequality (5.22) observe from the previous that $J_{\pi_0}(l, k) \geq J_{\pi_0}(l, k+m)$ holds for $m \to \infty$. We prove then that $J_{\pi_0}(l, k+m|_{m\to\infty}) \geq J_{\pi_0}(l-1, 1)$.

$$\begin{aligned} J_{\pi_0}(l, k+m|_{m\to\infty}) - J_{\pi_0}(l-1, 1) &= \\ 1 - \delta p_1 + \beta\lambda\left[J_{\pi_0}(l, 1) - J_{\pi_0}(l-1, 1)\right] &+ \\ \beta(1-\lambda)\left[J_{\pi_0}(l-1, 1) - J_{\pi_0}(l-2, 1)\right] &\stackrel{(a)}{\geq} \\ 1 - \delta p_1 + \beta(1 + \delta p_1) &\stackrel{(b)}{\geq} 0 \end{aligned}$$

where (a) comes from Theorem 20, since the difference $J_{\pi_0}(l, 1) - J_{\pi_0}(l-1, 1)$ is monotone non-decreasing and $J_{\pi_0}(l, 1) - J_{\pi_0}(l-1, 1) \geq J_{\pi_0}(1, 1) - J_{\pi_0}(0, 1) = 1 + \delta p_1$ and (b) holds for $\beta \geq 1 - 1/(1 + \delta p_1)$ which tends to 1 as $\delta \to \infty$.

Assume now that the policy iteration algorithm is initialized with policy π_0 and the above *two* inequalities hold for π_n. We will prove that the same holds for π_{n+1}, and hence

5.3. Design Rules for the Optimal Tradeoff

the inequalities also hold for the optimal policy π^* as $n \to \infty$. Let us first consider (5.22)

$$J_{\pi_{n+1}}(l,k) - J_{\pi_{n+1}}(l-1,1) =$$
$$\min\left\{C_1^{\pi_{n+1}}(l,k), C_2^{\pi_{n+1}}(l,k)\right\} - J_{\pi_{n+1}}(l-1,1) \stackrel{(c)}{\geq}$$
$$\min\left\{C_1^{\pi_{n+1}}(l,k), C_2^{\pi_{n+1}}(l,k)\right\} - J_{\pi_n}(l-1,1) \stackrel{(d)}{\geq} 0$$

where (c) follows from the property of the policy iteration algorithm that $J_{\pi_{n+1}} \leq J_{\pi_n}$ (for a proof the reader is referred to [Put05, Prop. 6.4.1, p. 175]) and (d) comes from the induction argument and is easy to verify for $\beta \to 1$.

We continue to (5.23) and consider the two cases where (i) $d_{\pi_{n+1}}(l,k) = 1$, or (ii) 0.

$$J_{\pi_{n+1}}(l,k) \stackrel{(i)}{=} C_2^{\pi_{n+1}}(l,k) \stackrel{(e)}{\geq} C_2^{\pi_{n+1}}(l,k+m) \geq J_{\pi_{n+1}}(l,k+m)$$

where (e) is for the case (i) due to the fact that $p_k \geq p_{k+m}$. For case (ii) we have the same as above by changing the indices 2 with 1 and (i) with (ii). Inequality (e) now follows from the fact that $p_k \geq p_{k+m}$ and $J_{\pi_n}(l,k) - J_{\pi_n}(l-1,1) \geq 0$ from the induction hypothesis.

For the *'Furthermore'* part of the Theorem, the proof follows the same lines as in that of Theorem 19 where inequality (5.23) is used in place of (5.13). □

5.3 Design Rules for the Optimal Tradeoff

The above theorems provide important structural properties of the optimal policy. We may identify two very important parameters that define the structure, namely the sequence of success probabilities per retransmission $\{q_n\}$ as well as the weighting factor $\delta > 0$, which plays the role of the penalty when dropping occurs. Especially δ has a crucial role in the upper bound for $l_{\pi^*}^{th}$ provided. Specifically, Theorem 20 suggests that it is optimal to use an ARQ protocol only up to a finite queue length $l_{\pi^*}^{th}$. When the queue exceeds the threshold the packet is removed from the queue after the first effort regardless of the result of decoding.

Since Bernoulli arrivals have been assumed, this keeps the queue finite for $\lambda \leq 1$ and the optimal policy truncates the buffer up to length $L = l_{\pi^*}^{th}$. This reduces our investigation to the family of **L-truncating** policies (see Def. 3). Theorem 20 (specifically inequality (5.17)) in the current chapter provide furthermore an upper bound for the queue length.

The importance of the penalty weight δ is emphasized by this expression. An increase in δ represents an increase of the dropping cost, which results in an increase of the optimal finite buffer length. In this case we prefer to increase system reliability and reduce the ratio of dropped packets at the cost of higher packet delay (measured as queue length). Theorem 21 presents a condition regarding δ for which dropping is always optimal.

Finally Theorems 19 and 22 prove the threshold behavior of the optimal policy on the k-axis. For $q_1 \geq q_2 \geq \ldots$ there exists a maximum positive integer $K = \max_l \hat{k}_l$ such that it is always optimal to drop for $k \geq K$ irrespective of l. This motivates the search over the optimal **K-retransmitting** policy (see Def. 2), which belongs to the family of policies for which retransmissions are allowed up to finite number of trials K. Observe by Theorem 22 that if $q_1 \leq q_2 \leq \ldots$ then K is always unbounded since after some l-dependent threshold $k \geq \hat{k}_l$ it is always optimal to continue.

Combining the two above suboptimal policies will provide a good approximation of the optimal strategy. Note that there will exist special values of δ and success probability sequences for which this is the optimal solution as well. The performance of the **L-truncating**, **K-retransmitting** policies, which will be from now on named $< \mathbf{L}, \mathbf{K} >$-policies, will be analyzed in the following paragraph.

5.4 Optimal and Suboptimal Delay-Dropping Tradeoffs

Since from Theorem 20 the maximum queue length and consequently the maximum number of retransmissions are always bounded, the state space is finite and standard algorithms such as policy iteration or value iteration can be implemented to determine the optimal solution. In the following, policy iteration for variable values of the dropping cost is used to provide the optimal delay and dropping tradeoff for decreasing in Fig.5.1.a and respectively for increasing success probabilities in Fig.5.1.b.

The behaviour of the delay - expressed as average queue length $\bar{u}$ - for both monotonicity cases is shown in Fig. 5.2. For the average dropping $\lim_{N \to \infty} \frac{1}{N} \sum_{n=1}^{N} A_n p(Z_n)$ the dependence on the dropping cost is illustrated in Fig.5.3. The scenario implemented has arrival rate $\lambda = 0.6$ and $\beta = 0.99$. The decreasing sequence of success probabilities equals $q_k = e^{-0.3k}$ with $\max_k q_k = 0.741$, the increasing sequence of success probabilities equals $q_k = 1 - e^{-0.5k}$ with $\min_k q_k = 0.394$, maximum retransmission number $K_{max} = 10$ and queue length $L_{max} = 40$.

5.4. Optimal and Suboptimal Delay-Dropping Tradeoffs

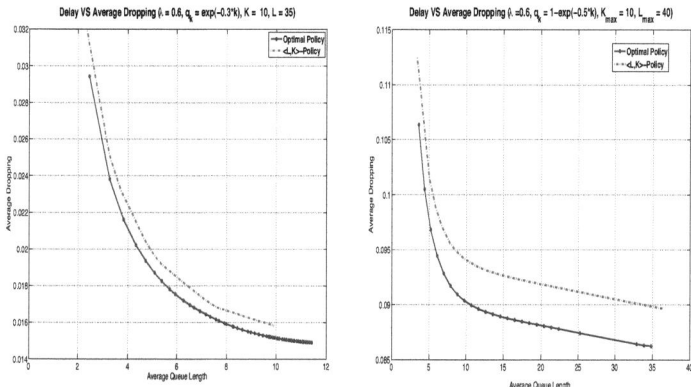

Figure 5.1: Optimal and $< L, K >$ delay-dropping tradeoff for (a)$q_k \downarrow$, (b)$q_k \uparrow$.

The results in all figures are compared to the $< L, K >$-policies suggested in the previous paragraph, where an algorithm similar to policy iteration but with certain adaptations is implemented to find the optimal L and K. The algorithm initializes with π_0 which is simply the policy which always choses drop as optimal action. At each step n the policy $\pi_n := \pi_{<L_n,K_n>}$ is evaluated (see [Put05, pp. 174-175]) where $< L_n, K_n >$ are the max queue length and retransmission number and $J_{\pi_{<L_n,K_n>}}$ is obtained. There are four options. Either end the algorithm or look for a lower $J_{\pi_{n+1}}$ by increasing K_n, L_n or both by 1. In this way comparing between these possibilities the algorithm evolves and terminates when $< L_n, K_n > = < L_{n+1}, K_{n+1} >$.

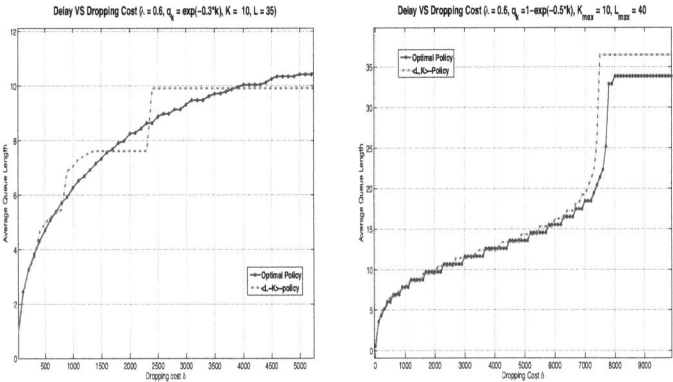

Figure 5.2: Average queue length vs dropping cost for the optimal and $<L, K>$ policy.

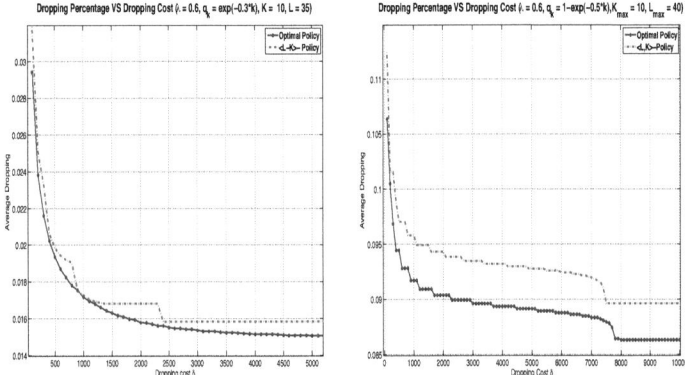

Figure 5.3: Average dropping vs dropping cost for the optimal and $<L, K>$ policy.

Part II

Multiuser Systems with ARQ

Chapter 6

Stability and Power Control in Downlink with ARQ

The ARQ protocols within multiuser systems bring a totally different research perspective. The interactions between users who compete for common resources such as power, time and frequency have a very large impact on delay and reliability. The application of retransmission protocols within such a framework is crucial. Interference not only influences the amount of data that a user may transmit but also the degree of reliability with which these data may be transmitted. In this sence, power control algorithms for interference have in this framework a totally different flare. The aim here is not only to find the optimal way to allocate resources among users so that an SINR threshold can be guaranteed [Yat95]. Since the transmission SINR of each user is related to a success probability function, the power should be optimally allocated so that the number of retransmissions and hence the system delay, in terms of average queue length, should be minimized. An optimal power control of the retransmission process can eventually maximize the amount of data that a multiuser system is able to reliably support.

The general problem of optimally allocating power and rate to a wireless buffered communication system so that stability can be guaranteed, has been a major topic of research during the recent years. Starting as a server allocation problem in [TE93], the investigation was generalized to the problem of a joint power/rate allocation for parallel queues in [NMR03] and resulted in a cross-layer analytical framework for systems with interference and buffered transmitters [YC03] where delay and throughput optimal allocations were provided. In the investigations mentioned above - and others following - transmission errors did not play an important role - not to mention having a direct impact - on the system model and the allocation policies introduced. The systems have either been considered error-free or in the case of errors the packets were simply discarded.

In the current chapter, errors are included in the analysis and ARQ protocols are incorporated for error correction. In the model under study the transmission rates are kept constant while the success probability of packets destined to each user depend on the level of SINR. The stability region of such a system is derived together with the power allocation policy that achieves it. Different power allocation algorithms for the policy implementation are suggested and their results are compared in the last section.

6.1 The Downlink Model under Study

We focus on a downlink scenario where a base station communicates with multiple access terminals $n = 1, \ldots, N$ with *constant* transmission rate per user n, given by the vector $\vec{\mu} = (\mu_1, \ldots, \mu_N)$ and determined by QoS requirements. Packets destined to each user arrive from an input stream α_n, $n = 1, \ldots, N$ with average arrival rates $\vec{\lambda} = (\lambda_1, \ldots, \lambda_N)$ and are buffered, waiting for processing at each server. Infinite buffer capacity is assumed. The feedback is given by the vector $\vec{X} = (X_1, \ldots, X_N)$, $X_n \in \{0, 1\}$, where 0 represents a NACK and 1 an ACK. The model under study is illustrated in Fig.6.1.

The method of imbedded Markov chains can be used to describe the evolution of queues in time [Kle75, p.174]. The queue backlog is observed at each time instant a packet transmission is *attempted*. If packets of equal length are considered, the duration of each slot equals $T_n^{slot} = \frac{1}{\mu_n}$ and is different for each user. On the other hand we may consider the slot duration constant and equal to T^{slot}, while the lengths of transmitted packets $T^{slot} \cdot \mu_n$ differ per user. In both cases the analysis is the same.

At each time slot t the base station decides over which transmission power level to assign to each user, under a short-term sum power constraint. The set of all possible power assignment vectors is $\mathcal{P}(P_{tot}) := \left\{ \vec{\rho} = (\rho_1, \ldots, \rho_N) : \sum_{n=1}^{N} \rho_n \leq P_{tot} \right\}$. We consider the class Π of stationary policies, that allocate the vector $\vec{\rho}(t)$ at slot t based on some higher layer system information available to the controller at this time, denoted by $\mathcal{I}(t)$. The mapping $\pi : \mathcal{I} \to \mathcal{P}$ is an element of Π. Since the transmission rates μ_n are considered constant, the allocation of different power levels per slot can solely affect the success transmission probabilities. This is stated by the notation $X_n(\vec{\rho}(t), \mathcal{I}(t))$. The queue evolution for user n

6.1. The Downlink Model under Study

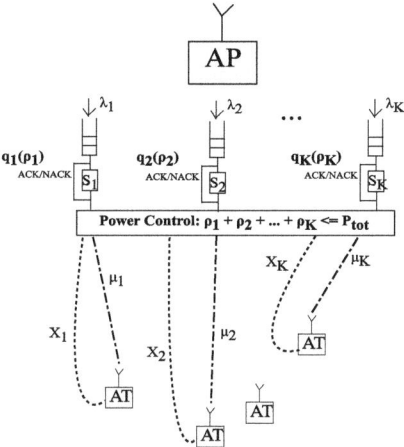

Figure 6.1: The downlink power allocation model under study

at slot t is given by the one-step recursion

$$u_n(t+1) = [u_n(t) - X_n(\vec{\rho}(t), \mathcal{I}(t))]^+ + \alpha_n(t+1) \tag{6.1}$$
$$= u_n(t) - X_n(\vec{\rho}(t), \mathcal{I}(t)) \cdot \mathbf{1}_{\{u_n(t)>0\}} + \alpha_n(t+1) \tag{6.2}$$

$$X_n = \begin{cases} 1 & \text{ACK, with prob. } q_n(\vec{\rho}(t), \mathcal{I}(t)) \\ 0 & \text{NACK, with prob. } 1 - q_n(\vec{\rho}(t), \mathcal{I}(t)) \end{cases} \tag{6.3}$$

The system of N queues described by (6.1) (or (6.2)) forms an N-dimensional Markov chain under the following three conditions:

1. The memoryless property holds for the inter-arrival intervals

2. The controller decides over the power allocation based on $\vec{u}(t)$, in other words $\mathcal{I}(t) \equiv \vec{u}(t)$ and

3. The random variables $X_n(1), \ldots, X_n(t)$ for each user are independent non-identically distributed, given the power allocations $\vec{\rho}(1), \ldots, \vec{\rho}(t)$.

Under these conditions the next queue state $\vec{u}(t+1)$ depends only on the previous queue states at slot t. Observe that the whole information over the arrivals and the success or failure of messages up to t is summarized in $\vec{u}(t)$. The average per slot arrivals are finite and equal $\mathbb{E}[\alpha_n(t)] = \lambda_n \cdot \frac{1}{\mu_n}$ [packets/sec][sec]. The second moment of the Poisson arrival processes is also finite.

Throughout the chapter, the only information fed back to the base station is the per slot ACK/NACK vector $\vec{X}(t)$. In particular, no channel state information is available at the transmitter. We assume however knowledge on the fading statistics to describe the success probability as a real valued function $q(\vec{\rho})$, which is a mapping $q : \mathbb{R}_+^N \to [0,1]$. The dependence of the success on the entire allocation vector is reasonable when interference is taken into account.

Examples of success probability functions for the downlink can be found for a flat block-fading Gaussian channel in which the user's fading at each slot h_n, $n = 1, \ldots, N$ is i.i.d. according to some distribution, say Rayleigh. In such cases $q_n(\vec{\rho}) = 1 - \mathcal{P}_{out,n}(\vec{\rho})$, where $\mathcal{P}_{out,n}$ is the outage probability given a threshold γ_n determined by μ_n

$$q_n(\vec{\rho}) = \mathbb{P}\left(\frac{\rho_n \cdot h_n}{\sigma^2 + h_n \cdot \sum_{k \neq n}^N \rho_k} \geq \gamma_n\right) \qquad (6.4)$$

where $\gamma_n := \gamma(\mu_n) = e^{\mu_n} - 1$ and σ^2 equals the noise variance.

Considering cases where the power allocation for each user solely affects his/her own success $q_n(\rho_n)$, e.g. for channels with no interference, we may obtain rather simple success functions as is the case of the expression for outage in parallel channels

$$q_n(\rho_n) = \mathbb{P}\left(\rho_n \cdot h_n/\sigma^2 \geq \gamma_n\right) \qquad (6.5)$$
$$\stackrel{Rayleigh}{=} \exp\left(\sigma^2 \frac{1 - e^{\mu_n}}{\rho_n}\right) \qquad (6.6)$$

The distribution function $q(\rho)$ has the properties of *right - continuity* and *monotonicity* (non-decreasing) with respect to power [Wil91]. Moreover $\lim_{\rho \to 0} q(\rho) = 0$ and $\lim_{\rho \to \infty} q(\rho) = 1$.

6.2 Notions of Stability

In the current section cetrtain stability notions used throughout will be presented. The unfinished work in a queue u_n at slot t is given in (6.1). We introduce, following [NMR03] and [NMR] the discrete "overflow" function and its stability definition

$$w(B) = \lim_{t\to\infty} \sup \frac{1}{t} \sum_{i=1}^{t} \mathbf{1}_{\{u(i)>B\}} \qquad (6.7)$$

where $\mathbf{1}_{\{u(t)>B\}}$ is the indicator function taking value 1, whenever the event $\{u(t) > B\}$ occurs. If we replace $u(t)$ by $\|\vec{u}(t)\|$, where $\|.\|$ denotes any vector norm, we get the expression of the "overflow" function for a system with N queues.

Definition 4. A queueing system is *"overflow" stable* if $w(B) \to 0$ as $B \to \infty$.

We define further the notion of *weak stability*, following [BW]

Definition 5. A queueing system is *weakly stable*, if $\forall \epsilon > 0$, $\exists B > 0$ and $\tau = \tau(\epsilon)$, such that $\forall t > \tau$

$$\mathbb{P}\left(\|\vec{u}(t)\| > B\right) < \epsilon \qquad (6.8)$$

Weak stability may be determined by the Foster-Lyapunov drift criteria [Asm00], [MT93], [Haj06] vastly used in the communications and control literature e.g. [TE93], [NMR03], [LMNM01]. Let $V(\vec{u}(t))$ be a lower bounded real function. The following theorem is based on Foster's stability criteria for Markov chains [Fos53] and extends Pakes' criterion [Pak69] to allow for the use of general test functions $V(\vec{u}(t))$.

Theorem 23. Given a system of N queues which forms an N-dimensional Markov chain $\vec{u}$, if there exists $B < \infty$ and $a > 0$, as well as a Lyapunov test function $V : \mathbb{R}^N \to \mathbb{R}$ such that

1. $\forall \vec{u}(t): \|\vec{u}(t)\| \leq B$

$$\mathbb{E}\left[V(\vec{u}(t+1))|\vec{u}(t)\right] < \infty \qquad (6.9)$$

2. $\forall \vec{u}(t): \|\vec{u}(t)\| > B$

$$\mathbb{E}\left[V\left(\vec{u}(t+1)\right) - V\left(\vec{u}(t)\right) | \vec{u}(t)\right] \leq -a \qquad (6.10)$$

the chain (such as the one defined in (6.1)) is *positive recurrent* and $\forall \epsilon$, $\exists B > 0$, such that

$$\lim_{t \to \infty} \mathbb{P}\left(\left\|\vec{u}(t)\right\| > B\right) < \epsilon \qquad (6.11)$$

In words, the criterion states that if a test function V of the queue lengths exists, with the property of having a negative drift - defined as $\mathbb{E}\left[\Delta V\left(\vec{u}(t)\right) | \vec{u}(t)\right]$ - for the entire state space except maybe for a closed and bounded (compact) set given by $\left\|\vec{u}(t)\right\| \leq B$ for which however the conditional expectation remains finite, the chain approaches a steady state with regards to the distribution. Of course (6.11) is simply the definition of weak stability given in Definition 5.

It is noted in [NMR03] and [NMR] that "*if sample paths of unfinished work in the queue are ergodic and a steady state exists, the overflow function $w(B)$ is simply the steady-state probability that the unfinished work exceeds the value B and is identical to the usual notion of stability defined in terms of a vanishing complementary occupancy distribution*". Based on the above, we provide the following theorem that expicitly connects the two notions of stability.

Theorem 24. If a system of N queues is "overflow" stable according to Definition 4 and $\forall B \geq 0$ the limit $\lim_{t \to \infty} \mathbb{P}\left(\left\|\vec{u}(t)\right\| > B\right) = c \in [0, 1]$ is well defined, the system is also *weakly stable* (Definition 5).

Proof. By Definition 4 we have that, given the overflow function for the N queue system

$$w(B) = \limsup_{t \to \infty} \frac{1}{t} \sum_{i=1}^{t} \mathbf{1}_{\{\|\vec{u}(i)\| > B\}}$$

and overflow stability implies:

$$\lim_{B \to \infty} w(B) = 0$$

6.2. Notions of Stability

The above means that $\forall \epsilon, \exists B_1$ such that for $B \geq B_1 : |w(B) - 0| < \epsilon$. We may upper bound

$$\limsup_{t \to \infty} v^{(t)}(B) < \epsilon$$

where $v^{(t)}(B) := \frac{1}{t}\sum_{i=1}^{t} \mathbf{1}_{\{\|\vec{u}(i)\| > B\}} \in [0, 1]$, $v^{(\infty)}(B) := \lim_{t \to \infty} \sup \frac{1}{t}\sum_{i=1}^{t} \mathbf{1}_{\{\|\vec{u}(i)\| > B\}}$ and hence bounded $\forall t$. We get $\mathbb{E}\left[\lim_{t \to \infty} \sup v^{(t)}(B)\right] = \mathbb{E}\left[v^{(\infty)}(B)\right] < \epsilon$. Using the reverse Fatou Lemma

$$\limsup_{t \to \infty} \mathbb{E}\left[v^{(t)}(B)\right] \leq \mathbb{E}\left[\limsup_{t \to \infty} v^{(t)}(B)\right] < \epsilon \tag{6.12}$$

But since

$$\mathbb{E}\left[v^{(t)}(B)\right] = \frac{1}{t}\sum_{i=1}^{t} \mathbb{P}\left(\|\vec{u}(i)\| > B\right)$$

inequality (6.12) can be written as

$$\limsup_{t \to \infty} \frac{1}{t}\sum_{i=1}^{t} \mathbb{P}\left(\|\vec{u}(i)\| > B\right) < \epsilon$$

The limit $\lim_{t \to \infty} \mathbb{P}\left(\|\vec{u}(t)\| > B\right) = c \in [0, 1]$ is by the Theorem's assumptions well defined, hence by using Cesàro's Lemma [Wil91], [Rud64], the limit $\lim_{t \to \infty} \frac{1}{t}\sum_{i=1}^{t} \mathbb{P}\left(\|\vec{u}(i)\| > B\right)$ exists and also equals c. Using these observations

$$c = \lim_{t \to \infty} \mathbb{P}\left(\|\vec{u}(t)\| > B\right) < \epsilon$$

and the weak stability is proved. □

The above theorem states that a weakly stable system is also overflow stable, but the converse does not necessarily hold.

6.3 Downlink Stability Region with Constant Transmission Rates

For the N user downlink system illustrated in Fig.6.1 stability may be achieved by the use of a power allocation policy $\pi \in \Pi$ which guarantees that none of the N queues explodes to infinity. The power allocation vector per time slot t is denoted by the vector $\vec{\rho}(t)$ under the constraint $\|\vec{\rho}(t)\|_1 = \sum_{n=1}^{N} \rho_n(t) \leq P_{tot}$, $\forall t$. We assume that the power vector may be chosen at each slot among a *countably infinite set* of possible choices $\mathcal{P}$, which all satisfy the short-term constraint. The elements of the set are denoted by $\vec{\rho}_j$, $j = 1, \ldots, \infty$ and $\rho_{j,n}$ is the allocated power to user n for choice of vector j.

For each one of the N system queues, the actual processing rate at slot t, equals $\mu_n(t) := \mu_n X_n(t) \cdot \mathbf{1}_{\{u_n(t)>0\}}$ and hence equals 0 whenever either the queue is empty or the transmission is not successful and the packet remains in queue. The symbols $\mathbf{1}_{\{u(t)>0\}}$ and $X(t)$ are explained in (6.2) and (6.3) respectively. Following [NMR03], since power control π may result in a nonergodic processing rate, the processing time-average is defined as

$$\bar{\mu}_n := \liminf_{t \to \infty} \frac{1}{t} \sum_{i=1}^{t} \mu_n(i) := \liminf_{t \to \infty} \frac{1}{t} \sum_{i=1}^{t} \mu_n X_n(i) \cdot \mathbf{1}_{\{u_n(i)>0\}} \qquad (6.13)$$

We first provide a necessary condition for the stability of an N user system.

Lemma 10. If the system of N queues in (6.1) is overflow stable under some policy $\pi \in \Pi$, the input rate vector $\vec{\lambda}$ belongs to the region Λ_D, given by

$$\Lambda_D = \mathbf{co} \bigcup_{\vec{\rho} \in \mathcal{P}(P_{tot})} \left\{ \vec{\lambda} \in \mathbb{R}_+^N : \lambda_n \leq \mu_n q_n(\vec{\rho}), \forall n \right\} \qquad (6.14)$$

where **co** denotes the convex hull of the set.

Proof. Stability of the N user system implies that each queue u_n, $n = 1, \ldots, N$ is overflow stable. From [NMR03] a necessary conditon for stability of a single queue is $\lambda_n \leq \bar{\mu}_n$, where $\bar{\mu}_n$ is the time average in (6.13). We may write

$$\lambda_n \leq \liminf_{t \to \infty} \frac{1}{t} \sum_{i=1}^{t} \mu_n X_n(i) \qquad (6.15)$$

6.3. Downlink Stability Region with Constant Transmission Rates

where we use the fact that $\mathbf{1}_{\{u_n(t)>0\}} \cdot X_n(t) \leq X_n(t)$. The equality cannot hold $\forall t$ since the queue is assumed stable and the empty queue state is visited infinitely often [Kle75, p.279]. Hence for arrival rates arbitrary close to the right handside stability depends on the frequency of visits to the empty state. Furthermore, since the random variables $|X_n(t)| \leq 1$, $\forall t$ are uniformly bounded, the weak law of large numbers for a sequence of independent non-identically distributed random variables [Fel68, pp.253-255] applies. Then $\forall \epsilon > 0$

$$\mathbb{P}\left(\left|\frac{\sum_{i=1}^{t} X_n(i)}{t} - \frac{\sum_{i=1}^{t} q_n(\vec{\rho}(i))}{t}\right| > \epsilon\right) \to 0$$

Combined with (6.15) it follows that

$$\begin{aligned}\lambda_n &\leq \liminf_{t\to\infty} \frac{1}{t}\sum_{i=1}^{t} \mu_n q_n(\vec{\rho}(i)) \\ &= \sum_{j=1}^{\infty} f_j \cdot \mu_n q_n(\vec{\rho}_j), \quad \forall n\end{aligned} \quad (6.16)$$

In the above, f_j is simply the fraction of time-slots that the power vector $\vec{\rho}_j \in \mathcal{P}$ is allocated to the users under some policy $\pi \in \Pi$. It holds $\sum_{j=1}^{\infty} f_j = 1$. From the right handside of (6.16) we deduce that if the system is stable, $\vec{\lambda}$ belongs to the interior of the convex hull of the set of vectors $(\mu_1 q_1(\vec{\rho}), \ldots, \mu_N q_N(\vec{\rho})), \vec{\rho} \in \mathcal{P}$ ([BV04, p.25]). □

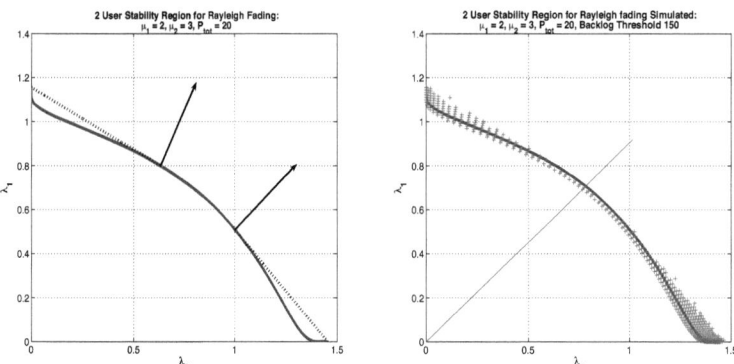

Figure 6.2: Two User Stability Region: (a) Calculated, (b) Simulated.

An illustration of the two user stability region given constant γ_n for $n = 1, 2$ and for the special case of Rayleigh fading statistics is provided in the above Fig.6.2.a. The convex hull is calculated by finding the strict supporting hyperplanes [BV04] that are tangential to the convex part and at the same time pass through the edge points $(0, \mu_1 q_1(P_{tot}))$ and $(\mu_2 q_2(P_{tot}), 0)$ respectively. Fig.6.2.b illustrates the stability region resulting from simulation of the two queue system. In this plot instability is declared if the backlog of at least one queue exceeds 150 packets. The solid line represents the set $\bigcup \{[\mu_2 q_2(\rho_2), \mu_1 q_1(\rho_1)], \rho_1 + \rho_2 = P_{tot}\}$.

As a *sufficient* condition, the following Lemma is provided.

Lemma 11. The system of N queues in (6.1) is overflow stable under some policy $\pi^* \in \Pi$, if the input rates belong to the region described in (6.14). The policy π^* to stabilize all $\vec{\lambda} \in \Lambda_D$ chooses at each slot t the power vector

$$\vec{\rho}^*(t) = \arg\max_{\vec{\rho} \in \mathcal{P}} \sum_{n=1}^{N} u_n(t) q_n(\vec{\rho}) \qquad (6.17)$$

Proof. We will use Theorem 23 for the proof of the Lemma, with $V(\vec{u}(t)) = \sum_{n=1}^{N} u_n^2(t)$ as a test function. The proof method follows closely [NMR03]. In what follows the dependence of variables on time will be shown only when necessary. From equation (6.1) we have for the n-th queue

$$\begin{aligned} u_n^2(t+1) &= \left([u_n(t) - X_n(\vec{\rho})]^+ + \alpha_n\right)^2 \\ &\overset{(a)}{\leq} [u_n(t) - X_n(\vec{\rho})]^2 + \alpha_n^2 + 2\alpha_n \cdot u_n(t) \\ &\overset{(b)}{\leq} u_n^2(t) + X_n(\vec{\rho}) + \alpha_n^2 - 2u_n(t)(X_n(\vec{\rho}) - \alpha_n) \end{aligned}$$

where (a) is due to the fact that $(x)^{+2} \leq x^2$ and that $[u_n - X_n]^+ \leq u_n$, (b) due to $X_n^2 = X_n$. The drift for a single queue of the system satisfies the following inequality

$$\mathbb{E}\left[u_n^2(t+1) - u_n^2(t) | u_n(t)\right] \leq \mathbb{E}\left[\alpha_n^2\right] + \mathbb{E}\left[X_n(\vec{\rho}) | u_n\right] - 2u_n \mathbb{E}\left[X_n(\vec{\rho}) - \alpha_n | u_n\right]$$

6.3. Downlink Stability Region with Constant Transmission Rates

Remember that by assumption $\mathbb{E}\left[\alpha_n^2\right] = \beta_n < \infty$. We further use the notation

$$C = \max_{\vec{p}_j \in \mathcal{P}} \sum_{n=1}^{N} q_n(\vec{p}_j)$$

Then the Lyapunov drift for the N users under the chosen test function will be

$$\mathbb{E}\left[V(\vec{u}(t+1)) - V(\vec{u}(t)) \mid \vec{u}(t)\right] \leq \sum_{n=1}^{N} \beta_n + C - 2 \sum_{n=1}^{N} u_n \left(\mathbb{E}\left[X_n(\vec{\rho}) \mid \vec{u}\right] - \frac{\lambda_n}{\mu_n}\right) \quad (6.18)$$

Using the description of the region given in (6.14) and using the inequality in (6.16) for all $\frac{\lambda_n}{\mu_n}$ that belong to the region Λ we have that

$$\sum_{n=1}^{N} u_n(t) \frac{\lambda_n}{\mu_n} \overset{(6.16)}{\leq} \sum_{n=1}^{N} u_n(t) \sum_{j=1}^{\infty} f_j \cdot q_n(\vec{p}_j)$$

$$= \sum_{j=1}^{\infty} f_j \sum_{n=1}^{N} u_n(t) q_n(\vec{p}_j)$$

$$\leq \sum_{j=1}^{\infty} f_j \max_{\vec{p}_j \in \mathcal{P}} \sum_{n=1}^{N} u_n(t) q_n(\vec{p}_j)$$

$$= \sum_{n=1}^{N} u_n(t) q_n(\vec{p}_{j^*}, \vec{u}(t)) \quad (6.19)$$

where $\vec{\rho}_{j^*}$ can be evaluated by (6.17), given the vector of current queue lengths $\vec{u}(t)$ and $\sum_{j=1}^{\infty} f_j = 1$. We have thus shown in (6.19) that the weighted sum $\sum_{n=1}^{N} u_n(t) \frac{\lambda_n}{\mu_n}$ is maximized by $\sum_{n=1}^{N} u_n(t) \mathbb{E}\left[X_n(\vec{\rho}^*(t)) \mid \vec{u}(t)\right]$, for any vector $\vec{\lambda}/\vec{\mu}$ chosen within Λ_D. But then for each $\vec{\lambda}/\vec{\mu} \in \Lambda_D$ we may choose an $N \times 1$ vector $\vec{\epsilon}$, $\epsilon > 0$ such that $\vec{\lambda}/\vec{\mu} + \vec{\epsilon} \in \Lambda_D$ and

$$\sum_{n=1}^{N} u_n(t) \left(\mathbb{E}\left[X_n(\vec{\rho}(t)) \mid \vec{u}(t)\right] - \frac{\lambda_n}{\mu_n}\right) \geq \epsilon \sum_{n=1}^{N} u_n(t)$$

Using the above inequality in (6.18) we obtain

$$\mathbb{E}\left[V(\vec{u}(t+1)) - V(\vec{u}(t)) \mid \vec{u}(t)\right] \leq \sum_{n=1}^{N} \beta_n + C - 2\epsilon \sum_{n=1}^{N} u_n(t) \leq -a$$

The righthand inequality, where $a > 0$ from Theorem 23 is satisfied for

$$\sum_{n=1}^{N} u_n(t) \geq \frac{a + \sum_{n=1}^{N} \beta_n + C}{2\epsilon}$$

Since the righthand side is finite, part 1) of Theorem 23 is also satisfied for $\sum_{n=1}^{N} u_n(t) \leq \frac{a + \sum_{n=1}^{N} \beta_n + C}{2\epsilon}$. We may directly deduce that $\mathbb{E}\left[V(\vec{u}(t+1))|\vec{u}(t)\right] < \infty$ for the latter set, using (6.18). □

Theorem 25. The necessary and sufficient condition for the system (6.1) of N queues with retransmissions to be overflow stable under some policy $\pi \in \Pi$ is that $\vec{\lambda} \in \Lambda_D$, where Λ_D is given in (6.14). As long as this condition holds, the policy $\pi^* \in \Pi$ that chooses per slot the power allocation vector $\vec{\rho}(t) = \vec{\rho}^*(t)$ according to (6.17) always stabilizes the system.

Observing the power control in (6.17) we conclude that the stability optimal power allocation policy aims to maximize the success probability of the longest queues. To further understand what this implies for the system, we may use (6.1) and write

$$u_n(t)\left[u_n(t+1) - u_n(t)\right] = -u_n(t) X_n(t) \mathbf{1}_{\{u_n(t)>0\}} + u_n(t) \alpha_n(t+1)$$

Since, $u_n(t) \mathbf{1}_{\{u_n(t)>0\}} = u_n(t)$ and taking expectations, we may write

$$u_n(t) q_n(\vec{\rho}(t)) = u_n(t) \frac{\lambda_n}{\mu_n} - \mathbb{E}\left[u_n(t) \Delta u_n(t) | u_n(t)\right]$$

Observe now from the above that

$$\max \sum_{n=1}^{N} u_n(t) q_n(\vec{\rho}(t)) \Rightarrow \min \sum_{n=1}^{N} u_n(t) \mathbb{E}\left[\Delta u_n(t) | u_n(t)\right]$$

Hence the stability optimal contol policy aims to minimize the weighted sum of the expected change of queue lengths from the current slot t to the next, where the current queue lengths play the role of the weights.

6.4 Optimal and Suboptimal Power Allocation Policies

The maximization of the weighted sum in (6.17) is a rather difficult task, due to the fact that the success functions $q_n(\vec{\rho})$ are generally non-concave. The problem may be cast in the general framework of non-concave utility maximization which has received much attention in the recent years, the reason being that most natural utility functions are nonconcave. The utility here is the success probability of each user. Starting with the seminal work by Kelly over Network Utility Maximization [KMT98] efforts on maximizing sums of nonconcave utilities include [FC05] where a convex sum-of-squares relaxation is employed and [LMS02] where a resource allocation problem for the downlink is posed and distributed algorithms based on the Lagrange dual function provide a rather satisfactory approximation to the social optimal solution. The works in [MB02] and [YL06] are also closely related. Conditions for convergence to the global optimal solution are presented in [CZH05], whereas in [LMS05] "self-regulating" heuristics which exclude some users with sigmoidal-like utilities from accessing the resources leads to algorithms that always converge to feasible but possibly not optimal allocations.

The downlink formulation in our context, together with the outage expression in (6.4) provides a rather important simplification summarized in the following

Theorem 26. If $\vec{\rho}$ is a power allocation vector such that $\sum_{n=1}^{N} \rho_n < P_{tot}$ then another vector $\vec{\hat{\rho}}$ can be always found such that $\sum_{n=1}^{N} \hat{\rho}_n = P_{tot}$ and $\sum_{n=1}^{N} u_n q_n(\vec{\hat{\rho}}) > \sum_{n=1}^{N} u_n q_n(\vec{\rho})$.

Proof. The outage probability for user n at the downlink is given in (6.4) where the $\gamma_n = e^{\mu_n} - 1 \geq 0$. Choose a power vector $\vec{\rho}$ that activates the short term power constraint $\sum_{n=1}^{N} \rho_n < P_{tot}$. The expression may be reformulated as

$$q_n(\vec{\rho}) \stackrel{z_n := \sigma^2/h_n}{=} \mathbb{P}\left(z_n \leq \frac{\rho_n}{\gamma_n} + \rho_n - \sum_{k=1}^{N} \rho_k\right)$$

z_n is a new random variable. Let us choose $\vec{\hat{\rho}} = c \cdot \vec{\rho}$ such that $\sum_{n=1}^{N} \hat{\rho}_n = P_{tot}$ and $\hat{\rho}_n = c \cdot \rho_n, \forall n = 1, \ldots, N, c > 1$. It can directly be seen that $q_n(\vec{\hat{\rho}}) \stackrel{c>1}{\geq} q_n(\vec{\rho})$, $\forall n$ □

For the vector $\vec{\hat{\rho}}$, we may write $SINR_n(\vec{\hat{\rho}}) = \frac{\hat{\rho}_n}{P_{tot} - \hat{\rho}_n + z_n}$. Observe that this last expression depends no more on the entire allocation vector but only on the value of the assigned individual power $\hat{\rho}_n$. That is: $q_n(\vec{\rho}) = q_n(\hat{\rho}_n)$ and the maximization problem in (6.17) is equivalent to

$$\begin{aligned} \text{maximize} \quad & \sum_{n=1}^{N} u_n(t) q_n(\rho_n) \\ \text{subject to} \quad & \sum_{n=1}^{N} \rho_n \leq P_{tot} \\ & \rho_n \geq 0, \, \forall n \end{aligned} \quad (6.20)$$

The distribution functions in the objective often admit a sigmoidal-like form with a single inflection point ρ_n^o which has the property that $q_n(\rho)$ is convex for $\rho < \rho_n^o$ and concave for $\rho > \rho_n^o$ as shown in fig. 6.3. Depending on the available P_{tot} and the transmission rate μ_n the function may by convex in the whole domain $[0, P_{tot}]$. The Lagrangian is

$$L(\vec{\rho}, \nu) = \sum_{n=1}^{N} u_n \hat{q}_n(\rho_n) + \nu \left(P_{tot} - \sum_{n=1}^{N} \rho_n \right) \quad (6.21)$$

where the non-negativity constraints are implicitly stated in the $\hat{q}_n$ ($\hat{q}_n = q_n$ for $0 \leq \rho_n \leq P_{tot}$, otherwise $-\infty$). In the above ν is the non-negative Lagrange multiplier related to the sum power constraint. In the following we omit the ^(hat) in the notation.

If the constraint $P_{tot} \geq \sum_{n=1}^{N} \rho_n$ in (6.21) is violated, users incur an extra charge proportional to the amount of violation with price ν. On the other hand users are rewarded proportional to the amount of under-used power. However, in such case, since the distribution functions are non-decreasing, the objective function will not attain its optimum. The Lagrange dual function is

$$L_{dual}(\nu) = \max_{0 \leq \rho_n \leq P_{tot}, \forall n} \left\{ \sum_{n=1}^{N} u_n q_n(\rho_n) + \nu \left(P_{tot} - \sum_{n=1}^{N} \rho_n \right) \right\}$$

$\vec{\rho}(\nu)$ is the optimizing variable for a certain shadow-price ν and will be called *price-based power allocation* [CZH05]. $L_{dual}(\nu)$ is always an upper bound for the primal optimum, which is achieved by allocating the power vector $\vec{\rho}^*$. The problem of maximizing the Lagrangian is *seperable*, due to the locality of each user's function to its individual power allocation and hence may be decomposed in N independent optimization problems, which are equivalent to finding the conjugate function of each utility $u_n q_n(\rho_n)$

6.4. Optimal and Suboptimal Power Allocation Policies

$$\rho_n(v) = \arg \max_{0 \leq \rho_n \leq P_{tot}} \{u_n q_n(\rho_n) - v\rho_n\} \tag{6.22}$$

Solving the following dual problem gives the best possible upper bound to the solution of the primal problem that we may obtain, for optimal price v^*.

$$\begin{aligned} \text{minimize} \quad & L_{dual}(v) = L(\vec{\rho}(v), v) \\ \text{subject to} \quad & v \geq 0 \end{aligned} \tag{6.23}$$

The dual function $L_{dual}(v)$ is always *convex* but may not be differentiable. The solution can be algorithmically attained using *bisection* [YL06], [LMS02] or an *iterative subgradient* method [YL06], [CZH05] that updates the dual variables in the direction of the subgradient $P_{tot} - \sum_{n=1}^{N} \rho_n(v)$.

Altogether, approaching the problem in (6.20) by its dual has several advantages. (6.23) is always a *convex* problem being the maximum of linear functions of the dual variables [BV04] while the maximization in (6.22) can be decomposed in K individual problems, easier to be solved. There are however certain drawbacks in the dual approach suggested. Most importantly, the *duality gap* defined as $L_{dual}(v^*) - \sum_{n=1}^{N} u_n q_n(\rho_n^*) \geq 0$ can be strictly positive. The sufficiency condition for zero duality gap in [CZH05] requires continuity of the price-based power allocation $\vec{\rho}(v)$ at the optimal prices v^* which unfortunately cannot be guaranteed for sigmoidal-like functions. This implies that even if the problem in (6.23) is solved we may obtain only an upper bound, given the price v^* and the price-based allocation $\vec{\rho}(v^*)$ may not provide the primal global optimum or may even be an infeasible allocation. What is more, for nonconcave utilities, there may be more than one solutions $\rho_n(v)$ for each of the N problems in (6.22).

We summarize, based on [LMS02], the properties of the power allocation $\vec{\rho}(v)$ solving (6.22). We have first to define

$$\begin{aligned} v_n^{\max} &= \arg \min_{v \geq 0} \left\{ \max_{\rho_n \geq 0} \{u_n q_n(\rho_n) - v\rho_n\} = 0 \right\} \\ v_n^{\min} &= \arg \max_{v \geq 0} \{\rho_n(v) = P_{tot}\} \end{aligned}$$

In other words $v_n^{\max}$ is the maximum price per user for which (6.22) yields $\max \{u_n q_n(\rho_n) - v\rho_n\} >$

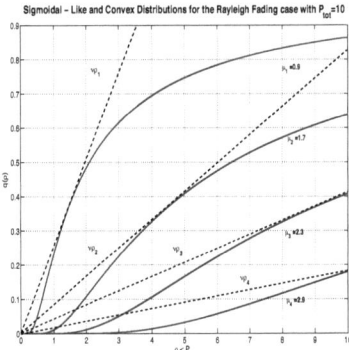

Figure 6.3: Convex and Sigmoidal-like distribution functions $q(\rho)$

0 and $v_n^{\min}$ is the highest price for which user n requires the total power. For sigmoidal-like functions $\rho_n(v)$ is

- discontinuous at $v = v_n^{\max}$
- positive and decreasing for $v_n^{\min} \leq v \leq v_n^{\max}$
- equal to 0 for $v > v_n^{\max}$
- equal to P_{tot} for $v \leq v_n^{\min}$

The properties are illustrated in Fig. 6.4 for the Rayleigh fading case, $P_{tot} = 10$ and different choices of transmission rates μ. Observe in the figure the discontinuity for $v^{\max}$ and the monotonicity.

Algorithm 1: For the solution of the maximization problem in (6.20) we will follow the algorithmic suggestion in [LMS02] and apply it for simplicity to the specific case of Rayleigh fading statistics and parallel channels. The algorithm involves two steps. In the first one a subset M out of the N users is selected to allocate power. The $N - M$ users left out are excluded from the power allocation. In the next step a utility maximization problem is solved among the M users which always provides a Pareto optimal allocation and can be solved by a simple bisect algorithm. The solution is either the exact social optimal power allocation or a rather satisfactory approximation.

For the user selection part, the users are ordered first in descending order based on the value of their $v_n^{\max}$. For the Rayleigh fading case it can be shown that $v_n^{\max} = \frac{1}{e} \frac{\mu_n}{e^{\mu_n}-1}$.

6.4. Optimal and Suboptimal Power Allocation Policies

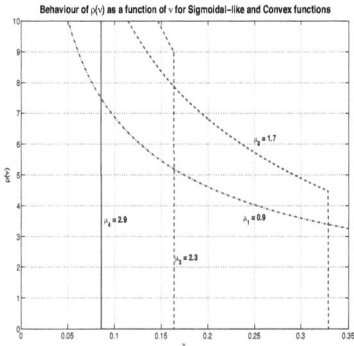

Figure 6.4: Price-based Power Allocation (6.22) for Sigmoidal-Like distributions.

$$\frac{u_{1'}}{e^{\mu_{1'}}-1} \geq \frac{u_{2'}}{e^{\mu_{2'}}-1} \geq \ldots \geq \frac{u_{N'}}{e^{\mu_{N'}}-1} \quad (6.24)$$

where n' is the index of the ordered users. The decomposed problems in (6.22) can be shown to attain at most one solution for $0 < \rho_n < P_{tot}$ which may be estimated algorithmically (e.g. Newton's method). The idea of sorting is based on the facts that each user has the maximum willingness to pay per unit power and also that as the price decreases the requested per user power increases (see properties). Starting from the highest $v_{1'}^{max} = v$ the required power only for the first user is estimated. For all other users it holds $v_{n'}^{max} < v$ and from the properties $\rho_{n'}(v) = 0$, $\forall n' \neq 1$. If the price-based power is less that P_{tot}, both the first and second user in order are considered with $v = v_{2'}^{max}$, else the algorithm ends with $M = 1$ and $v^* = v_{1'}^{max}$. Remember that the power of the first user increases as the price decreases. Hence for the second iteration, if the sum of power allocations equals P_{tot} the algorithm ends with $v^* = v_{2'}^{max}$ and $M = 2$. If it is higher than P_{tot} then the algorithm stops and only the first user is selected. The optimal price then lies between $v_{2'}^{max} < v^* < v_{1'}^{max}$. If the sum is lower, another user (third) is considered and the price decreases, and so on.

Based on this ordering, *if all users were to transmit with equal rate μ, users with higher queue lengths are preferred compared to those with lower queue lengths. For equal queue lengths u, users with lower transmission rate are prefered to those with higher rates.* The reason for the latter is that users with lower rates have a higher inter-service interval $1/\mu$

and hence higher expected number of arrivals which tend to increase their queue length relatively faster. After the M users are selected the following problem should be solved

$$\begin{aligned}\text{maximize} \quad & \sum_{n=1}^{M} u_n(t)\, q_n(\rho_n) \\ \text{subject to} \quad & \sum_{n=1}^{M} \rho_n \leq P_{tot} \\ & \rho_n \geq 0, \; \forall n = 1, \ldots, M\end{aligned} \qquad (6.25)$$

This can be shown to be equivalent to a convex programming problem, since the M users selected require power that always lies in the concave part of the sigmoidal-like functions. For more details on the algorithm the reader is referred to [LMS02].

Algorithm 2: An alternative algorithm to be used is based on an iterative subgradient method that updates the dual variable ν to solve the problem in (6.23). The subgradient for the dual function $L_{dual}(\nu)$ is $P_{tot} - \sum_{n=1}^{N} \rho_n(\nu)$ [YL06]

$$\nu(t+1) = \left[\nu(t) - s(t)\left(P_{tot} - \sum_{n=1}^{N} \rho_n(\nu(t))\right)\right]^{+} \qquad (6.26)$$

Certain selection of step sizes such as $s(t) = \beta/t$ or $\beta/\sqrt{t}$ or β, where β is a real positive constant, guarantee that the sequence of dual variables converges to the dual optimal ν^* as $t \to \infty$ [CZH05]. After initializing ν, the sequence of actions:

- Solve (6.22) and

- Update the price at the direction of the subgradient using (6.26) until the price converges

forms a *Canonically Distributed Algorithm* (CDA) that globally solves the primal and dual problems in case the utilities are concave. For non-concave utilities the solutions produced may be infeasible or suboptimal, since the duality gap can be strictly positive. A sufficient condition for the convergence of the CDA to the global optimal solution is provided in [CZH05] and it requires continuity of the price-based allocation at all optimal prices, which can unfortunately not be guaranteed for the sigmoidal-like functions under investigation.

We provide in the following some numerical evaluation for the power allocation prob-

6.4. Optimal and Suboptimal Power Allocation Policies

lem solved using the algorithm in [LMS02]. We consider a four user scenario where the service rates equal $\vec{\mu} = [0.9\ 1.7\ 2.3\ 2.9]$. A power vector $\vec{\rho} = [\rho_1, \rho_2, \rho_3, \rho_4]$ is chosen, that satisfies the constraint $P_{tot} = 20$ with equality and vector $\vec{\lambda} = [\mu_1 q_1(\rho_1), \ldots, \mu_4 q_4(\rho_4)]$ is taken as a reference.

For different values of $c \in [0, 1.2]$ and $T_{all} = 50000$ the time average $\frac{1}{T_{all}} \sum_{t=1}^{T_{all}} \sum_{n=1}^{4} u_n(t)$ is calculated through simulations for a system with arrival rates $c \cdot \vec{\lambda}$. The results are shown in Fig. 6.5 where the two curves are produced using a brut force method to find the optimal power allocation that solves (6.17) as well as the suggested Algorithm 1. The suboptimality of the power allocation using Algorithm 1 results in instability of the system for arrival rates that actually belong to the stability region (see $1.05 \leq c \leq 1.1$).

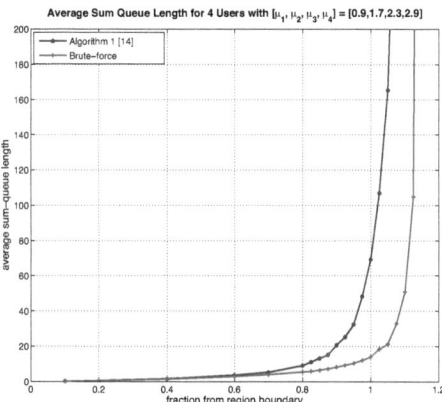

Figure 6.5: Average sum of queue lengths for 4 queues: Algorithm 1 vs Brut Force.

We further compare in Tables 6.1-6.3 the algorithm in [LMS02] with Algorithm 2 for the case of Rayleigh Fading, where 7 users compete for the short-term power budget $P_{tot} = 20$ and use different transmission rates.

The example in Table 6.2 shows that the CDA is possible to produce infeasible solutions. In Table 6.2 the queue lengths are kept equal for all users, where the solution of the algorithm 1 and 2 show that users with higher rates are preferred but the power allocation is not necessarily proportional to the rate. The same results for the two algorithms are shown in Table 6.3 where all users transmit with the same rate but the current queue lengths are here different. The algorithms choose users with higher queue lengths and the higher the actual queue length the higher the allocated power. Finally Table 6.1 illustrates a scenario where users have different queue lengths and transmission rates. The v_n^{max} values are calculated and it is explicitly shown that both algorithms choose users with highest maximum prices. Hence the tables support the conclusions derived from the ordering in (6.24) that users with higher backlog and lower rates are preferred for power allocation.

μ_n	1.9	2.7	1.4	1.1	2.9	1.9	2.3
u_n	10	7	3	3	2	3	15
λ_n^{max}	0.65	0.19	0.36	0.55	0.04	0.19	0.62
ρ_k (CDA)	6.5	0	1.6	2	0	0	9.9
ρ_k ([LMS02])	7.1	0	0	2.2	0	0	10.7

Table 6.1: Algorithm comparison: different queue lengths and different rates

μ_n	1.9	2.7	1.4	1.1	2.9	1.9	2.3
u_n	4	4	4	4	4	4	4
λ_n^{max}	0.26	0.11	0.48	0.73	0.09	0.26	0.16
ρ_n (CDA)	5.23	0	4.81	4.22	0	5.23	5.37
ρ_k ([LMS02])	7.85	0	6.55	5.60	0	0	0

Table 6.2: Algorithm comparison: constant queue lengths and different rates.

μ_n	1.9	1.9	1.9	1.9	1.9	1.9	1.9
u_n	10	7	3	3	2	3	15
λ_n^{max}	0.65	0.45	0.19	0.19	0.13	0.19	0.97
ρ_n (CDA)	6.52	4.46	0	0	0	0	9.02
ρ_k ([LMS02])	8.59	0	0	0	0	0	11.41

Table 6.3: Algorithm comparison: constant rates and different queue lengths.

Chapter 7

Stability and Distributed Power Control in MANETs with ARQ

The current chapter considers a Mobile Ad-hoc NETwork (MANET) where data flows entering from a set of source nodes should be routed to their destinations. In such networks a major concern is the maximum set of incoming rates that can be supported, since interference is the bottleneck. If a utility function is related to each incoming flow a very interesting problem is to maximize the sum of all utilities under the constraint that the queues of all nodes remain stable. Such problems have been addressed in [TE92], [NMR05], [NML08], [LS], [SWB09] and algorithms that optimally adapt the incoming rates and the transmission powers of each node have been suggested.

Here we are interested in bringing these models a step further and investigate how the stability regions and the optimal policies for congestion control, routing and power allocation vary, when the queues of each node use ARQ protocols to repeat transmissions of erroneous packets due to outages. In the current literature, investigations already addressing the network utility maximization (NUM) problem with erroneous transmissions through the links consider mainly fixed routing. In [PDE] the model does not consider queueing aspects and a NUM problem with rate-outage constraints per link is approximately solved. In [LCC06] the effect of end-to-end error probability is included in the utility of each source. The same problem with average power and reliability requirements is posed and algorithmically solved in [OTGB08]. Furthermore, in [ACAB09] a single hop ad-hoc network with outages is considered where a solution for joint admission control, rate and power allocation is derived based on a stochastic game formulation. Other contributions that investigate the effect of retransmissions in MANETs incorporating Random Access MAC protocols include [MFK08], [EKEA08].

Motivated by a comment in [XJB04] where it is stated that "*in practical communication systems, the link capacity should be defined appropriately, taking packet loss and retransmissions into account, hence the flow conservation law holds for goodputs instead of rates*", and after a presentation of the model under study, we derive the goodput capacity region. The success probability for the transmission over a wireless link depends on the entire power allocation and the scheduled transmission rate. We constrain our investigations to functions with specific properties, where it is shown that these also hold for the expression with Rayleigh fading [KB02]. The NUM problem naturally decomposes into the input rate control and the scheduling problem.

At this point a major challenge is to achieve a decentralized solution of the second problem. This is always possible of course for the case of parallel channels (see also [XJB04] and [CB04]). Algorithmic suggestions can be found in [NMR05] for zero-full power allocations and in [CLCD] by solving a maximum weighted matching problem over a conflict graph. In our work fully distributed implementation is achieved by approaching the second problem with the arsenal of supermodular game theory - an idea appearing in [HBH06] and [SMG02] - and result to the suggestion of a price based algortithm that achieves almost optimal solutions with minimum information exchange between the nodes.

7.1 The MANET Model under Study

We consider a wireless network consisting of N nodes $\mathcal{N} = \{1, \ldots, N\}$, while $\mathcal{L}$ is the set of all possible $L_{links} = N \cdot (N-1)$ links. The time is divided into slots of equal duration T^{slot} (normalized to 1) and $t = \{0, 1, \ldots\}$ is the time index. Data flows enter the network at source nodes and are removed at destination nodes $\mathcal{D} = \{1, \ldots, D\}$. The set of data flows (*commodity flows*) injected into the network at a source node with a predefined destination is denoted by $\mathcal{S} = \{1, \ldots, S\}$. The routes of the data flows through the network are not fixed. Furthermore, each link $l \in \mathcal{L}$ is characterized by an origin node $b(l)$ (begin) and an end node $e(l)$ (end). At each node n, a total of D buffers - one for each commodity flow - are reserved (see also Fig.7.1).

In the general case investigated, each node $n \in \mathcal{N}$ chooses at slot t a power $\rho_l(t)$ as well as a rate $\mu_l(t)$ to transmit data through link l, as long as $n = b(l)$. The total transmission

7.1. The MANET Model under Study

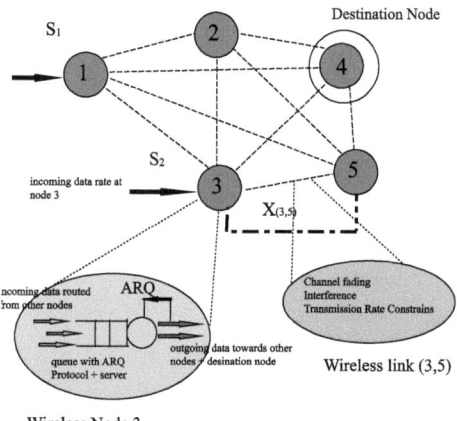

Figure 7.1: An example of the wireless network with a single destination $d = 4$.

rate of packets through link l at some time slot t is the sum of the transmission rates of the individual commodities sharing the link meaning $\mu_l(t) = \sum_{d=1}^{D} \mu_l^d(t)$. Scheduled packets of variable length $\mu_l^d(t)$ for each commodity d are combined into a common packet of length $\mu_l(t)$ and sent through the link. The resulting long packet may be received at node $e(l)$ with errors due to fading and interference. The probability of successful transmission is then a real valued function $q(\vec{\rho}, \mu) : \mathbb{R}_+^{N \cdot (N-1)} \times \mathcal{M} \to [0, 1]$ of the entire power allocation at slot t, $\vec{\rho}(t) \in \mathcal{P} \subseteq \mathbb{R}_+^{N \cdot (N-1)}$ and the scheduled rate $\mu_l(t)$. The set of all possible scheduling rates is denoted by $\mathcal{M}$. The nodes have power restrictions, e.g. $\forall n, \sum_{l:n=b(l)} \rho_l(t) \leq P_n$ and $\mathcal{P}$ is the convex compact set of all feasible power allocations.

Examples of such success probability functions for flat block-fading channels can be found - as in the previous chapter - using the outage probability definition [7]. Given an $SINR_l$ threshold value $\gamma(\mu_l) = e^{\mu_l} - 1$ of link l (we often simply write $\gamma_l := \gamma(\mu_l)$)

$$q_l(\vec{\rho}, \mu_l) = \mathbb{P}(SINR_l(\vec{\rho}) \geq e^{\mu_l} - 1), \quad SINR_l(\vec{\rho}) = \frac{G_{ll} F_{ll} \rho_l}{\sum_{j \neq l} G_{lj} F_{lj} \rho_j + \sigma_{e(l)}^2} \quad (7.1)$$

where Y_{lj} stands for $Y_{b(j)e(l)}$, μ_l is the scheduled transmission rate through the link, $G_{b(j)e(l)}$ is the slow varying path gain and $F_{b(j)e(l)}$ is the associated flat fading component of the channel. For the case of Rayleigh/Rayleigh fading (meaning Rayleigh slow fading for both the desired and interference signals), a closed form expression of (7.1) can be found in [KB02] and [PED05]

$$q_l(\vec{\rho}, \mu_l) = \exp\left(\frac{-\sigma^2 \gamma_l}{G_{ll}\rho_l}\right) \prod_{j \neq l} \left(1 + \frac{\gamma_l G_{lj}\rho_j}{G_{ll}\rho_l}\right)^{-1}. \quad (7.2)$$

Observe that the success functions used imply that only the channel fast fading *statistics* are known and the nodes have no other instantaneous channel state information (CSI) over the fading gains, except - possibly - the slow varying path gains. The actual amount of data transmitted through each link equals $\mu_l(t) \cdot X_l(t)$. $X_l(t)$ is a binary random variable which equals 1 for success (with prob. q_l) and 0 for failure (with prob. $1 - q_l$). The expected transmission rate through link l is then

$$g_l(\vec{\rho}, \mu_l) := \mu_l \cdot q_l(\vec{\rho}, \mu_l) \quad (7.3)$$

and is called the *goodput* of link l [AB03], [BS06]. Furthermore, in the analysis that follows we often encounter a quantity called *maximum goodput* defined as (see [AB03] and [5] for parallel Rayleigh fading channels)

$$g_l(\vec{\rho}) = \max_{\mu_l \in \mathcal{M}} \mu_l \cdot q_l(\vec{\rho}, \mu_l). \quad (7.4)$$

In case a packet of length $\mu_l(t)$ is received at node $e(l)$ with errors, we assume that this can always be detected during decoding. When reception is correct an ACK is fed back otherwise a NACK signal is transmitted to $b(l)$ via a reliable zero-delay wireless feedback link. In the latter case the packets of all transmitted commodities are then not removed from the buffer but wait for a future retransmission (Stop-and-Wait ARQ) under some new scheduling decision. The queue evolution for each node n and commodity flow d at slot t, is given by

7.2 Network Capacity Region and Variations with Dropping

$$u_n^d(t+1) = \left[u_n^d(t) - \sum_{k:n=b(k)} \mu_k^d(t) X_k(t)\right]^+ + \sum_{l:n=e(l)} \mu_l^d(t) X_l(t) + \alpha_n^d(t+1). \quad (7.5)$$

The success probability of the transmission through link l is equal for all commodities d, since it depends on the sum rate μ_l. In the expression (7.5), $\sum_{k:n=b(k)} \mu_k^d(t) X_k(t)$ is the actual outgoing data ("actual" meaning "error free") from node n, $\sum_{l:n=e(l)} \mu_l^d(t) X_l(t)$ is the actual incoming data from links $l \in \mathcal{L} : n = e(l)$, $n \neq d$ and $\alpha_n^d(t+1)$ is the amount of commodity d bits arriving exogenously to the network at node n during t.

We associate each incoming flow to the network at node n with destination $d \in \mathcal{D}$, $\alpha_n^d = \alpha_s$, with a utility function $U_s : \mathbb{R}_+ \to \mathbb{R}_+$. The utility function takes as argument the average incoming data rate $\mathbb{E}[\alpha_s] = \lambda_s$ and is non-decreasing, strictly concave and continuously differentiable over the range $\lambda_s \geq 0$ (*elastic traffic*, [Kel97]). The utilities describe the satisfaction received by transmitting data from node $s \in \mathcal{S}$ to $d \in \mathcal{D}$.

The aim here is to find an incoming rate vector $\vec{\lambda} = (\lambda_1, \ldots, \lambda_S)$ to maximize the sum of the utilities $\sum_{s \in \mathcal{S}} U_s(\lambda_s)$ subject to the constraint that the system remains stable and furthermore explicitly provide the stabilizing scheduling policy $\forall \vec{\lambda} \in \Lambda$. Λ denotes the *capacity region* of the system, the largest set of $\vec{\lambda}$ for which the system remains stable. Formally we write

$$\max \sum_{s \in \mathcal{S}} U_s(\lambda_s) \quad \text{subject to} \quad \vec{\lambda} \in \Lambda. \quad (7.6)$$

7.2 Network Capacity Region and Variations with Dropping

The problem posed so far is similar to the models investigated in [NMR05], [NML08], [LS] and [CLCD]. Due to the occurence of errors and the use of retransmissions, the capacity region of the model under investigation is definitely reduced and has a different expression compared to the works mentioned. The proof follows the same lines as for the derivation of the network capacity region in [NMR05].

Theorem 27. *The capacity region Λ of the wireless network under study is the set of all non-negative vectors $\vec{\lambda} = (\lambda_1, \ldots, \lambda_S)$ such that there exist multicommodity **goodput** flow variables $\{g_l^d\}_{l \in \mathcal{L}}^{d \in \mathcal{D}}$, satisfying*

Chapter 7. Stability and Distributed Power Control in MANETs with ARQ

- $g_l^d \geq 0$, $\forall l \in \mathcal{L}, d \in \mathcal{D}$ and $g_l^d = 0$ if $e(l) = d$
- $\forall n \in \mathcal{N}, d \in \mathcal{D}$: $\sum_{l:e(l)=n} g_l^d + \lambda_n^d \leq \sum_{k:b(k)=n} g_k^d$
- $\sum_{d \in \mathcal{D}} g_l^d \leq g_l$, $\vec{g} = \{g_l\} \in \Gamma$, where $\Gamma = \mathbf{co}\left(\hat{\Gamma}\right)$ and

$$\hat{\Gamma} = \bigcup_{\vec{p} \in \mathcal{P}} \left\{ \vec{g} \in \mathbb{R}_+^{N \cdot (N-1)} : \forall l \in \mathcal{L}, g_l \leq \bar{\mu}_l(\vec{p}) \cdot q_l(\vec{p}, \bar{\mu}_l(\vec{p})), \bar{\mu}_l(\vec{p}) = \arg\max_{\mu_l \in \mathcal{M}} \mu_l \cdot q_l(\vec{p}, \mu_l) \right\} \quad (7.7)$$

Proof. • Necessary condition. If the network is stable then $\vec{\lambda} \in \Lambda$

Let us consider a system with rate convergent inputs and input rate vector $\vec{\lambda} = (\lambda_s)_{s \in \mathcal{S}}$. Then $\lim_{t \to \infty} \frac{1}{t} \sum_t \alpha_s(t) = \lambda_s$. The process $\alpha_s(t)$ has been defined in (7.5) to be the amount of commodity bits exogenously entering the network at node s during timeslot t. We further define $u_n^d(t)$ (see (7.5)) as the current length of the buffer reserved at node n for commodity d and $\hat{g}_l^d(t)$ the *actual* number of bits of commodity d *correctly* transmitted over the link l to node $e(l)$ for the time period $[0,t]$. We note here that the latter is less or equal to the goodput $\sum_t \mu(t) \cdot q(\vec{p}(t), \mu(t))$ up to t since the potential rate scheduled at some time slot $\mu(t)$ may be larger than the available bits waiting in queue.

The first property for the g_l^d's can be directly verified. Using now the *conservation law* for each queue, we have that the actual unfinished work equals the number of bits arrived minus those that have been correctly served, up to time t.

$$\sum_t \alpha_n^d(t) + \sum_{l \in \mathcal{L}: n = e(l)} \hat{g}_l^d(t) = u_n^d(t) + \sum_{k \in \mathcal{L}: n = b(k)} \hat{g}_k^d(t), \quad \forall n \in \mathcal{N}, \forall d \in \mathcal{D}$$

and $\sum_t \alpha_n^d(t) = 0$ if $n \notin \mathcal{S}$. Argumenting as in [NMR05] we may find arbitrarily large time instants $\hat{t}$ such that there exists a positive probability for the events $u_n^d(\hat{t})/\hat{t} \leq V/\hat{t} \leq \epsilon$ and $\sum_t \alpha_n^d(\hat{t})/\hat{t} \geq \lambda_n^d - \epsilon$, $\forall n \in \mathcal{N}, d \in \mathcal{D}$. V is some finite level of unfinished work. Setting $g_l^d = \hat{g}_l^d(\hat{t})/\hat{t}$

$$\lambda_n^d + \sum_{l \in \mathcal{L}: n = e(l)} g_l^d(t) \leq \sum_{k \in \mathcal{L}: n = b(k)} g_k^d(t) + 2\epsilon$$

7.2. Network Capacity Region and Variations with Dropping

and the second property of the multicommodity goodput flow variables is satisfied. Finally we have that $\sum_{d \in \mathcal{D}} g_l^d = \frac{1}{\hat{t}} \sum_{d \in \mathcal{D}} \hat{g}_l^d(\hat{t})$ and

$$\sum_{d \in \mathcal{D}} \frac{\hat{g}_l^d(\hat{t})}{\hat{t}} \leq \frac{1}{\hat{t}} \sum_{t=1}^{\hat{t}} \mu_l(t) \cdot q_l(\vec{p}(t), \mu_l(t))$$

$$\stackrel{(a)}{=} \sum_{j=1}^{\infty} \frac{T_{\vec{p}^j}}{\hat{t}} \frac{1}{T_{\vec{p}^j}} \sum_{\tau_j=1}^{T_{\vec{p}^j}} \mu_l(\tau_j) \cdot q_l(\vec{p}^j, \mu_l(\tau_j))$$

$$\leq \sum_{j=1}^{\infty} \frac{T_{\vec{p}^j}}{\hat{t}} \max_{\mu_l} \mu_l \cdot q_l(\vec{p}^j, \mu_l)$$

$$\stackrel{\hat{t} \to \infty}{\to} \sum_{j=1}^{\infty} f_j \cdot \bar{\mu}_l(\vec{p}^j) \cdot q_l(\vec{p}^j, \bar{\mu}_l(\vec{p}^j))$$

where (a) comes from the fact that the power allocation vector $\vec{p}^j$ is used $T_{\vec{p}^j}$ out of the total $\hat{t}$ slots under some policy π, f_j is the limit $T_{\vec{p}^j}/\hat{t} \stackrel{\hat{t} \to \infty}{\to} f_j$, $\sum_{j=1}^{\infty} f_j = 1$ and $\bar{\mu}_l(\vec{p}^j) = \arg\max_{\mu_l} \mu_l \cdot q_l(\vec{p}^j, \mu_l)$. Then if the system is stable $\forall l \in \mathcal{L}$, $\sum_{d \in \mathcal{D}} g_l^d \leq g_l$, where g_l is written as a convex combination of all possible values of goodput $\bar{\mu}_l(\vec{p}^j) \cdot q_l(\vec{p}^j, \bar{\mu}_l(\vec{p}^j))$ produced by allocating $\vec{p}^j \in \mathcal{P}$ (we consider only a countably infinite number of different possible power allocations). This equals to the convex hull of the set $\hat{\Gamma}$, by [Roc70, p.18, Th. 3.3] Hence the last property holds.

- Sufficient Condition. If $\vec{\lambda} \in \Lambda$ then the system is stable under the goodput backpressure policy

The proof utilizes the Foster - Lyapunov stability criteria [Asm00], [LMNM01]. We have to assume as in [7] and the previous chapter that

1. The data arrivals per slot $\alpha_n^d(t+1)$ are realizations of i.i.d. random variables,

2. The power allocation is based solely on the information on the current queue lengths and

3. The random variables $X_l(t)$ are independent $\forall l \in \mathcal{L}, t = \{0, 1, \ldots\}$

so that the equations in (7.5) form an $N \cdot D$-dimensional Markov Chain. The test function is the sum of queue backlog squares $\sum_{n,d} u_n^d(t)^2$ where $u_n^d(t)$ is given in (7.5). Omitting the details we have $\forall n, d$ and $n \neq d$ (the dependence on time is also omitted when it is obvious from the context)

Chapter 7. Stability and Distributed Power Control in MANETs with ARQ

$$u_n^d(t+1)^2 - u_n^d(t)^2 \leq \left(\sum_{k:n=b(k)} \mu_k^d X_k\right)^2 + \left(\sum_{l:n=e(l)} \mu_l^d X_l + \alpha_n^d\right)^2$$
$$- 2u_n^d \left(\sum_{k:n=b(k)} \mu_k^d X_k - \sum_{l:n=e(l)} \mu_l^d X_l - \alpha_n^d\right)$$

If the maximum transmission rate and the second moment of the arrival processes are bounded, then the first two terms of the righthand side above are less than equal to a positive constant K and the Lyapunov drift $\Delta\left((u)_n^d\right)$ of the network satisfies

$$\mathbb{E}\left[\sum_{n,d} u_n^d(t+1)^2 - \sum_{n,d} u_n^d(t)^2 \,|\, u_n^d(t)\right] \leq KND -$$
$$-2 \sum_{n,d} u_n^d \mathbb{E}\left[\sum_{k:n=b(k)} \mu_k^d X_k - \sum_{l:n=e(l)} \mu_l^d X_l - \alpha_n^d \,|\, u_n^d(t)\right]$$
$$= KND + \sum_{n,d} u_n^d x_n^d$$
$$-2 \sum_{n,d} u_n^d \left(\sum_{k:n=b(k)} \mu_k^d q_k(\vec{p}, \mu_k) - \sum_{l:n=e(l)} \mu_l^d q_l(\vec{p}, \mu_l)\right)$$

Choose now an arrival rate vector $\vec{\lambda}$ such that $\vec{\lambda} + \vec{\epsilon} \in \Lambda$, where $\vec{\epsilon}$ is an S-dimensional vector whose entries all equal $\epsilon > 0$. Since $\vec{\lambda} + \vec{\epsilon}$ belongs to the capacity region the second property in Theorem 27 holds and $\lambda_n^d \leq -\epsilon + \sum_{k:b(k)=n} g_k^d - \sum_{l:e(l)=n} g_l^d$.

$$\Delta\left((u)_n^d\right) = KND - \sum_{n,d} u_n^d \epsilon -$$
$$-2 \sum_{n,d} u_n^d \left(\sum_{k:n=b(k)} \mu_k^d q_k(\vec{p}, \mu_k) - \sum_{k:b(k)=n} g_k^d\right)$$
$$+2 \sum_{n,d} u_n^d \left(\sum_{l:n=e(l)} \mu_l^d q_l(\vec{p}, \mu_l) - \sum_{l:e(l)=n} g_l^d\right)$$

By rearranging the summation over n, d for the last two terms we get

7.2. Network Capacity Region and Variations with Dropping

$$\Delta\left((u)_n^d\right) = KND - \sum_{n,d} u_n^d \epsilon -$$
$$-2 \sum_{l \in \mathcal{L}, d \in \mathcal{D}} \left(u_{b(l)}^d - u_{e(l)}^d\right)\left(\mu_l^d q_l(\vec{p}, \mu_l) - g_l^d\right) \tag{7.8}$$

We show in the following that the last term is always negative under the *goodput backpressure policy* π_{g-bp} (see [TE92] and [NMR05]). Based on this policy the single commodity $d^*(l) = \arg\max_d (u_{b(l)} - u_{e(l)})$ is chosen to be routed through each link $l \in \mathcal{L}$. Now define $w_l = \max(u_{b(l)} - u_{e(l)}, 0)$. The policy π_{g-bp} maximizes the sum $\sum_{l \in \mathcal{L}, d \in \mathcal{D}} w_l \mu_l^{d^*} q_l(\vec{p}, \mu_l)$ over $\vec{p} \in \mathcal{P}$ and $\mu_l \in \mathcal{M}$. Then we have

$$\max_{\vec{p}, \mu_l} \sum_l w_l \mu_l q_l(\vec{p}, \mu_l) = \max_{\vec{p}} \sum_l w_l \bar{\mu}_l q_l(\vec{p}, \bar{\mu}_l) \stackrel{(a)}{=}$$
$$\stackrel{(a)}{=} \max_{(g_l) \in \Gamma} \sum_l w_l g_l \geq \sum_l w_l g_l$$

For equality (a) we may argue as follows. We use the notation $r_l(\vec{p}) = \bar{\mu}_l q_l(\vec{p}, \bar{\mu}_l)$ and $\vec{r}(\vec{p})$ is a length L_{link} goodput vector. The set of achievable values of $\vec{r}(\vec{p})$ is the set $\hat{\Gamma}$ defined in Theorem 27. Then $\vec{p}^*$ maximizes $\sum_l w_l \bar{\mu}_l q_l(\vec{p}, \bar{\mu}_l)$ over the feasible set $\vec{p} \in \mathcal{P}$ (in other words is a Pareto optimal point) if and only if $\{\vec{z} | \vec{w}^T (\vec{z} - \vec{r}(\vec{p}^*)) = 0\}$, ($\vec{w}^T$ is the transpose vector of $\vec{w}$) is a supporting hyperplane to the set $\hat{\Gamma}$ of achievable values at the point $\vec{r}(\vec{p}^*)$ [BV04, p.179]. But of course this will also be a supporting hyperplane to the convex hull Γ of the above set at the same point.

Since the third term in (7.8) is negative, we conclude that there exists a $B \geq 0$ such that the drift is always negative for $\|\vec{u}\|_2^2 > B$, where $\|\vec{u}\|_2^2 = \sum_{n,d} u_n^{d2}$ is the square of the 2-norm of $\vec{u} = \left(u_1^1, \ldots, u_1^D, \ldots, u_N^1, \ldots, u_N^D\right)$ (which is simply the test function) and the network is *strongly stable* [LMNM01, Th.2] under the policy π_{g-bp}.

□

In the above $\{g_l^d\}_{l \in \mathcal{L}}^{d \in \mathcal{D}}$ is the $D \cdot N \cdot (N-1)$ size vector of goodput flow variables for all commodities through the network. An optimal policy achieving stability for all vectors within Λ is a variation of the well-known backpressure policy [TE92], [NMR05] where goodputs replace the rate vectors. This is named here **goodput** backpressure policy. We further denote with Γ the *goodput region* of the network, which equals the convex hull (co) of $\hat{\Gamma}$ given in (7.7). Comparing this region to the ones appearing in [NMR05] and [CB04] the rate-power mapping $r_l(\vec{\rho}) = \log(1 + SINR_l(\vec{\rho}))$ is replaced here by the maximum goodput-power mapping $g_l(\vec{\rho})$.

Let us now assume that the nodes can decide, in addition to the transmission power ρ_l and rate μ_l over the link $l \in \mathcal{L} : n = b(l)$, whether the possibly erroneous packet at time slot t should be dropped or should be held in the node's queues and wait to be retransmitted at the next time slot $t+1$. We use the binary decision variable $A_l(t)$ taking values $A_l(t) = 0$ for dropping decision and $A_l(t) = 1$ for a decision to continue. The single queue evolution will be the same as in (7.5) where X_l (and similarly X_k) should be replaced by the expression $1 - A_l(t)(1 - X_l(t))$ which equals $X_l(t)$ when $A_l(t) = 1$ and 1 when $A_l(t) = 0$.

If the decisions on dropping are randomized, with a fixed probability of dropping per link equal to $1 - \delta_l \in [0, 1]$ (and hence $\mathbb{E}[A_l(t)] = \delta_l$), the network capacity region $\Lambda_{\vec{\delta}}$, $\vec{\delta} = (\delta_1, \ldots, \delta_{L_{links}})$, will be the same as in Theorem 27 with a modification on the region $\hat{\Gamma}$. In this case we have that

$$\hat{\Gamma}_{\vec{\delta}} = \bigcup_{\vec{\rho} \in \mathcal{P}} \left\{ \vec{g} \in \mathbb{R}_+^{N \cdot (N-1)} : \forall l \in \mathcal{L}, g_l \leq \bar{\mu}_l^{\delta_l} \left(1 - \delta_l \cdot \left(1 - q_l\left(\vec{\rho}, \bar{\mu}_l^{\delta_l}\right)\right)\right) \right\} \quad (7.9)$$

$\bar{\mu}_l^{\delta_l} := \bar{\mu}_l(\vec{\rho}, \delta_l) = \arg\max_{\mu_l \in \mathcal{M}} \mu_l \cdot (1 - \delta_l \cdot (1 - q_l(\vec{\rho}, \mu_l)))$. Choice of the vector $\vec{\delta} = \vec{1} := (1, \ldots, 1)$ results in the region of Theorem 27 where no dropping takes place, while for $\vec{\delta} = \vec{0} := (0, \ldots, 0)$, dropping always takes place after an erroneous transmission and this provides the maximum network capacity region with $\hat{\Gamma}_{\vec{\delta}}$ equal to

$$\hat{\Gamma}_{\vec{\delta}=\vec{0}} = \left\{ \vec{g} \in \mathbb{R}_+^{N \cdot (N-1)} : \forall l \in \mathcal{L}, g_l \leq \mu_l^* \right\} \quad (7.10)$$

where $\mu_l^* = \arg\max_{\mu_l \in \mathcal{M}} \mu_l$ is the maximum allowable transmission rate per link. We can then obtain different regions $\Lambda_{\vec{\delta}}$ between these two extremes by varying the dropping probabilities per link. To understand why this is important suppose that a network user transmitting a data flow with source node $s \in \mathcal{S}$ has a higher data rate than that offered by the actual error free network capacity region $\Lambda_{\vec{\delta}=\vec{1}}$. We may then vary the vector $\vec{\delta}$ so that the network will fit the requirements of the user. Of course the *average* rate of *correctly* transmitted packets through the network will not change. What will happen is that, instead of removing part of the user's packets at entering the network (admission control), the network will offer per link at least one chance for all packets to be correctly transmitted through the network, hence will be able to provide *unreliable* service to the *entire* required high data rate, with index of reliablity $\vec{\delta}$.

7.3 Properties of the Success Function and Maximum Goodput Function

The success probability function $q_l(\vec{\rho}, \mu_l)$ for transmission over link $l \in \mathcal{L}$ considered in this work, has the following properties[*].

- **P.1** q_l is strictly *increasing* in ρ_l and the log of the function is concave in ρ_l

- **P.2** q_l is strictly *decreasing* and *convex* in ρ_k, $\forall k \neq l, k \in \mathcal{L}$

- **P.3** q_l is strictly *decreasing* in μ_l

- **P.4** The log of the function has *increasing differences* for the pair of variables (ρ_l, μ_l) meaning that

$$\log q_l\left(\rho_l^+, \mu_l\right) - \log q_l(\rho_l, \mu_l) \leq \log q_l\left(\rho_l^+, \mu_l^+\right) - \log q_l\left(\rho_l, \mu_l^+\right) \quad (7.11)$$

where $\rho_l^+ \geq \rho_l$ and $\mu_l^+ \geq \mu_l$.

- **P.5** The log of the function has *increasing differences* for each pair of variables (ρ_l, ρ_j), $\forall j \neq l$, meaning

$$\log q_l\left(\rho_l^+, \rho_j\right) - \log q_l\left(\rho_l, \rho_j\right) \leq \log q_l\left(\rho_l^+, \rho_j^+\right) - \log q_l\left(\rho_l, \rho_j^+\right) \quad (7.12)$$

where $\rho_l^+ \geq \rho_l$ and $\rho_j^+ \geq \rho_j$. The differences are *constant* for all pairs (ρ_i, ρ_j), where $i \neq j$ and $i, j \in \mathcal{L} \setminus \{l\}$.

---

[*]The game-theoretic notation $q_l(\rho_l, \vec{\rho}_{-l}, \mu_l)$ is often used, where $\vec{\rho}_{-l}$ is the entire power vector excluding the l-th element ρ_l. Furtermore, the dependence of the success function on variables that do not influence certain properties, as in (7.11) and (7.12) may be omitted for convinience of the presentation.

122 Chapter 7. Stability and Distributed Power Control in MANETs with ARQ

The last property actually implies - using [Top98, Corollary 2.6.1] - that the function is log-*supermodular*. By property **P.4** a positive change on the transmission power ρ_l has a greater impact on the increase of the (logarithm of the) success probability, the higher the rate of transmission. If we e.g. transmit with 16-QAM modulation, an increase of power by $\Delta \rho_l > 0$ will increase $\log q$ much more than in the case of transmission with BPSK.

Theorem 28. *The success probability function for the Rayleigh/Rayleigh fading case, given in (7.2) satisfies properties* **P.1-P.5**.

Proof. For the proof, the expressions (7.13) - (7.17) of first and second order partial derivatives are required. Specifically, from (7.13) and (7.14) the function is increasing in ρ_l and decreasing in ρ_j (strictly if $\rho_l \geq P_l^{\min} > 0$ and same for j). From (7.16) the logarithm of the function is concave in ρ_l. The convexity in **P.2** comes directly from the partial derivative of (7.14) over ρ_j which is easily shown to be positive. **P.3** is shown in (7.15), whereas **P.4** comes directly by derivating (7.15) w.r.t. ρ_l. Finally, **P.5** is a direct consequence of the fact that - in (7.17) - $\frac{\partial^2 \log q_l(\vec{\rho}, \mu_l)}{\partial \rho_l \partial \rho_j} \geq 0$ and $\frac{\partial^2 \log q_l(\vec{\rho}, \mu_l)}{\partial \rho_i \partial \rho_j} = 0$ (see [Top98, p.42]).

$$\frac{\partial q_l(\rho_l, \vec{\rho}_{-l}, \mu_l)}{\partial \rho_l} = q_l(\rho_l, \vec{\rho}_{-l}, \mu_l) \cdot \left[\frac{\sigma^2 \gamma_l(\mu_l)}{G_{ll} \rho_l^2} + \sum_{j \neq l} \frac{1}{\frac{G_{ll} \rho_l^2}{\gamma_l(\mu_l) G_{lj} \rho_j} + \rho_l} \right] \geq 0 \quad (7.13)$$

$$\frac{\partial q_l(\rho_l, \vec{\rho}_{-l}, \mu_l)}{\partial \rho_j} = -q_l(\rho_l, \vec{\rho}_{-l}, \mu_l) \cdot \frac{1}{\frac{G_{ll} \rho_l}{\gamma_l(\mu_l) G_{lj}} + \rho_j} \leq 0 \quad (7.14)$$

$$\frac{\partial q_l(\rho_l, \vec{\rho}_{-l}, \mu_l)}{\partial \mu_l} = q_l(\rho_l, \vec{\rho}_{-l}, \mu_l) \cdot \left[\frac{-\sigma^2 e^{\mu_l}}{G_{ll} \rho_l} - \sum_{j \neq l} \frac{e^{\mu_l} G_{lj} \rho_j}{G_{ll} \rho_l + \gamma_l(\mu_l) G_{lj} \rho_j} \right] \leq 0 \quad (7.15)$$

$$\frac{\partial^2 \log q_l(\rho_l, \vec{\rho}_{-l}, \mu_l)}{\partial \rho_l^2} = -\frac{2\sigma^2 \gamma_l(\mu_l)}{G_{ll} \rho_l^3} - \sum_{j \neq l} \frac{\frac{2 \rho_l G_{ll}}{\gamma_l(\mu_l) G_{lj} \rho_j} + 1}{\left(\frac{G_{ll} \rho_l^2}{\gamma_l(\mu_l) G_{lj} \rho_j} + \rho_l \right)^2} \leq 0 \quad (7.16)$$

$$\frac{\partial^2 \log q_l(\rho_l, \vec{\rho}_{-l}, \mu_l)}{\partial \rho_l \partial \rho_j} = \frac{\frac{G_{ll}}{\gamma_l(\mu_l) G_{lj}}}{\left(\frac{G_{ll} \rho_l}{\gamma_l(\mu_l) G_{lj}} + \rho_j \right)^2} \geq 0. \quad (7.17)$$

□

Using the above properties we can derive important properties for the maximum goodput function in (7.4), which as seen in (7.7) plays a critical role in the definition of the system capacity region.

7.3. Properties of the Success Function and Maximum Goodput Function

Theorem 29. If the success probability function satisfies **P.1-P.5** then the *maximum goodput function* in (7.4) has the following properties (where $\bar{\mu}_l(\vec{\rho}) = \arg\max_{\mu_l \in \mathcal{M}} \mu_l q_l(\vec{\rho}, \mu_l)$)

- **P'.1** $g_l(\vec{\rho})$ is *strictly increasing* in ρ_l
- **P'.2** $g_l(\vec{\rho})$ is *strictly decreasing* and *convex* in ρ_k, $\forall k \neq l$
- **P'.3** $\bar{\mu}_l(\vec{\rho})$ is *non-decreasing* in ρ_l
- **P'.4** $\bar{\mu}_l(\vec{\rho})$ is *non-increasing* in ρ_k, $\forall k \neq l$

Proof.
- **P'.1**: Suppose $\rho_l^+ > \rho_l$ and let $\mu_l^+ := \arg\max_{\mu_l \in \mathcal{M}} \mu_l q_l(\rho_l^+, \mu_l)$, and also $\bar{\mu}_l := \arg\max_{\mu_l \in \mathcal{M}} \mu_l q_l(\rho_l, \mu_l)$. Then $\forall \mu_l \in \mathcal{M}$

$$\mu_l^+ q_l\left(\rho_l^+, \mu_l^+\right) \stackrel{(a)}{\geq} \mu_l q_l\left(\rho_l^+, \mu_l\right) \stackrel{(b)}{>} \mu_l q_l(\rho_l, \mu_l)$$

In the above, (a) comes from the definition of μ_l^+ and (b) from **P.1** of the success probability function. Since the inequality holds $\forall \mu_l$ it also holds for $\mu_l = \bar{\mu}_l$, hence $g_l\left(\rho_l^+, \vec{\rho}_{-l}\right) > g_l(\rho_l, \vec{\rho}_{-l})$.

- **P'.2**: For the monotonicity we proceed as above, where $\rho_k^+ > \rho_k$, $\mu_l^+ := \arg\max_{\mu_l \in \mathcal{M}} \mu_l q_l\left(\rho_k^+, \mu_l\right)$, and also $\bar{\mu}_l := \arg\max_{\mu_l \in \mathcal{M}} \mu_l q_l(\rho_k, \mu_l)$. Then $\forall \mu_l \in \mathcal{M}$

$$\bar{\mu}_l q_l(\rho_k, \bar{\mu}_l) \stackrel{(c)}{\geq} \mu_l q_l(\rho_k, \mu_l) \stackrel{(d)}{>} \mu_l q_l\left(\rho_k^+, \mu_l\right)$$

where (c) comes from the definition of μ_l^+ and (d) from the monotonicity in **P.2**. Since the inequality holds $\forall \mu_l$ it also holds for $\mu_l = \mu_l^+$, hence $g_l\left(\rho_k^+, \vec{\rho}_{-k}\right) < g_l(\rho_k, \vec{\rho}_{-k})$. For the convexity we write for $\rho_k^{(1)} \neq \rho_k^{(2)}$

$$\begin{aligned}
g_l\left(\theta\rho_k^{(1)} + (1-\theta)\rho_k^{(2)}\right) &= \max_{\mu_l} \mu_l q_l\left(\theta\rho_k^{(1)} + (1-\theta)\rho_k^{(2)}, \mu_l\right) \\
&\stackrel{(P.2)}{\leq} \max_{\mu_l}\left\{\theta\mu_l q_l\left(\rho_k^{(1)}, \mu_l\right) + (1-\theta)\mu_l q_l\left(\rho_k^{(2)}, \mu_l\right)\right\} \\
&\leq \max_{\mu_l} \theta\mu_l q_l\left(\rho_k^{(1)}, \mu_l\right) + \max_{\mu_l}(1-\theta)\mu_l q_l\left(\rho_k^{(2)}, \mu_l\right) \\
&= \theta g_l\left(\rho_k^{(1)}, \vec{\rho}_{-k}\right) + (1-\theta) g_l\left(\rho_k^{(2)}, \vec{\rho}_{-k}\right)
\end{aligned}$$

124   Chapter 7. Stability and Distributed Power Control in MANETs with ARQ

- **P'.3** Choose $\rho_l^b \geq \rho_l^a$ and denote $\mu_l^b := \arg\max_{\mu_l \in \mathcal{M}} \mu_l q_l(\rho_l^b, \mu_l)$, and also $\mu_l^a := \arg\max_{\mu_l \in \mathcal{M}} \mu_l q_l(\rho_l^a, \mu_l)$. By definition

$$\mu_l^b q_l(\rho_l^b, \mu_l^b) \geq \mu_l^a q_l(\rho_l^b, \mu_l^a) \quad \Rightarrow \quad \frac{\mu_l^b}{\mu_l^a} \geq \frac{q_l(\rho_l^b, \mu_l^a)}{q_l(\rho_l^b, \mu_l^b)} \tag{7.18}$$

We prove the property by contradiction. Suppose that $\mu_l^b < \mu_l^a$. From the log-supermodularity property **P.4**

$$\frac{q_l(\rho_l^b, \mu_l^a)}{q_l(\rho_l^a, \mu_l^a)} > \frac{q_l(\rho_l^b, \mu_l^b)}{q_l(\rho_l^a, \mu_l^b)} \tag{7.19}$$

Combining (7.18) and (7.19)

$$\frac{\mu_l^b}{\mu_l^a} \overset{(7.18)}{\geq} \frac{q_l(\rho_l^b, \mu_l^a)}{q_l(\rho_l^b, \mu_l^b)} \overset{(7.19)}{>} \frac{q_l(\rho_l^a, \mu_l^a)}{q_l(\rho_l^a, \mu_l^b)} \quad \Rightarrow \quad \mu_l^b q_l(\rho_l^a, \mu_l^b) > \mu_l^a q_l(\rho_l^a, \mu_l^a) \tag{7.20}$$

But (7.20) is impossible from the definition of $\mu_l^a := \arg\max_{\mu_l \in \mathcal{M}} \mu_l q_l(\rho_l^a, \mu_l)$ hence $\mu_l^b \geq \mu_l^a$.

- **P'.4**: We make use of the fact that given a pair $(\rho_l^{(1)}, \mu_l^{(1)})$ there always exists another one $(\rho_l^{(2)}, \mu_l^{(2)})$, with $\rho_l^{(1)} \neq \rho_l^{(2)}$ and $\mu_l^{(1)} \neq \mu_l^{(2)}$ such that $q_l(\rho_l^{(1)}, \vec{\rho}_{-l}, \mu_l^{(1)}) = q_l(\rho_l^{(2)}, \vec{\rho}_{-l}, \mu_l^{(2)})$. This is because $\forall \mu_l \in \mathcal{M}$, the success probability function $q_l(\rho_l, \mu_l) \in [0, 1]$ is strictly increasing in ρ_l and strictly decreasing in μ_l by **P.1** and **P.3** (here $\rho_l \in \mathbb{R}_+$).

Denote by $\mu_l^b := \arg\max_{\mu_l \in \mathcal{M}} \mu_l q_l(\rho_l^b, \mu_l)$, and also $\mu_l^a := \arg\max_{\mu_l \in \mathcal{M}} \mu_l q_l(\rho_k^a, \mu_l)$. Using the above fact we can write $q_l(\rho_l, \rho_k^a, \mu_l^a) = q_l(\rho_l^a, \rho_k^a, \mu_l)$ and $q_l(\rho_l, \rho_k^b, \mu_l^b) = q_l(\rho_l^b, \rho_k^b, \mu_l)$, e.g. for some $\mu_l \geq \max\{\mu_l^a, \mu_l^b\}$, $\rho_l^a \geq \rho_l$ and $\rho_l^b \geq \rho_l$. By definition

$$\frac{\mu_l^b}{\mu_l^a} \geq \frac{q_l(\rho_l, \rho_k^b, \mu_l^a)}{q_l(\rho_l, \rho_k^b, \mu_l^b)} = \frac{q_l(\rho_l^a, \rho_k^b, \mu_l)}{q_l(\rho_l^b, \rho_k^b, \mu_l)} \tag{7.21}$$

7.3. Properties of the Success Function and Maximum Goodput Function

The property is proven by contradiction.. Choose $\rho_k^b \geq \rho_k^a$ and suppose that

$$\mu_l^b \geq \mu_l^a \overset{(P.3)}{\Leftrightarrow} q_l\left(\rho_l, \rho_k^b, \mu_l^b\right) \leq q_l\left(\rho_l, \rho_k^b, \mu_l^a\right) \Leftrightarrow$$
$$q_l\left(\rho_l^b, \rho_k^b, \mu_l\right) \leq q_l\left(\rho_l^a, \rho_k^b, \mu_l\right) \overset{(P.1)}{\Leftrightarrow} \rho_l^b \leq \rho_l^a \qquad (7.22)$$

From the log-supermodularity property **P.5** we reach the inequality $\mu_l^b q_l\left(\rho_l, \rho_k^a, \mu_l^b\right) \geq \mu_l^a q_l\left(\rho_l, \rho_k^a, \mu_l^a\right)$ which is impossible by the definition of $\mu_l^a \Rightarrow \rho_l^b \leq \rho_l^a$ is impossible $\Leftrightarrow \mu_l^b \geq \mu_l^a$ is impossible.

□

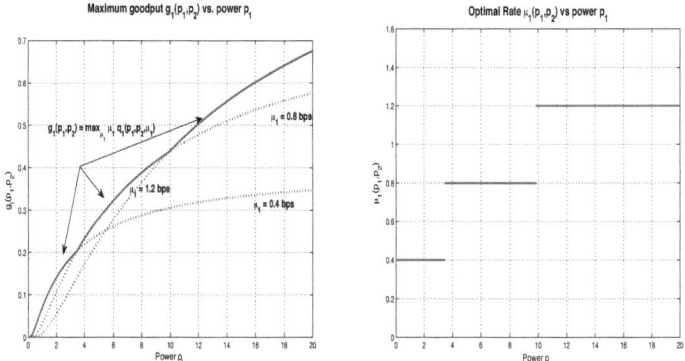

Figure 7.2: a. Max Goodput $g_1(\rho_1, \rho_2)$ vs power ρ_1, b. Max rate $\bar{\mu}_1 (\rho_1, \rho_2)$ vs power ρ_1.

The above properties are illustrated in Fig.7.2 and Fig.7.3 using a success probability function with the expression in (7.2) for the 2-user Rayleigh/Rayleigh fading case. These properties will not be directly used in what follows but are rather useful for the characterisation of the stability region and the optimal scheduling policies of such systems. More specifically, in Fig.7.2 we simulate a 2-user Rayleigh/Rayleigh fading channel with set of rates $\mathcal{M} = \{0.4, 0.8, \ldots, 2\}$ and $\rho_2 = 5$ Watt, $P_1 = 20$ Watt. Properties **P'.1** and **P'.3** are illustrated in the left and right plot respectively. In Fig.7.3 a 2-user Rayleigh/Rayleigh fading channel is again simulated with set of rates $\mathcal{M} = \{0.4, 0.8, \ldots, 2\}$ and $\rho_1 = 20$ Watt, $P_2 = 25$ Watt. Properties **P'.2** and **P'.4** are illustrated in the left and right plot respectively.

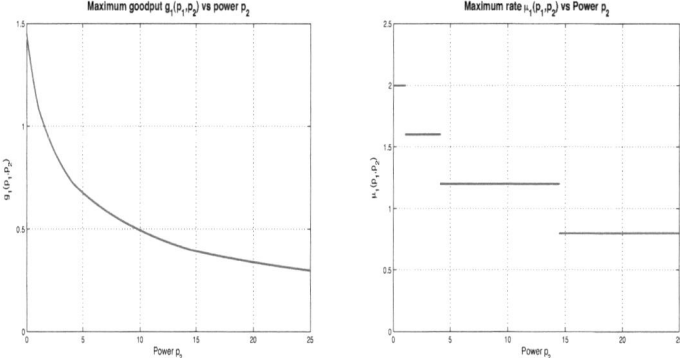

Figure 7.3: a. Max Goodput $g_1(\rho_1, \rho_2)$ vs power ρ_2, b. Max rate $\bar{\mu}_1(\rho_1, \rho_2)$ vs power ρ_2.

Remark 9. In economic terms, we can interpret the success probability function q_l as the *demand* of product l in a market of L_{link} firms. In this framework μ_l is the *product's price* and g_l is the *firm's revenue*. Then $g_l(\rho_l, \vec{\rho}_{-l}, \mu_l) = \mu_l \times q_l(\rho_l, \vec{\rho}_{-l}, \mu_l)$ is firm's l (*revenue*) = (*price*)×(*demand*). The demand is by **P.3** a decreasing function of the price, is increasing by **P.1** in ρ_l and decreasing by **P.2** in ρ_k, $k \neq l$. Then ρ_l can be interpreted as a variable valuating product's l quality (or maybe the money spent by firm l in advertisement) and ρ_k as the quality (or money for advertisement) of products from competitors $k \neq l$. Then the maximum goodput $g_l(\vec{\rho})$ is the *maximum revenue* that a firm l can obtain by choosing an *optimal price* $\bar{\mu}_l(\vec{\rho})$, given a vector $\vec{\rho}$. By properties **P'.1** and **P'.2** the maximum revenue is increasing in ρ_l and decreasing in ρ_k, $k \neq l$, whereas by **P'.3** and **P'.4** the optimal price is also increasing in ρ_l and decreasing in ρ_k. Notice that if in **P.4** log-supermodularity would be replaced by log-submodularity the optimal price would be a decreasing function of ρ_l.

7.4 Examples of the Goodput Region for some Simple Network Topologies

In the current paragraph we investigate two simple characteristic network topologies, illustrate their goodput region and derive some important properties used in the solution of the utility optimization problem that follows. These topologies are

- 2 Transmitting Nodes and 1 Receiving Node

7.4. Examples of the Goodput Region for some Simple Network Topologies

- 1 Transmitting Node and 2 Receiving Nodes

We first consider a network having two transmitting nodes $\mathcal{N} = \{1, 2\}$ with power constraints per node $0 \leq \rho_n \leq P_n^{\max}$, $n = 1, 2$ and a single receiver node. Using the properies **P'.1** and **P'.2** from Theorem 29 we obtain $\forall \rho_1, \rho_2$ the inequalities

$$g_1\left(P_1^{\max}, \rho_2\right) \geq g_1(\rho_1, \rho_2) \geq g_1\left(\rho_1, P_2^{\max}\right)$$
$$g_2\left(\rho_1, P_2^{\max}\right) \geq g_2(\rho_1, \rho_2) \geq g_2\left(P_1^{\max}, \rho_2\right)$$

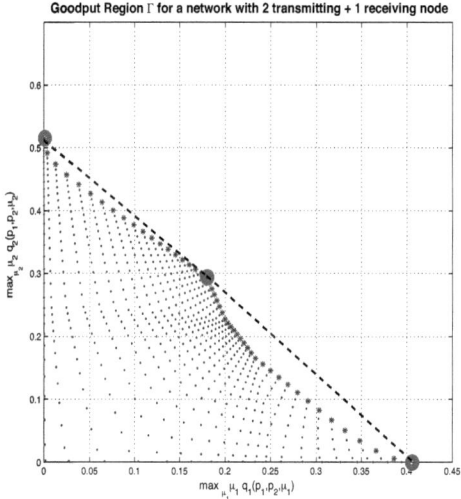

Figure 7.4: Two-user Rayleigh goodput region for the network of 2 T_X and 1 R_X.

In Fig.7.4 the 2-user Rayleigh/Rayleigh goodput region $\hat{\Gamma}_1$ and Γ_1 for the network of 2 transmitters and a single receiver is plotted. The convex hull is shown with the dashed dot lines. For the illustration $\mathcal{M} = \{0.4, 0.8, \ldots, 1.8\}$, $P_1^{\max} = 2$ Watt, $P_2^{\max} = 3$ Watt and the success probability function in (7.2) has been used with $G_{1,1} = G_{1,2} = 1, G_{2,2} = G_{2,1} = 1$.

We further consider the network having two receiving nodes $\mathcal{N} = \{1, 2\}$ and one transmitting with sum power constraints $\rho_1 + \rho_2 \leq P$. We can write similarly to the above inequalities

$$0 = g_1(0, P) \le g_1(\rho_1, P - \rho_1) \le g_1(P, 0)$$
$$g_2(0, P) \ge g_2(\rho_1, P - \rho_1) \ge g_2(P, 0) = 0$$

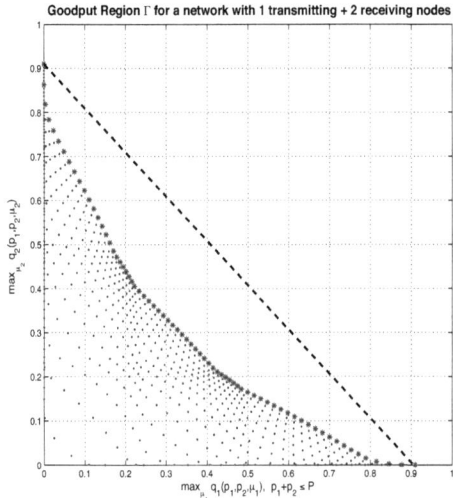

Figure 7.5: Two-user Rayleigh goodput region for the network of 1 T_X and 2 R_X.

Fig. 7.5 illustrates the 2-user Rayleigh/Rayleigh goodput region $\hat{\Gamma}_2$ and Γ_2 for this second topology. The convex hull is again shown with the dashed dot lines. For this topology, $\mathcal{M} = \{0.2, 0.4, 0.6\}$, $\rho_1 + \rho_2 \le P = 10$ Watt and the success probability function in (7.2) has been used with $G_{1,1} = G_{2,2} = 1, G_{1,2} = 0.5, G_{2,1} = 0.8$.

We call an *operating point*, a Pareto optimal point [BV04] $\left(\rho_1^*, \rho_2^*\right)$ of the region that solves the weighted sum goodput maximization problem

$$\max_{(\rho_1, \rho_2) \in \mathcal{P}} w_1 g_1(\rho_1, \rho_2) + w_2 g_2(\rho_1, \rho_2) = \max_{(g_1, g_2) \in \hat{\Gamma}} w_1 g_1 + w_2 g_2 \qquad (7.23)$$

where w_1, w_2 are non-negative weights and $\left(g_1^*, g_2^*\right)$ is the related Pareto optimal value. We will prove in the following that the 2-user region $\hat{\Gamma}$ of the example under study has at most

7.4. Examples of the Goodput Region for some Simple Network Topologies 129

three operating points. We first define Pareto dominant and Pareto optimal power allocations

Definition 6 ([SMG02]). A power vector $\vec{\rho}$ *Pareto dominates* another $\vec{\rho}$, if $\forall l \in \mathcal{L}$, $g_l(\vec{\rho}) \geq g_l(\vec{\rho})$ and for some $k \in \mathcal{L}$, $g_k(\vec{\rho}) > g_k(\vec{\rho})$.

A power vector $\vec{\rho}^*$ is *Pareto-optimal* if there exists no other power vector $\vec{\rho}$ such that $g_l(\vec{\rho}) \geq g_l(\vec{\rho}^*)$ $\forall l \in \mathcal{L}$ and $g_k(\vec{\rho}) > g_k(\vec{\rho}^*)$ for some $k \in \mathcal{L}$.

We can prove the following Theorem for the example topologies discussed. The result generalizes trivially to the cases of more than two transmitting (resp. receiving) nodes.

Theorem 30. *The Pareto-optimal frontier of the goodput region for the 3-node topology, with two transmitting nodes and one receiving node $\hat{\Gamma}_1$ (single transmitting node and two receiving nodes $\hat{\Gamma}_2$ resp.), denoted by $\mathcal{P}_1^{opt}$ (resp. $\mathcal{P}_2^{opt}$) is the set of points $(g_1(\rho_1, \rho_2), g_2(\rho_1, \rho_2))$ for which at least one of the two constraints $0 \leq \rho_j \leq P_j^{\max}$, $j = 1, 2$ is satisfied with equality (for which the sum power constraint $\rho_1 + \rho_2 \leq P$ is satisfied with equality).*

Proof. We first consider the case of two transmitters with individual power constraints and single receiver. Fix initially a rate pair (μ_1, μ_2), $\mu_j \in \mathcal{M}$, $j = 1, 2$ and choose a pair of power allocations (ρ_1, ρ_2) with $\rho_1 < P_1$ and $\rho_2 < P_2$, which maps to the point $(g_1(\rho_1, \rho_2, \mu_1), g_2(\rho_1, \rho_2, \mu_2))$ of the goodput region. Use the success probability function with the general form in (7.1). Then $\forall a > 1$, $(\rho_1', \rho_2') := (a\rho_1, a\rho_2) > (\rho_1, \rho_2)$

$$\frac{G_{1,1}F_{1,1}a\rho_1}{G_{1,2}F_{1,2}a\rho_2 + \sigma^2} \geq \frac{G_{1,1}F_{1,1}\rho_1}{G_{1,2}F_{1,2}\rho_2 + \sigma^2} \Leftrightarrow$$
$$g_1(\rho_1', \rho_2', \mu_1) \geq g_1(\rho_1, \rho_2, \mu_1)$$

where $g_1(\rho_1, \rho_2, \mu_1)$ is defined in (7.3) and the same inequality holds for $g_2(\rho_1, \rho_2, \mu_2)$. Then $(a\rho_1, a\rho_2)$ always Pareto dominiates (ρ_1, ρ_2) and the Pareto optimal vector is one for which one of the two constraints is satisfied with equality. Hence the Lemma holds for the set $(g_1(\rho_1, \rho_2, \mu_1), g_2(\rho_1, \rho_2, \mu_2))$, $(\rho_1, \rho_2) \in \mathcal{P}$ and $\forall (\mu_1, \mu_2) \in \mathcal{M} \times \mathcal{M}$.

Now for each pair (μ_1, μ_2) denote by $\mathcal{B}_{(\mu_1, \mu_2) \in \mathcal{M} \times \mathcal{M}}$ the set

$$\mathcal{B}_{(\mu_1, \mu_2)} = \bigcup_{(\rho_1, \rho_2) \in \mathcal{P}} \{(g_1, g_2) : g_1 \leq \mu_1 q_1(\rho_1, \rho_2, \mu_1), g_2 \leq \mu_2 q_2(\rho_1, \rho_2, \mu_2)\}$$

It is easy to verify that the union of all possible sets $\mathcal{B}_{(\mu_1,\mu_2)}$, $(\mu_1,\mu_2) \in \mathcal{M} \times \mathcal{M}$ equals the set $\hat{\Gamma}$

$$\hat{\Gamma} = \bigcup_{\mathcal{M} \times \mathcal{M}} \mathcal{B}_{(\mu_1,\mu_2)} \tag{7.24}$$

and hence the property holds for the goodput region. This is also illustrated in fig. 7.6 where the set $\hat{\Gamma}$ as well as $\mathcal{B}_{(1.2,1.6)}$ and $\mathcal{B}_{(0.4,0.4)}$ are plotted.

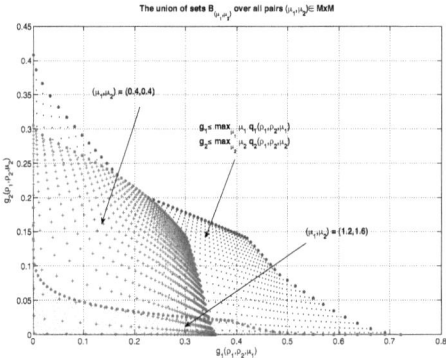

Figure 7.6: Illustration of the property (7.24)

The case of one transmitter and two receivers with sum power constraints can be similarly proved. □

Observe in fig. 7.4, 7.5 that the set of points forming the Pareto-optimal frontier of set $\hat{\Gamma}$ are marked with an asterisk (*).

In the analysis that follows the problem of maximizing the weighted sum of the goodputs is very important. This can be written for both topologies as

$$\begin{aligned} \max \quad & \omega_1 g_1(\rho_1,\rho_2) + \omega_2 g_2(\rho_1,\rho_2) \\ \text{s.t.} \quad & (\rho_1,\rho_2) \in \mathcal{P} \end{aligned} \tag{7.25}$$

7.4. Examples of the Goodput Region for some Simple Network Topologies

where (ω_1, ω_2) are pairs of nonnegative weights and the constraint set is $\mathcal{P}^1 = \{(\rho_1, \rho_2) : \rho_j \in [0, P_j^{\max}], j = 1, 2\}$ for the 2 transmitter case and $\mathcal{P}^2 = \{(\rho_1, \rho_2) : \rho_1 + \rho_2 \in [0, P]\}$ for the 2 receiver case. We can provide the following conditions for the first scenario so that the optimal power allocation solving (7.25) to be on/off, meaning $(0, P_2^{\max})$, $(P_1^{\max}, 0)$ or $(P_1^{\max}, P_2^{\max})$.

Theorem 31. *The optimal solution of the problem in* (7.25) *for the* $\mathcal{P}^1$ *constraint set is the on/off allocation, meaning that each of the two nodes transmits either with full power or does not transmit at all, if*

$$\mathcal{R}^r_{g_2(P_1^{\max}, \rho_2)} < \mathcal{R}^r_{-g_1(P_1^{\max}, \rho_2)} \quad \& \quad (7.26)$$

$$\mathcal{R}^r_{g_1(\rho_1, P_2^{\max})} < \mathcal{R}^r_{-g_2(\rho_1, P_2^{\max})} \quad (7.27)$$

where $\mathcal{R}^r_{f(x)}$ *is the Absolute Risk Aversion Coefficient of the function* $f(x)$.

Proof. From Theorem 30 we have that the Pareto optimal frontier is the set $C_1 \cup C_2$, where

$$C_1 = \{(g_1(P_1^{\max}, \rho_2), g_2(P_1^{\max}, \rho_2)), \rho_2 \in [0, P_2^{\max}]\}$$
$$C_2 = \{(g_1(\rho_1, P_2^{\max}), g_2(\rho_1, P_2^{\max})), \rho_1 \in [0, P_1^{\max}]\}$$

Let us first focus on C_1 and give a mapping $h_1 : g_1 \to g_2$ for the curve. By property **P'.2**, since $g_1(P_1^{\max}, \rho_2)$ is strictly decreasing and convex in ρ_2, then it is a *1-1* mapping of $\mathcal{P}^1 = \{\rho_2 : 0 \le \rho_2 \le P_2^{\max}\}$ into $\mathcal{G} = \{g_1(P_1^{\max}, \rho_2), \rho_2 \in [0, P_2^{\max}]\}$. The inverse function $f(g_1)$ is well defined since for each $g_1 \in \mathcal{G}$, $f(g_1)$ consists of at most one element of $\mathcal{P}^1$. Then we have

$$f(g_1(P_1^{\max}, \rho_2)) = \rho_2, \ \rho_2 \in \mathcal{P}^1$$

Furthermore $f(g_1)$ is also *strictly decreasing* and *convex*. To see this choose $g_1, g_2 \in \mathcal{G}$, $g_1 \ge g_2 \overset{P'.2}{\Leftrightarrow} \rho_1 \le \rho_2 \Leftrightarrow f(g_1) \le f(g_2)$. For the convexity we have

$$\theta f\left(g_1^A\right) + (1-\theta)f\left(g_1^B\right) = \theta \rho_2^A + (1-\theta)\rho_2^B = \rho_2^\theta =$$
$$f\left(g_1\left(P_1^{\max}, \rho_2^\theta\right)\right) \geq f\left(\theta g_1\left(P_1^{\max}, \rho_2^A\right) + (1-\theta)g_1\left(P_1^{\max}, \rho_2^B\right)\right) = f\left(\theta g_1^A + (1-\theta)g_1^B\right)$$

where the above inequality comes from **P'.2** (g_1 is convex in ρ_2) and the property that f is decreasing. Using this we can write g_2 as a function h_1 of g_1 for $(g_1, g_2) \in C_1$, that is

$$g_2\left(P_1^{\max}, \rho_2\right) = g_2\left(P_1^{\max}, f(g_1)\right) \Leftrightarrow g_2 = h_1(g_1) \qquad (7.28)$$

From the first derivative we get that the curve is decreasing

$$\frac{dg_2\left(P_1^{\max}, f(g_1)\right)}{dg_1} = \underbrace{\frac{dg_2\left(P_1^{\max}, f(g_1)\right)}{df(g_1)}}_{>0 \text{ (\textbf{P'}.1)}} \cdot \underbrace{\frac{df(g_1)}{dg_1}}_{<0} < 0$$

The second derivative of the mapping in (7.28) equals

$$\frac{d^2 g_2\left(P_1^{\max}, f(g_1)\right)}{dg_1^2} = \underbrace{\frac{d^2 g_2\left(P_1^{\max}, f(g_1)\right)}{df(g_1)^2}}_{(?)} \cdot \underbrace{\left(\frac{df(g_1)}{dg_1}\right)^2}_{>0} + \underbrace{\frac{dg_2\left(P_1^{\max}, f(g_1)\right)}{df(g_1)}}_{>0 \text{ (\textbf{P'}.1)}} \cdot \underbrace{\frac{d^2 f(g_1)}{dg_1^2}}_{>0}$$

and observe that the sign of the expression in $\frac{d^2 g_2(P_1^{\max}, f(g_1))}{df(g_1)^2}$ can be positive or negative. The condition for the expression to be positive and hence for the curve to be convex is

$$-\frac{\frac{d^2 g_2(P_1^{\max}, f(g_1))}{df(g_1)^2}}{\frac{dg_2(P_1^{\max}, f(g_1))}{df(g_1)}} < \frac{\frac{d^2 f(g_1)}{dg_1^2}}{\left(\frac{df(g_1)}{dg_1}\right)^2}$$

In the right handside of the expression above the first and second derivative of the inverse function $f(g_1)$ appears. Using the Lagrange forms for the derivatives [CJ89] $\frac{d^2 f(g_1)}{dg_1^2} = -\frac{\frac{d^2 g_1(P_1^{\max}, f(g_1))}{df(g_1)^2}}{\left(\frac{dg_1(P_1^{\max}, f(g_1))}{df(g_1)}\right)^3}$ and $\frac{df(g_1)}{dg_1} = \frac{1}{\frac{dg_1(P_1^{\max}, f(g_1))}{df(g_1)}}$ we can rewrite (7.29) as follows

$$-\frac{\frac{d^2 g_2(P_1^{\max},\rho_2)}{d\rho_2^2}}{\frac{dg_2(P_1^{\max},\rho_2)}{d\rho_2}} < -\frac{\frac{d^2 g_1(P_1^{\max},\rho_2)}{d\rho_2^2}}{\frac{dg_1(P_1^{\max},\rho_2)}{d\rho_2}}$$

The left handside equals the *absolute risk aversion coefficient* [Pra64] of the function $g_2\left(P_1^{\max},\rho_2\right)$, denoted by $\mathcal{R}^r_{g_2(P_1^{\max},\rho_2)}$ while the right hand side is the coefficient for the function $-g_1\left(P_1^{\max},\rho_2\right)$. We can then write $\mathcal{R}^r_{g_2(P_1^{\max},\rho_2)} < \mathcal{R}^r_{-g_1(P_1^{\max},\rho_2)}$. Following the same steps for the set C_2 we reach the conditon $\mathcal{R}^r_{g_1(\rho_1,P_2^{\max})} < \mathcal{R}^r_{-g_2(\rho_1,P_2^{\max})}$ for the curve $g_1 = h_2(g_2)$ to be decreasing and convex.

Since both parts of the frontier are convex and decreasing, and $C_1 \cap C_2 = \{\left(g_1\left(P_1^{\max},P_2^{\max}\right), g_2\left(P_1^{\max},P_2^{\max}\right)\right)\}$ then the Pareto optimal allocation pairs solving the problem in (7.25) can at most be three and specifically the pairs $\left(P_1^{\max},0\right)$, $\left(0,P_2^{\max}\right)$ or $\left(P_1^{\max},P_2^{\max}\right)$. □

The above theorem practically states that the on/off power allocation is optimal if the function $-g_1\left(P_1^{\max},\rho_2\right)$ is "more" concave compared to $g_2\left(P_1^{\max},\rho_2\right)$ and similarly for the case with $\rho_2 = P_2^{\max}$. This comes directly from Pratt's theorem [Pra64] under the condition that $-g_1\left(P_1^{\max},\rho_2\right)$ and $g_2\left(P_1^{\max},\rho_2\right)$ are both increasing (from **P'.1** and **P'.2**), continuous and twice differentiable functons of ρ_2. Then if (7.26) holds there exists a concave function T such that $-g_1\left(P_1^{\max},\rho_2\right) = T\left(g_2\left(P_1^{\max},\rho_2\right)\right)$. A similar result can also be shown for the case of the $\mathcal{P}^2$ constraint set.

7.5 NUM Problem Dual Decomposition

The utility maximization problem in (7.6) given the network capacity region in Theorem 27 takes the form

$$\begin{aligned}\max_{\lambda_s \geq 0,\, g_l^d \geq 0} \quad & \sum_{s \in S} U_s(\lambda_s) \\ \text{subject to} \quad & \sum_{l:e(l)=n} g_l^d + \lambda_n^d \leq \sum_{k:b(k)=n} g_k^d \quad \forall n,d \\ & \vec{g} \in \mathbf{co}\left(\hat{\Gamma}\right) = \Gamma \end{aligned}$$

and $\hat{\Gamma}$ is given in (7.7). The constraint set is convex and compact (see [Nee03, Appendix 4.C]), the objective function is concave and Slater's condition can be shown to hold, hence strong duality also holds and known distributed algorithms, like the one following, can solve the Lagrange dual problem $\min_{\vec{v} \geq 0} L_{dual}(\vec{v})$ which involves the $(N \cdot D)$-vector $\vec{v}$ of dual variables v_n^d. The Lagrangian associated with the primal NUM problem is denoted by $L(\vec{\lambda}, \vec{v})$ while the dual function $L_{dual}(\vec{v})$ yields, due to the linearity of the differential operator (see [Kel97], [LS], [CLCD])

$$L_{dual}(\vec{v}) = \sum_{s \in S} \max_{\lambda_s \geq 0} \{U_s(\lambda_s) - v_s \lambda_s\} + \max_{\vec{g} \in \Gamma} \sum_{n,d} v_n^d \left(\sum_{k:b(k)=n} g_k^d - \sum_{l:e(l)=n} g_l^d \right)$$

and $v_s = v_n^d$, $\lambda_s = \lambda_n^d$ for the flow s with source node n and destination d. We can interpret v_n^d as the implicit cost per pair (n,d). Thus, the NUM problem is decomposed into:

(a) *The input rate control problem*

$$\textbf{Prob.1}: \quad \sum_{s \in S} \max_{\lambda_s \geq 0} \{U_s(\lambda_s) - v_s \lambda_s\} \qquad (7.29)$$

solved for each commodity flow at the incoming nodes independently $\lambda_s = U_s'^{-1}(v_s)$. Observe that by assumption $U_s'(\lambda_s)$ is continuous and monotone decreasing in $\mathbb{R}_+$ (thus a bijection) and the inverse of the function exists. Since $U_s(\lambda_s)$ is strictly concave the solution is unique for each v_s.

(b) *The scheduling problem*

$$\textbf{Prob.2}: \quad \max_{\vec{g} \in \Gamma} \sum_{n,d} v_n^d \left(\sum_{k:b(k)=n} g_k^d - \sum_{l:e(l)=n} g_l^d \right) = \max_{\vec{g} \in \Gamma} \sum_{l,d} g_l^d \cdot \left(v_{b(l)}^d - v_{e(l)}^d \right)$$

$$\leq \max_{\vec{g} \in \Gamma} \sum_l w_l \cdot g_l \qquad (7.30)$$

Through each link l the commodity $d^* = \arg\max_d \left(v_{b(l)}^d - v_{e(l)}^d \right)$ is scheduled to be routed with goodput rate g_l and $w_l = \max_d \left(v_{b(l)}^d - v_{e(l)}^d, 0 \right)$. This is the well known *backpressure policy* [TE92]. The solution of (7.30) further provides the optimal multicommodity goodput flow variables $\{g_l^*\}$. The optimal solution described is very similar to the DRPC policy in [NMR05].

If we can solve (7.30) distributedly, then algorithms can be provided, that solve the dual problem $\min L_{dual}(\vec{v})$ also in a distributed manner, and converge to the optimal average incoming rate vector $\vec{\lambda}^*$ and average price vector $\vec{v}^*$. The dual problem can be solved by the subgradient method. The prices v_n^d for each node-destination pair (n,d) are step-wise adjusted by

$$v_n^d(t+1) = [v_n^d(t) + s(t) \cdot (\lambda_n^d(t) - \sum_{k:b(k)=n} g_k^d(t) + \sum_{l:e(l)=n} g_l^d(t))]^+. \quad (7.31)$$

In the above $s(t)$ is a positive scalar stepsize, $[\ldots]^+$ denotes the projection onto the set $\mathbb{R}_+$ and for each t the values $\lambda_n^d(t)$ and $g_n^d(t)$ are calculated by solving problems (7.29) and (7.30) respectively and using prices $\vec{v}(t)$. As noted in the aforementioned works, in practice a constant stepsize is used for implementation purposes, although the convergence of the algorithm is guaranteed for $s(t) \xrightarrow{t \to \infty} 0$. For constant stepsizes statistical convergence to $\vec{v}^*, \vec{\lambda}^*$ is guaranteed as shown in [CLCD, Def.1,Th.2].

7.6 The Scheduling Problem

7.6.1 Relaxation

As was mentioned previously it is very important that the problem in (7.30) is solved in a *distributed* manner. To this aim the theory of *supermodular games* can be used. We make the following three assumptions

1. *Assumption 1*: Each origin node chooses a *single* end node to transmit

2. *Assumption 2*: Each node can transmit and receive at the same time

3. *Assumption 3*: Fixed scheduled rates per link μ_l are considered.

Specifically the last assumption constraints the generality of the initial model but is necessary for the approach that follows. Variable scheduled rates would involve a joint maximization over power allocation and rates. This would complicate the analysis, but is a rather important topic for future research. The maximization in (7.30) can be written as

136   Chapter 7. Stability and Distributed Power Control in MANETs with ARQ

$$\max_{\vec{g} \in \Gamma} \sum_l w_l \cdot g_l \stackrel{(a)}{=} \max_{\vec{g} \in \hat{\Gamma}} \sum_l w_l \cdot g_l = \max_{\vec{p} \in \mathcal{P}} \sum_{n:n=b(l)} \sum_{n:n=e(l)} w_l \cdot \mu_l q_l(\vec{\rho}, \mu_l)$$
$$\stackrel{(b)}{=} \max_{\rho_n \in [P_n^{\min}, P_n^{\max}]} \sum_{n:n=b(l)} w_n \cdot \mu_n q_n(\vec{\rho}, \mu_n) \quad (7.32)$$

where (a) comes from the fact that the objective function is linear and the supporting hyperplanes to the sets $\hat{\Gamma}$ and $\Gamma = \mathbf{co}\{\hat{\Gamma}\}$ are the same, while (b) from Assumption 1. The latter simplifies the problem to a weighted sum maximization problem with number of summants equal to the number of nodes and allows the formulation of a noncooperative game in the following subsections, where each node decides independently over its transmitting power through a single chosen link. The capacity region of the system in Theorem 27 is of course reduced. An important question is how each node choses the optimal single link to transmit.

The number of links with node n as origin are all links $\{l \in \mathcal{L} : n = b(l) \ \& \ w_l > 0\}$. This is the *connectivity set* of node n. The optimal link is obviously the one which provides maximum weighted goodput to the above summation, for a given power allocation $\rho_n \in [P_n^{\min}, P_n^{\max}]$.

Departing here briefly from the main line of the analysis, we end this subsection with a heuristic suggestion for an almost optimal choice of a single receiver node, using low information exchange between the network nodes. Applying Markov's inequality in (7.1)

$$\omega_l \mu_l \mathbb{P}(SINR_l(\vec{\rho}) \geq e^{\mu_l} - 1) \leq \frac{\omega_l \mu_l}{e^{\mu_l} - 1} \mathbb{E}(SINR_l(\vec{\rho})).$$

Suppose that the end node $e(l)$ of each link l measures the received level of interference, the latter denoted by $\mathcal{E}_l$. This is not any more a random variable with unknown realization but rather a known deterministic quantity. The right handside then reduces to

$$\frac{\omega_l \mu_l}{e^{\mu_l} - 1} \frac{\mathbb{E}(G_{l,l} F_{l,l} \rho_l)}{(\mathcal{E}_l + \sigma^2_{e(l)})} = \frac{\omega_l \mu_l}{e^{\mu_l} - 1} \frac{G_{l,l} \rho_l}{(\mathcal{E}_l + \sigma^2_{e(l)})}. \quad (7.33)$$

This is an upper bound on the actual error probability. The process of the sub-optimal choice then is as follows. Each destination node of links belonging to the connectivity set of node n, informs the origin node over $\mathcal{E}_l + \sigma^2_{e(l)}$ and afterwards n chooses to transmit over the link

7.6. The Scheduling Problem

with the maximum ratio (7.33), since $G_{l,l}$, ω_l and μ_l are known to n.

An alternative way to choose a single receiver node could be by assigning to each element of the connectivity set a probability, with sum equal to one per transmitting node, and the choice will then be a random process.

7.6.2 Optimality conditions

Using the Karush-Kuhn-Tucker (KKT) optimality conditions and observing that the active inequality constraint gradients are linearly independent [Ber, pp.315-317] all feasible vectors $\vec{\rho}$ are regular and we have the following *necessary conditions* for $\vec{\rho}^*$ to be a local maximizer of the objective function in (7.32).

$$0 = \frac{\partial}{\partial \rho_n} L\left(\vec{\rho}^*, \vec{\kappa}^l, \vec{\kappa}^u\right) = \kappa_n^l - \kappa_n^u + \omega_n \cdot \mu_n \frac{\partial q_n\left(\vec{\rho}^*, \mu_n\right)}{\partial \rho_n} + \sum_{m \neq n} \omega_m \cdot \mu_m \frac{\partial q_m\left(\vec{\rho}^*, \mu_m\right)}{\partial \rho_n} \quad (7.34)$$

for each n and the complementary slackness conditions satisfy

$$\kappa_n^l \cdot \left(P_n^{\min} - \rho_n^*\right) = 0 \quad \& \quad \kappa_n^u \cdot \left(\rho_n^* - P_n^{\max}\right) = 0 \quad (7.35)$$

$L\left(\vec{\rho}^*, \vec{\kappa}^l, \vec{\kappa}^u\right)$ is the Lagrangian of the problem in (7.32). The conditions are only necessary and **not** sufficient. We make here the remark that if the objective function were concave, the dual gap would be zero and any local maximizer would also be global for the problem at hand. In this case the conditions would also be sufficient. Unfortunately this generaly does not hold for the specific objective function.

Divide (7.34) and (7.35) by $q_n\left(\vec{\rho}^*, \mu_n\right)$ (which is definitely positive if we choose $P_n^{\min} > 0$, $\forall n \in \mathcal{N}$) and then - approching the problem similarly to [HBH06] - set

$$0 \geq \omega_m \cdot \mu_m \frac{\partial q_m\left(\vec{\rho}, \mu_m\right)}{\partial \rho_n} \frac{1}{q_n\left(\vec{\rho}, \mu_n\right)} = \frac{\pi_{m,n}\left(\vec{\rho}\right)}{q_n\left(\vec{\rho}, \mu_n\right)} \quad (7.36)$$

$$= \hat{\pi}_{m,n}\left(\vec{\rho}\right) \quad (7.37)$$

and for the Lagrange multipliers

$$\hat{\kappa}_n^u = \frac{\kappa_n^u}{q_n\left(\vec{\rho}^*, \mu_n\right)} \geq 0 \quad \& \quad \hat{\kappa}_n^l = \frac{\kappa_n^l}{q_n\left(\vec{\rho}^*, \mu_n\right)} \geq 0. \quad (7.38)$$

With the above substitutions the per node condition in (7.34) is rewritten as

$$\omega_n \cdot \mu_n \frac{1}{q_n(\vec{\rho}^*, \mu_n)} \frac{\partial q_n(\vec{\rho}^*, \mu_n)}{\partial \rho_n} + \sum_{m \neq n} \hat{\pi}_{m,n}(\vec{\rho}^*) = \hat{\kappa}_n^u - \hat{\kappa}_n^l. \qquad (7.39)$$

Then (7.39) with the related complementary slackness conditions are the necessary and sufficient conditions for ρ_n^* to be the global maximizer of the problem

$$\max_{\rho_n} \quad \omega_n \mu_n \log\left(q_n(\rho_n, \vec{\rho}_{-n}^*, \mu_n)\right) + \rho_n \sum_{m \neq n} \hat{\pi}_{m,n}(\vec{\rho}^*) \qquad (7.40)$$

since by property **P.1** of the success function, $\log q_n(\vec{\rho}, \mu_n)$ is concave in ρ_n, the constraint set $\rho_n \in \left[P_n^{\min}, P_n^{\max}\right]$ is convex and compact and Slater's condition holds true. This explains now why the division in (7.36) and (7.38) was required.

7.6.3 A Supermodular Game

If we view $-\hat{\pi}_{m,n}(\vec{\rho})$ as the price charged by user m to user n for affecting its goodput by creating interference, we can approach the solution to the optimal power allocation problem in a distributed fashion with the use of game theory. We denote the non-cooperative game by the triple $\mathcal{G} = (\mathcal{N}, \Pi, \{J_n(\cdot), n \in \mathcal{N}\})$ where $\mathcal{N}$ are the players, Π is the set of feasible joint strategies and J_n is the payoff function for user n.

We distinguish between two types of players. First, the *power players* who belong to the set $\mathcal{N}^p$, each one of which represents a node and the set of feasible joint strategies Π^p is identical to the set $\mathcal{P}$ of feasible power allocations. Their payoff function equals

$$J_n(\rho_n, \vec{\rho}_{-n}, (\hat{\pi}_{m,n})) = \omega_n \mu_n \log\left(q_n(\rho_n, \vec{\rho}_{-n}, \mu_n)\right) + \rho_n \cdot \sum_{m \neq n} \hat{\pi}_{m,n} \qquad (7.41)$$

We often set $c_n := \sum_{m \neq n} \hat{\pi}_{m,n}$ to emphasize the dependence of J_n on the sum instead of the individual prices. The *best response correspondence for player n* is the set

$$Y_n(\vec{\rho}_{-n}) = \arg\max_{\rho_n \in \mathcal{P}_n(\vec{\rho}_{-n})} J_n(\rho_n, \vec{\rho}_{-n}, (\hat{\pi}_{m,n})) \qquad (7.42)$$

7.6. The Scheduling Problem

where $\mathcal{P}_n(\vec{\rho}_{-n}) = \{\rho_n : (\rho_n, \vec{\rho}_{-n}) \in \Pi^p\}$.

Second, the *price players* who belong to the set $\mathcal{N}^{pr} := \{(m,n) : m \neq n, \, m, n \in \mathcal{N}\}$ with cardinality $N \cdot (N-1)$. The feasible set of strategies for player (m,n) is

$$\Pi_{m,n}^{pr} = \left\{\hat{\pi}_{m,n} \in \left[\min_{\vec{\rho} \in \mathcal{P}} \hat{\pi}_{m,n}(\vec{\rho}), 0\right]\right\} \tag{7.43}$$

where $\hat{\pi}_{m,n}(\vec{\rho})$ is given in (7.37). The best response for a price player is denoted by (following [HBH06])

$$Y_{m,n}^{pr} = \arg\max_{\hat{\pi}_{m,n} \in \Pi_{m,n}^{pr}} -(\hat{\pi}_{m,n} - \hat{\pi}_{m,n}(\vec{\rho}))^2 \tag{7.44}$$

and $\Pi^{pr} = \{\Pi_{(2,1)}, \ldots, \Pi_{(N-1,N)}\}$ is the joint feasible set.

A *Nash equilibrium* (NE) for the game $\mathcal{G}$ is defined as the set of power vectors $\vec{\rho}^e = \left(\rho_1^e, \ldots, \rho_N^e\right)$ and price vectors $\vec{\hat{\pi}}^e = \left(\hat{\pi}_{2,1}^e, \ldots, \hat{\pi}_{n,1}^e, \ldots, \hat{\pi}_{1,n}^e, \ldots, \hat{\pi}_{n-1,n}^e\right)$ with the property for every $n, m \in \mathcal{N}^p$ and every $(m,n) \in \mathcal{N}^{pr}$

$$J_n\left(\rho_n^e, \vec{\rho}_{-n}^e, (\hat{\pi}_{m,n}^e)\right) \geq J_n\left(\rho_n, \vec{\rho}_{-n}^e, (\hat{\pi}_{m,n}^e)\right), \, \& \, \hat{\pi}_{m,n}^e = \hat{\pi}_{m,n}(\vec{\rho}^e), \, \forall \rho_n \in \mathcal{P}_n(\vec{\rho}_{-n}^e) \tag{7.45}$$

Hence ρ_n^e belongs to the best response correspondence of player n, $\forall n \in \mathcal{N}^p$, given the equilibrium prices, whereas $\hat{\pi}_{m,n}^e$ belongs to the best response correspondence of player $(m,n) \in \mathcal{N}^{pr}$ given the equilibrium powers.

The existence and uniqueness of the NE when the prices do not take part as players in the game has been proven in [ABD06, Th.III.1] under mild assumptions on the problem parameters usually satisfied in practice. In our case however with $N + N \cdot (N-1) = N^2$ players the uniqueness of a Nash equilibrium is not guaranteed. We can however make use of the theory of *supermodular games*, exploiting the structure of the payoff function in (7.41) to find algorithms that converge to one of the Nash Equilibria. We first give the definition of a supermodular game from Topkis [Top98]

Definition 7. A noncooperative game with N players $\{\mathcal{N}, \Pi, \{f_n : n \in \mathcal{N}\}\}$, each having strategy x_n belonging to the feasible set of strategies $\Pi_n(\vec{x}_{-n})$, is supermodular if the set

140 Chapter 7. Stability and Distributed Power Control in MANETs with ARQ

Π of feasible joint strategies is a sublattice of $\mathbb{R}^N$ and for each n the payoff function f_n is supermodular in player n's strategy x_n and has increasing differences for all pairs $(x_i, x_j) \in \Pi_i \times \Pi_j$, $i \neq j$, $i, j \in \mathcal{N}$.

Theorem 32. The noncooperative game with N power players and $N \cdot (N-1)$ price players is a supermodular game [Top98, p.178]. Furthermore, the set of equilibrium points is a nonempty complete lattice and a greatest and least equilibrium point exist.

Proof. The set of joint feasible strategies $\Pi^p \times \Pi^{pr} \in \mathbb{R}^{N^2}$ is a sublattice of $\mathbb{R}^{N^2}$. The set is also compact since for a power player $n \in \mathcal{N}^p$, $\rho_n \in \left[P_n^{\min}, P_n^{\max}\right]$ while for a price player $\pi_{m,n} \in \left[\min_{\vec{\rho} \in \Pi^p} \hat{\pi}_{m,n}(\vec{\rho}), 0\right]$ and the lowest endpoint of the interval is $> -\infty$ for $P_n^{\min} \geq \epsilon > 0$, $\forall n$ (see the expression for the success probability (7.2) and its derivative (7.13)).

Since the set of feasible strategies for power player n is a compact subset of $\mathbb{R}^1$ the payoff function in (7.41) is supermodular in ρ_n. We have further seen in property **P.5** that the logarithm of the success probability function of user n has increasing differences for each pair (ρ_n, ρ_m), $\forall m \neq n$ and constant differences for each pair (ρ_{m_1}, ρ_{m_2}), $m_1 \neq n$, $m_2 \neq n$. Then $\log q_n(\vec{\rho}, \mu_n)$ is supermodular in $\vec{\rho} \in \Pi^p$. Observe that $\rho_n \cdot \sum_{m \neq n} \hat{\pi}_{m,n}$ is also supermodular and by property [Top98, Lemma 2.6.1(b)] the sum of supermodular functions is supermodular. We reach the conclusion that $J_n = \omega_n \mu_n \cdot \log q_n(\vec{\rho}, \mu_n) + c_n \rho_n$ has increasing differences in all pairs (ρ_i, ρ_j) for distinct $i, j \in \mathcal{N}^p$.

The expression for J_n in (7.41) is a valuation (has constant differences) for each pair $(\hat{\pi}_{i,n}, \hat{\pi}_{j,n})$, $i, j \neq n$. Finally for the pairs $(\rho_i, \hat{\pi}_{j,n})$ the function has also increasing differences if $i = n$ and is a valuation for $i \neq n$. Then we reach the conclusion that J_n has increasing differences for each pair (x_i, x_j), $i, j \in \mathcal{N}^p \cup \mathcal{N}^{pr}$. By definition 7 the game is supermodular.

The set of feasible joint startegies $\Pi^p \times \Pi^{pr}$ is shown to be compact. Observing that the expression in (7.2) and hence J_n is continuous in ρ_n and having proven that the game is supermodular, the 'Furthermore' part of the theorem comes from [Top98, Th.4.2.1]. □

After proving that the problem at hand has the desired properties so that supermodular game theory can be applied we prove in the following that the Nash Equilibria of the game are exactly the power allocations that satisfy the KKT necessary optimality conditions of the original sum weighted maximization problem.

7.6. The Scheduling Problem

Theorem 33. Under the condition that $\forall n$, $P_n^{\min} > 0$, a power vector $\vec{\rho}^e$ is a Nash Equilibrium of the supermodular power-price game if and only if it satisfies the necessary optimality conditions (7.34)-(7.35).

Proof. The 'if' part comes directly from the way the extended supermodular game was formulated. For the 'only if' part we argue as follows. Suppose $\vec{\rho}^e$ is a Nash Equilibrium of the problem. Then for each n

$$\begin{aligned}
\rho_n^e &= \arg\max_{\rho_n \in [P_n^{\min}, P_n^{\max}]} \left\{ \omega_n \mu_n \log q_n(\rho_n, \vec{\rho}_{-n}^e, \mu_n) + \rho_n \sum_{m \neq n} \hat{\pi}_{m,n}^e \right\} \\
&= \arg\max_{\rho_n} \left\{ \omega_n \mu_n \log q_n(\rho_n, \vec{\rho}_{-n}^e, \mu_n) + \rho_n \sum_{m \neq n} \frac{\omega_m \mu_m}{q_n(\vec{\rho}^e, \mu_n)} \frac{\partial q_m(\vec{\rho}^e, \mu_m)}{\partial \rho_n} \right\} \\
&= \arg\max_{\rho_n} \left\{ \omega_n \mu_n \log q_n(\rho_n, \vec{\rho}_{-n}^e, \mu_n) \cdot q_n(\vec{\rho}^e, \mu_n) + \rho_n \sum_{m \neq n} \omega_m \mu_m \frac{\partial q_m(\vec{\rho}^e, \mu_m)}{\partial \rho_n} \right\}
\end{aligned}$$

The necessary and sufficient optimality conditions for the above problem are

$$\omega_n \mu_n \frac{\partial q_n(\rho_n, \vec{\rho}_{-n}^e, \mu_n)}{\partial \rho_n} \cdot \frac{q_n(\vec{\rho}^e, \mu_n)}{q_n(\rho_n, \vec{\rho}_{-n}^e, \mu_n)} + \sum_{m \neq n} \omega_m \mu_m \frac{\partial q_m(\vec{\rho}^e, \mu_m)}{\partial \rho_n} + v_n^l - v_n^u = 0$$

$$v_n^l \cdot (P_n^{\min} - \rho_n) \geq 0 \ \& \ v_n^u \cdot (\rho_n - P_n^{\max}) \geq 0$$

Since ρ_n^e is the global maximizer (remember that the objective function is concave) the necessary conditions (7.34)-(7.35) of the scheduling problem are satisfied $\forall n$. □

The above theorem is rather important because it shows that the formulated game leads to one of the solutions of the scheduling problem. If the objective function in (7.32) is concave then the NE is also unique and the game converges to the unique global maximizer. The suboptimality of the proposed scheme in the current work thus lies solely on the fact that the KKT conditions are only necessary but not sufficient. If we can define the region of $\mathcal{P}$ for which the objective function is concave and restrict the feasible power allocations to that, the suggested distributed solution is the optimal one. This can be a topic for future investigations.

7.6.4 The Scheduling Algorithm

In the current paragraph we provide an algorithm which updates for each player the power allocation ρ_n and the price $\pi_{m,n}$. Starting from any initial point within the joint feasible region, the algorithm will eventually converge to a NE bounded component-wise by the greatest and least NE. It is related to the Round-Robin optimization for supermodular games [Top98, Ch. 4.3.1], versions of which are suggested in [HBH06] and [SMG02].

The algorithm has two phases for each iteration t. The *power update phase* calculates the best response for each user n by (7.41) given fixed prices $\hat{\pi}_{m,n}^{(t)}$ and the opponents' decisions $\vec{\rho}_{-n}^{(t)}$.

During the *price update phase* each user m calculates $(N-1)$ new prices $\pi_{m,n}^{(t)}$ (without the hat) by (7.36) given the updated power vector. Then all users $m \neq n$ communicate the values $\pi_{m,n}^{(t)}$ to user n, who divides their sum by $q_n(\vec{\rho}, \mu_n)$ to form the new sum price $c_n^{(t+1)}$ for the next power update phase.

Observe that for each iteration, user n should know: (a) Its own rate of transmission μ_n (which defines q_n) and weight ω_n, (b) the power profile of the other users $\vec{\rho}_{-n}$, (c) the prices $\pi_{m,n}$ communicated by the interfering users and (d) the slow fading coefficients $G_{m,n}$ which depend on the distance between the nodes.

7.6.5 Implementation Issues

Considering implementation issues of the algorithm, information (b) and (c) should be communicated to node n, while (d) should be globally known. Notice that communicating the information over the power profile of the interfering users will violate the distributed nature of the algorithm. Instead of the power vector $\vec{\rho}_{-n}$ however, it suffices for each user to measure the current level of interference $\mathcal{E}_n = \sum_{m \neq n} G_{mn} F_{mn} \rho_m$ in which case we write

$$\hat{q}_n(\rho_n, \mathcal{E}_n, \mu_n) = \mathbb{P}\left(\frac{G_{nn} F_{nn} \rho_n}{\mathcal{E}_n + \sigma_{e(l)}^2} \geq \gamma_n(\mu_n)\right) \stackrel{Rayl.}{=} \exp\left(\frac{-\left(\mathcal{E}_n + \sigma_{e(l)}^2\right)\gamma_n(\mu_n)}{G_{nn}\rho_n}\right)$$

where $l : b(l) = n$ and the second equality holds for Rayleigh fading. The payoff function will change accordingly. In the price update phase observe that the partial derivative of $\hat{q}_m$

7.6. The Scheduling Problem

Distributed Algorithm for the Scheduling Problem

INITIALIZE

- Choose the least element of $\Pi^p \times \Pi^{pr}$: $\left(P_n^{\min}\right)$ for the *power* players and $\left(\min_{\vec{\rho} \in \Pi^p} \hat{\pi}_{m,n}(\vec{\rho})\right)$ for the *price* players.
- Set $t = 0$, $k = 0$.

REPEAT

1. **Power Update:** For $k = 1, \ldots, N$

   - Given $\left(\hat{\pi}_{m,n}^{(t)}\right)$ and $\vec{\rho}^{(t,k-1)}$

   $$\rho_k^{(t,k)} = \arg\max_{\rho_k \in \left[P_k^{\min}, P_k^{\max}\right]} J_k^{(t)}\left(\rho_k, \vec{\rho}_{-k}^{(t,k-1)}\right)$$

   where J_k is given in (7.41).
   - $\vec{\rho}_{-k}^{(t,k)} = \vec{\rho}_{-k}^{(t,k-1)}$

2. **Price Update:**

   - For $k = 1, \ldots, N$. Given $\vec{\rho}^{(t,N)}$ each user k updates the $N - 1$ prices $\pi_{k,n}$ for $k \neq n$

   $$\pi_{k,n}\left(\vec{\rho}^{(t,N)}\right) = \omega_k \cdot \mu_k \frac{\partial q_k\left(\vec{\rho}^{(t,N)}, \mu_k\right)}{\partial \rho_n}$$

   and communicates them to user n
   - Each user n receives $N - 1$ prices $\pi_{k,n}$ and calculates

   $$\hat{\pi}_{k,n}\left(\vec{\rho}^{(t,N)}\right) = \frac{\pi_{k,n}\left(\vec{\rho}^{(t,N)}\right)}{q_n\left(\vec{\rho}^{(t,N)}, \mu_k\right)}$$

   $$c_n^{(t+1)} = \sum_k \hat{\pi}_{k,n}\left(\vec{\rho}^{(t,N)}\right) \qquad (7.46)$$

3. Increase t by 1
   - Set $\vec{\rho}^{(t,0)} = \vec{\rho}^{(t-1,N)}$. Set $\left(\hat{\pi}_{m,n}^{(t)}\right) = \left(\hat{\pi}_{m,n}\left(\vec{\rho}^{(t-1,N)}\right)\right)$

UNTIL $\vec{\rho}^{(t,0)} = \vec{\rho}^{(t-1,0)}$ and $\left(\hat{\pi}_{m,n}^{(t)}\right) = \left(\hat{\pi}_{m,n}^{(t-1)}\right)$

---

with respect to ρ_n will be given by

$$\frac{\pi_{m,n}}{\omega_m \mu_m} = \frac{\partial \hat{q}_m(\rho_m, \mathcal{E}_m, \mu_m)}{\partial \rho_n} = \frac{\partial \hat{q}_m(\rho_m, \mathcal{E}_m, \mu_m)}{\partial \mathcal{E}_m} \frac{\partial \mathcal{E}_m}{\partial \rho_n} = -\frac{\phi_m(\rho_m, \mathcal{E}_m)}{\omega_m \mu_m} G_{nm} F_{nm} \quad (7.47)$$

The new values ϕ_m can be computed by each user m and are independent of the destination user n.

$$\phi_m(\rho_m, \mathcal{E}_m) \stackrel{Rayl.}{=} \omega_m \mu_m \hat{q}_m(\rho_m, \mathcal{E}_m, \mu_m) \left(\frac{\gamma(\mu_m)}{G_{mm} P_m} \right)$$

In the form (7.47) observe that the actual realization of the random variable F_{nm} appears. Remember that F_{nm} is the fast fading channel power coefficient. This information is unknown. But node n is interested in the sum c_n of the prices $\hat{\pi}_{m,n}$ (see (7.46)) which can be written as

$$c_n = -\frac{1}{q_n(\rho_n, \mathcal{E}_n, \mu_n)} \sum_{m \neq n} G_{nm} F_{nm} \phi_m(\rho_m, \mathcal{E}_m) \quad (7.48)$$

If each node $m \neq n$ broadcasts a sequence of random symbols S_m, $|S_m|^2 = 1$ with power $\sqrt{\phi_m(\rho_m, \mathcal{E}_m)}$ the received signal at node n will be (assuming reciprocity of the channel gains)

$$Y_n = \sum_{m \neq n} H_{nm} \sqrt{\phi_m(\rho_m, \mathcal{E}_m)} S_m + Noise \quad (7.49)$$

and its power is $|Y_n|^2 = \sum_{m \neq n} G_{nm} F_{nm} \phi_m(\rho_m, \mathcal{E}_m) + \sigma_n^2$. If the receiving node n divides by $-q_n(\rho_n, \mathcal{E}_n, \mu_n)$ we get a noisy version of the expression in (7.48).

The above idea is borrowed from recent works that deal with ways to use the Wireless Multiple Access Channel (MAC) in order to compute general functions of data among which is also addition [NG07]. The above method using power to convey information can be found specifically in [GSK09]. From the above we realize that although the fast fading coefficients are not known to the users m that have to calculate the prices $\pi_{m,n}$ these can be revealed to the receiver n within the sum signal in (7.48).

Finally rather important is the fact that for the implementation of the algorithm, each user m has to be aware of *its received interference* $\mathcal{E}_m$ and actually calculate only a *single price* ϕ_m. Then *in a single step* during the price update phase each player/node broadcasts its price ϕ_m, while acting simultaneously as a receiver (remember Assumption 2) to obtain the channel-power-weighted sum of the prices of the other $N-1$ users. The entire network topology is not any more necessary to be known to each user m, *only the slow fading gain* G_{mm}. This allows the scheduling algorithm to have as well application in cases where the topology possibly changes due to user mobility.

7.7 Simulations

Simulation results of the proposed scheme for congestion control, routing and distributed power allocation when hop-by-hop retransmissions are taken into account are presented in Fig.7.7. We used a four node topology having two commodity flows with source node 1 and destination nodes 3 and 4 respectively. The congestion control requires the solution of the subproblems (7.29) and (7.30) respectively with prices $\vec{v}(t)$. The prices are updated per node using the expression in (7.31). The optimal links per node are chosen at each step using (7.33). The scheduling problem in (7.32) is solved initially by brut force search (left column) which finds the global optimum of the weighted sum maximization problem (7.32) in order to provide a comparison with the results obtained when the price based algorithm is used (right column). We notice that although the uniqueness of the Nash Equilibrium cannot be guaranteed the results of the suggested algorithm considering the maximum supported incoming rate as well as the queue length (price v_1) are almost optimal. An important remark is that the two solutions would be exactly the same if the objective function in (7.32) would be concave.

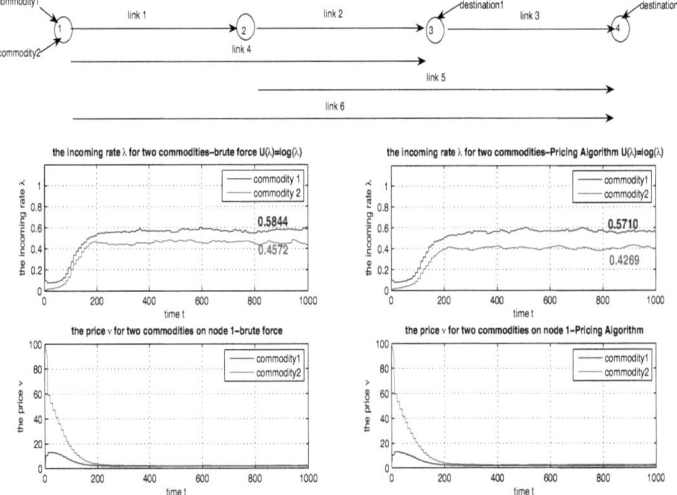

Figure 7.7: Congestion control for a four node topology with two commodity flows.

Chapter 8

Conclusions

The current thesis is an analytical approach to retransmission protocols and their control as part of a wireless communications system. The aim of using such protocols is the detection and correction of errors in order to guarantee reliability in communications. The protocol itself is a practical application that has been proven rather effective and has been widely used in the Internet and more recently in mobile networks. It is based on the very simple idea that a packet received in error should be retransmitted until its success. In a way ARQ protocols are nothing but a direct application of human behavior in a communications system. They are based on a binary answer from the receiver side, which does not provide more information to the transmitter on how to correct the errors occured through the channel. Even simple intuition suggests that restricting the design to this binary information makes the correction of the message difficult, especially in wireless environments where a deep fade can persist for long time intervals and errors can occur in bursts.

The first chapters of the thesis have the aim to provide a solid mathematical modeling of the communications protocol so that analysis can be as general as possible without being restricted to specific expressions for the success probabilities. This approach resulted in difficulties especially since the availability of channel fading at the receiver could not easily fit in a general analysis. A higher channel gain with a specific modulation leads to a higher success probability than a lower fading state. But other than this monotone increasing property the expressions for different communication modes do not follow a general rule. It is for example very common to model channel capacity by an increasing concave function with respect to the channel gain. The success probability however generally does not assume a concave form in the entire domain. To the author's knowledge certain exponential increasing functions, as well as sigmoidal like functions are available in the literature but these do not directly lead to a generalized expression, as the Shannon capacity does, where power, rate, channel gain and success probability can be put together.

The lack of a well accepted formula for the success probabilities led the author to focus his investigations on types of problems without channel state information available at the receiver. This had another simplifying impact on the entire analysis since it removed from the framework the problematic of what kind of extra information - other than the binary ARQ feedback - is required at the transmitter to achieve higher performance gains. The author does not agree with approaches in the literature that utilize both the binary ARQ feedback as well as full channel state information at the transmitter for the following reason. The full CSI is impossible to be available exactly at the transmitter, but even if it would be then no error should be expected since the scheduler can transmit error-free at the Shannon rate. Furthermore the presence of binary ARQ feedback together with CSI leads to an overuse of communication resources at the feedback link due to redundances that should be explored. A related discussion can be also found in the Introduction.

The entire work was based solely on the use of binary ACK/NACK feedback and although the approach is analytical, the aim of the investigations where to provide design patterns for practical communications systems and performance gains based solely on the protocol under study. Even in this overly simplified framework, the author realized that the simplest notions such as goodput and the measures of ARQ performance and reliability where not well defined.

For this reason, after the introduction, chapter 2 was focused on the discussion of what kind of measures are actually appropriate to use in order to describe the rate of correctly transmitted data over a wireless link. The use of the renewal-reward theorem in many published works assumes constant statistics and i.i.d. renewal epochs. A more thorough analysis should focus on the statistics of the channel and define measures that depend on correlation of data as well as ergodicity or not of the fading processes. The author suggested a practical short-term measure to estimate the expected goodput up to a predefined number of accepted packets. It was interestingly observed that the suggested measure leads to higher expected performance. The answer can be found in the fact that the renewal-reward theorem is not appropriate for the ARQ channel in the case of finite backlog, when the process is finalized under some stopping criterion and is not left to infinitely evolve.

The next chapter presented a definition of reliable communications as well as the problem of stability of an ARQ protocol which are closely related. The investigation considers only fixed markovian policies. If a packet is accepted the same probability transition matrix will describe the evolution of the next retransmission process as well. A reliable protocol is such that the instantaneous goodput falls under a strictly positive threshold only a finite number of times. In other words, the goodput will almost surely stay over this rate and the latter is an equivalent notion of delay limited capacity, since it is a minimum positive rate that can always be guaranteed irrespective of the channel realization, under the assumption that the channel fading state is i.i.d. per retransmission effort. The main theorem of the chapter is that a protocol which falls into this definition for reliability should be described by an ergodic matrix and vice versa. In the last paragraph power control is also put into the investigation and families of asymptotic power policies that lead to ergodic and non-ergodic protocols were described. The most interesting part of this last section is the realization that actually a strictly positive goodput can be guaranteed even with finite expected power consumption per packet.

Chapter 4 where the optimal stopping arguments define the optimal truncation time of a protocol was the first attempt to actually approach the ARQ problem in a sequential analytic way and solve a problem with general rewards and costs instead of using specific expressions for the delay and power. The results are rather general and can be applied to various scenarios by just adapting the values of costs and penalties to the requirements of each. The result could as well be extended to a multiuser scheme similar to the draining problem, where a single receiver has to provide service to a certain number of customers in a time division fashion, but can also decide at each time in addition to drop some user if the delay cost incurred from its service becomes high.

Chapter 5 considered the problem of a single queue and the analysis concluded to certain dropping policies that achieve an optimal linear combination of average delay and dropping. The problems here would definitely be more interesting if the power control also came into play. In this case the choice of dropping a packet would influence the power control policy, since the entire power budget utilized for the packet that is finally dropped would be wasted.

The mutliuser problems of chapters 6 and 7 are based on same assumptions and way of thought applied to two different communication scenarios. The assumptions are that the rate remains fixed and the protocols are controlled by optimal power allocation policies. The first remark here is that the policies would definitely be more interesting if the rate would also take part in the optimization problem. Furthrmore, the game theoretic investigations brought to the surface once again the importance of the kind of information exchange required, when one designs decentralized algorithms. To this we should add that each communication entity can also perform self-measurements, such as the level of received intereference, to estimate certain parameters that would be difficult to be communicated precisely from neighbouring nodes.

The problem of reliablity with ARQ protocols is an extremely broad and interesting topic and the author has to admit that the current thesis covers but a small part of what can be investigated. Further suggested topics are for example

- Routing in networks where the average number of NACKs per hop or end-to-end can be an indicator of congestion.

- Use of relays in a network that provide spatial and time diversity by transmitting a second copy of a message to the receiver through a different route. The messages from both routes can then be optimally combined at the destination.

- Design of control algorithms that can adapt the transmission process to errors in communications by exploiting the binary feedback and forming a closed loop system.

- Utilization of the ACK/NACK feedback in order to learn the unknown channel fading through each retransmission of the system, using Bayesian updates.

- Investigation of control algorithms to maximize the throughput or minimize the delay of ALOHA-type protocols, which are simply a variation of the ARQ principle (where the simultaneous transmission of packets from different users leads to collisions)

- Find optimal low cost correcting strategies that minimize the spread of an erroneous message within a network - similarly to gossip and consensus algorithms - as well as the amount of cooperation between neighbouring nodes required to achieve this.

Publication List

[1] A. Giovanidis and S. Stanczak, "Stability and Distributed Power Control in MANETs with Outages and Retransmissions," *submitted to the IEEE Trans. on Communications*, 2009.

[2] A. Giovanidis, G. Wunder, and J. Buehler, "Optimal Control of a Single Queue with Retransmissions: Delay Dropping Tradeoffs," *IEEE Trans. on Wireless Communications*, vol. 8, no. 7, pp. 3736–3746, July 2009.

[3] A. Giovanidis and S. Stanczak, "Retransmission Aware Congestion Control and Distributed Power Allocation in MANETs," *Proc. 5th Int. Workshop on Resource Allocation, Cooperation and Competition in Wireless Networks (RAWNET/WNC3), Seoul, Korea*, June 2009.

[4] ——, "Conditions for the Stability of Wireless ARQ Protocols and Reliable Communications," in *15th European Wireless Conference, Aalborg, Denmark*, May 2009.

[5] A. Giovanidis, G. Wunder, and H. Boche, "A short-term throughput measure for communications using ARQ protocols," *Proc. 7th ITG Conf. on SCC*, 2008.

[6] M. Wiese, A. Giovanidis, and G. Wunder, "Optimal Power Allocation Policies for the Reliable Transmission of a Single Packet via ARQ Protocols," *Asilomar Conf. on Sign. Sys. and Comp.*, 2008.

[7] A. Giovanidis, G. Wunder, H. Boche, and S. Stefanov, "Optimal Control of Transmission Errors with Power Allocation and Stability in ARQ Downlink," *CISS'08, Princeton, USA*, mar. 2008.

[8] A. Giovanidis, G. Wunder, and H. Boche, "An Optimal Stopping Approach to ARQ Protocols with Variable Success Probabilities per Retransmission," *45th Ann. Allerton Conf.*, 2007.

[9] A. Giovanidis, A. Sezgin, U. Mönich, and D. Kim, "Dynamic User Grouping and Shared Frequency Resource Assignment Strategies for OFDMA," in *IEEE 65th Vehicular Technology Conference VTC2007-Spring, Dublin, Ireland*, Apr. 2007.

[10] A. Giovanidis, T. Haustein, E. Jorswieck, and D. Kim, "Maximization of the Single User Rate in OFDMA Assuming Equal Power on Allocated Subcarriers," in *IEEE 65th Vehicular Technology Conference VTC2007-Spring, Dublin, Ireland*, Apr. 2007.

[11] A. Giovanidis, T. Haustein, Y. Hadisusanto, A. Sezgin, and D. Kim, "Multiuser Scheduling using Equal Power in Allocated Subcarriers for OFDM Uplink," in *40th Annual Asilomar Conference on Signals, Systems and Computers, Monterey, USA*, Nov. 2006.

Bibliography

[AB02] N. Arulselvan and R. Berry. Efficient Power Allocations in Wireless ARQ Protocols. In *Wireless Personal Multimedia Communications*, Nov. 2002.

[AB03] N. Ahmed and R.G. Baraniuk. Throughput Measures for Delay-Constrained Communications in Fading Channels. *41st Annual Allerton Conference on Communications, Control and Computing*, Oct. 2003.

[AB05] N. Arulselvan and R. Berry. Energy-throughput optimization for wireless ARQ protocols. In *IEEE ICASSP*, March 2005.

[AB06] N. Arulselvan and R. Berry. Joint Power-Error Control Schemes for Time-Varying Wireless Channels. *Proc. 40th Annual CISS, Princeton*, 2006.

[ABD06] T. Alpcan, T. Basar, and S. Dey. A Power Control Game Based on Outage Probabilities for Multicell Wireless Data Networks. *IEEE Trans. on Wireless Communications*, 5, no. 4, Apr. 2006.

[ABFG+93] A. Arapostathis, V.S. Borkar, E. Fernandez-Gaucherand, M.K. Ghosh, and S.I. Markus. Discrete-time control Markov processes with average cost criterion: A survey. *SIAM J. Control and Opt.*, 31, no.2, March 1993.

[ACAB09] Sara Akbarzadeh, Laura Cottatellucci, Eitan Altman, and Christian Bonnet. Distributed Communication Control Mechanisms for Ad hoc Networks. In *ICC*, 2009.

[Aig99] Martin Aigner. *Diskrete Mathematik*. Vieweg Verlag, 1999.

[AKB04] N. Ahmed, M. A. Khojestapour, and R. G. Baraniuk. Delay-Limited Throughput Maximization for Fading Channels using Rate and Power Control. *Proc. of IEEE Globecom*, 2004.

[AP86]   M.E. Anagnostou and E.N. Protonotarios. Performance Analysis of the Selective Repeat ARQ Protocol. *IEEE Trans. on Communications*, COM-34, no.2:127 – 135, 1986.

[Asm00] S. Asmussen. *Applied Probability and Queues*. Springer, NY, 2000.

[ASP84] M. E. Anagnostou, E. D. Sykas, and E. N. Protonotarios. Steady-State and Transient Analysis of ARQ Protocols. *Comput. Commun.*, 7:23–30, Feb. 1984.

[Ber]   Dimitri P. Bertsekas. *Nonlinear Programming*. Athena Scientific.

[Ber03] D. Bertsekas. *Dynamic Programming and Optimal Control Vol. I and II*. Athena Scientific, 2003.

[BG92]   D. Bertsekas and R. Gallager. *Data Networks*. Prentice-Hall, 1992.

[BG02]   R. A. Berry and R. G. Gallager. Communications over fading channels with delay constraints. *IEEE Trans. on Inf. Theory*, May 2002.

[BKP05] V.S. Borkar, A.A. Kherani, and B.J. Prabhu. Closed and open loop optimal control of buffer and energy of a wireless device. In *WIOPT*, 2005.

[BLZ08] L. Badia, M. Levorato, and M. Zorzi. Markov analysis of Selective Repeat Type-II Hybrid ARQ using Block Codes. *IEEE Trans. on Communications*, 56, no. 9:1434–1441, Sept. 2008.

[BM86]   H. Bruneel and M. Moeneclaey. On the Throughput Performance of Some Continuous ARQ Strategies with Repeated Transmissions. *IEEE Trans. on Communications*, 34, no. 3, March 1986.

[Bre99] Pierre Bremaud. *Markov Chains: Gibbs Fields, Monte Carlo Simulations and Queues*. Springer, 1999.

[BS00]   Ido Bettesh and Shlomo Schamai (Shitz). Queuing Analysis of the Single User Fading Channel. *Proc. 21st IEEE Conv. Electrical and Electronic Engineers in Israel*, pages 274 – 277, 2000.

[BS01]   Ido Bettesh and Shlomo Shamai (Shitz). Optimal Power and Rate Control for Fading Channels. *VTC 2001, Spring*, 2:1063–1067, 2001.

BIBLIOGRAPHY

[BS06] I. Bettesh and S. Shamai (Shitz). Optimal Power and Rate Control for Minimal Average Delay: The Single-User Case. *IEEE Trans. on Inf. Theory*, Sep. 2006.

[BV04] S. Boyd and L. Vandenberghe. *Convex Optimization*. Cambridge University Press, 2004.

[BW] H. Boche and M. Wiczanowski. Optimal Scheduling for High Speed Uplink Packet Access - A Cross-Layer Approach. *VTC 2004*.

[BY04] R. A. Berry and E. M. Yeh. Cross-Layer Wireless Resource Allocation. *IEEE Signal Processing Magazine*, 21, no. 5, Sept. 2004.

[CB04] M. Chiang and J. Bell. Balancing supply and demand of Bandwidth in Wireless cellular Networks: Utility Maximization over Powers and Rates. *Proc. INFOCOM*, 2004.

[CCJ84] R.A. Comroe and D.J. Costello-Jr. ARQ Schemes for Data Transmission in Mobile Radio Systems. *IEEE JSAC*, July 1984.

[CGH$^+$96] R.M. Corless, G.H. Gonnet, D.E.G. Hare, D.J. Jeffrey, and D.E. Knuth. On the Lambert W function. *Advances in Computational Mathematics*, 5:329–359, 1996.

[Cha85] D. Chase. Code Combining - A Maximum-Likelihood Approach for Combining an Arbitrary Number of Noisy Packets. *IEEE Trans on Comm*, 33, no.5, 1985.

[CJ89] R. Courant and F. John. *Introduction to Calculus and Analysis, Vol I*. Springer, 1989.

[CJHIW98] D. J. Costello-Jr., J. Hagenauer, H. Imai, and S. B. Wicker. Applications of Error-Control Coding. *IEEE Trans. on Information Theory*, 44, no. 6:2531–2560, Oct. 1998.

[CLCD] L. Chen, S.H. Low, M. Chiang, and J.C. Doyle. Cross-layer Congestion Control, Routing and Scheduling Design in Ad Hoc Wireless Networks. *Proc. INFOCOM 2006*.

[CR63]   Y.S. Chow and H. Robbins. On Optimal Stopping Rules. *Z. Wahrscheinlichkeitstheorie*, 2, 33-49, 1963.

[CRS71] Y.S. Chow, H. Robbins, and D. Siegmund. *Great Expectations: The Theory of Optimal Stopping*. Houghton Mifflin Company, 1971.

[CT01]   G. Caire and D. Tuninetti. The Throughput of Hybrid-ARQ Protocols for the Gaussian Collision Channel. *IEEE Trans. on Information Theory*, 47, No.5:1971–1988, July 2001.

[CZH05] M. Chiang, S. Zhang, and P. Hande. Distributed Rate Allocation for Inelastic Flows: Optimization Frameworks, Optimality Conditions and Optimal Algorithms. *IEEE INFOCOM*, 2005.

[DK94]   M.H.A. Davis and I. Karatzas. A deterministic approach to optimal stopping. *Prob., Stat. and Optimization (F.P. Kelly, ed.)*, 1994.

[DKB07] D.V. Djonin, A.K. Karmokar, and V.K. Bhargava. Joint Rate and Power Adapatation for Type-i Hybrid ARQ Systems over Correlated Fading Channels under Different Buffer Cost Constraints. *IEEE Trans. on Veh. Techn.*, 56, Mar. 2007.

[DSZ04] G. Dimic, N. D. Sidiropoulos, and R. Zhang. Medium Access Control - Physical Cross-Layer Design. *IEEE Signal Processing Magazine*, 4, Sep. 2004.

[EKEA08] Ralph El-Khoury and Rachid El-Azouzi. Dynamic Retransmission Limit Scheme in MAC Layer for Routing in Multihop Ad hoc Networks. *Hindawi Publishing Corporation, Journal of Computer Systems, Networks and Communications*, 2008.

[ER75]   P. Erdös and P. Révész. On the Length of the Longest Head-Run. *Colloq. Math. Soc. J. Bolyai, Topics in Information Theory, Keszthely (Hungary)*, 1975.

[FC05]   M. Fazel and M. Chiang. Network Utility Maximization With Nonconcave Utilities Using Sum-of-Squares Method. *44th IEEE Conf. on Dec. and Control*, Dec 2005.

BIBLIOGRAPHY

[Fel68]   W. Feller. *An Introduction to Probability Theory and Its Applications, Volume I*. John Wiley & Sons, 1968.

[Fer00]   T.S. Ferguson. *Optimal Stopping and Applications*. UCLA Lecture Notes, 2000.

[Fos53]   F. G. Foster. On the Stochastic Matrices Associated with Certain Queuing Processes. *Ann. Math. Stat.*, 26:355–360, 1953.

[Gal96]   R. G. Gallager. *Discrete Stochastic Processes*. Kluwer Academic Publishers, 1996.

[GKS03]   M. Goyal, A. Kumar, and V. Sharma. Power constrained and delay optimal policies for scheduling over a fading channel. *IEEE INFOCOM*, 2003.

[GKS08]   M. Goyal, A. Kumar, and V. Sharma. Optimal Cross-Layer Scheduling of Transmissions Over a Fading Multiaccess Channel. *IEEE Trans. on Information Theory*, 54, no. 8:3518–3537, Aug. 2008.

[GNG]   P.K. Gopala, Y.-H. Nam, and H. El Gamal. On the Error Exponents of ARQ Channels with Deadlines. *Submitted to Trans on Inf Theory arXiv:cs.IT/0610106v1 18 Oct 2006*.

[GO80]   L. J. Guibas and A. M. Odlyzko. Long Repetitive Patterns in Random Sequences. *Z. Wahrscheinlichkeitstheorie verw. Gebiete, Springer-Verlag*, 53:241–262, 1980.

[GSK09]   M. Goldenbaum, S. Stanczak, and M. Kaliszan. On Function Computation via Wireless Sensor Multiple-Access Channels. *Proc. IEEE WCNC*, 2009.

[GSW86]   L. Gordon, M. F. Schilling, and M. S. Waterman. An Extreme Value Theory for Long Head Runs. *Probab. Th. Rel. Fields, Springer Verlag*, 72:279–287, 1986.

[Haj06]   B. Hajek. *Lecture Notes on Communication Network Analysis*. UIUC, 2006.

[HBH05]   J. Huang, R.A. Berry, and M.L. Honig. Wireless Scheduling with Hybrid ARQ. *IEEE Trans. on Wireless Communications*, 4, no. 6, Nov. 2005.

[HBH06] J. Huang, R. Berry, and M.L. Honig. Distributed Interference Compensation for Wireless Networks. *JSAC*, 24, May 2006.

[HGG02] T. Holliday, A. Goldsmith, and P. Glynn. Wireless link adaptation policies: QoS for deadline constrained traffic with imperfect channel estimates. In *Proc. ICC*, 2002.

[HT98] S. Hanly and D. Tse. Multiaccess Fading Channels - Part II: Delay-Limited Capacities. *IEEE Trans. on Information Theory*, 44, no. 7, Nov. 1998.

[JHM06] K. Jacobsson, H. Hjalmarsson, and N. Moller. ACK-clock Dynamics in Network Congestion Control - An Inner Feedback Loop with Implications on Inelastic Flow Impact. In *45th IEEE Conf. on Decision and Control*, Dec. 2006.

[Kal94] S. Kallel. Efficient Hybrid ARQ Protocols with Adaptive Forward Error Correction. *IEEE Trans. on Comm.*, 42, no 2/3/4, 1994.

[Kap79] M. Kaplan. A Sufficient Condition for Nonergodicity of a Markov Chain. *IEEE Trans. on Information Theory*, 25, no. 4:470 – 471, July 1979.

[KB02] S. Kandukuri and S. Boyd. Optimal Power Control in Interference-Limited Fading Wireless Channels with Outage-Probability Specifications. *IEEE Trans. on Wireless Comm.*, 1, No. 1, Jan. 2002.

[KDB06a] A. K. Karmokar, D. V. Djonin, and V. K. Bhargava. POMDP-based coding rate adaptation for Type-I Hybrid ARQ systems over fading channels with memory. *IEEE Trans. on Wireless Communications*, vol. 5:3512–3523, Dec. 2006.

[KDB06b] A.K. Karmokar, D.V. Djonin, and V.K. Bhargava. Delay-aware Power Adapatation for Incremental Redundancy Hybrid ARQ over Fading Channels with Memory. *Proc. ICC '06*, 2006.

[KDB08] A. K. Karmokar, D. V. Djonin, and V. K. Bhargava. Cross-Layer Rate and Power adaptation Strategies for IR-HARQ Systems over Fading Channels with Memory: A SMDP-Based Approach. *IEEE Trans. on Communications*, 56, no. 8:1352–1365, Aug. 2008.

BIBLIOGRAPHY

[Kel97] F. Kelly. Charging and rate control for elastic traffic. *European Transactions on Telecommunications*, 8:33–37, 1997.

[Kle75] L. Kleinrock. *Queueing Systems Volume I: Theory*. John Wiley & Sons, 1975.

[KMT98] F.P. Kelly, A. Maulloo, and D. Tan. Rate Control in Communication Networks: Shadow Prices, Proportional Fairness and Stability. *Journal of the Operational Research Society*, 1998.

[LCC06] J.-W. Lee, M. Chiang, and A.R. Calderbank. Price-Based Distributed Algorithms for Rate-Reliability Tradeoff in Network Utility Maximization. *IEEE JSAC*, 24, no. 5, May 2006.

[LHJL$^+$08] D.J. Love, R.W. Heath-Jr, V.K.N. Lau, D. Gesbert, B.D. Rao, and M. Andrews. An Overview of Limited Feedback in Wireless Communication Systems. *IEEE Journal on Selected Areas in Communications*, 26, issue: 8:1341–1365, Oct. 2008.

[LJM84] S. Lin, D.J. Costello Jr, and M.J. Miller. Automatic-Repeat-Request Error-Control schemes. *IEEE Communications Magazine*, 22, no. 12, Dec. 1984.

[LK84] W. Lin and P. R. Kumar. Optimal control of a Queueing System with Two Heterogeneous Servers. *IEEE Trans. on Autom. Control*, Aug. 1984.

[LMNM01] E. Leonardi, M. Mellia, F. Neri, and M.A. Marson. Bounds on Average Delays and Queue Size Averages and Variances in Input-queued Cell-based Switches. *IEEE INFOCOM*, 2:1095–1103, 2001.

[LMS02] J. Lee, R. Mazumdar, and N. Shroff. Downlink Power Allocation for Multi-class CDMA Wirelss Networks. *IEEE INFOCOM*, 2002.

[LMS05] J.-W. Lee, R. R. Mazumdar, and N. B. Shroff. Non-Convex Optimization and Rate Control for Multi-Class Services in the Internet. *IEEE/ACM Trans. on Networking*, 13, no. 4, Aug 2005.

[LS] X. Lin and N.B. Shroff. Joint Rate Control and Scheduling in Multihop Wireless Networks. *Proc. IEEE CDC 2004*.

[LWZ04]   B. Lu, X. Wang, and J. Zhang. Throughput of CDMA Data Networks with Multiuser Detection, ARQ, and Packet Combining. *IEEE Trans. on Wireless Comm.*, 3, no. 5, Sept 2004.

[LY82]   S. Lin and P.S. Yu. A Hybrid-ARQ scheme with parity retransmission for error control of satellite channels. *IEEE Trans. on Communications*, COM-30:1701–1719, July 1982.

[LZG04]   Q. Liu, S. Zhou, and G. B. Giannakis. Cross-Layer Combining of Adaptive Modulation and Coding With Truncated ARQ Over Wireless Links. *IEEE trans. on Wireless Comm*, 3, Sept. 2004.

[MB02]   P. Marbach and R. Berry. Downlink Resource Allocation and Pricing for Wireless Networks. *IEEE INFOCOM*, 2002.

[MBBC86] M. Moeneclaey, H. Bruneel, I. Bruyland, and D.-Y. Chung. Throughput Optimization for a Generalized Stop-and-Wait ARQ Protocol. *IEEE Trans. on Communications*, 34, no 2, Feb. 1986.

[MFK08]   Robert J. McCabe, Nikolaos M. Freris, and P. R. Kumar. Controlled Random Access MAC for Network Utility Maximization in Wireless Networks. In *CDC*, 2008.

[ML00]   E. Malkamäki and H. Leib. Performance of Truncated Type-II Hybrid ARQ Schemes with Noisy Feedback over Block Fading Channels. *IEEE Trans. on Communications*, 48, Sept. 2000.

[MMS86]   D.-J. Ma, A.M. Makowski, and A. Shwartz. Estimation and Optimal Control of constrained Markov Chains. *Proc. IEEE Conf. on Dec. and Control*, Dec. 1986.

[Mod99]   E. Modiano. An adaptive algorithm for optimizing the packet size used in wireless ARQ protocols. *Wireless Networks 5*, 1999.

[MT93]   S. P. Meyn and R. L. Tweedie. *Markov Chains and Stochastic Stability*. Springer-Verlag London, 1993.

BIBLIOGRAPHY

[Nee03]   M.J. Neely. *Dynamic power allocation and routing for satellite and wireless networks with time varying channels.* Ph.D. dissertation, LIDS, Mass. Inst. Technology, Cambridge, MA, 2003.

[NG07]   B. Nazer and M. Gastpar. Computation over Multiple-Access Channels. *IEEE Trans. on Inf. Theory*, 53, no. 10, Oct. 2007.

[NML08]   M.J. Neely, E. Modiano, and C.-P. Li. Fairness and Optimal Stochastic Control for Heterogeneous Networks. *IEEE/ACM Trans. on Networking*, 16, No. 2, Apr. 2008.

[NMR]   M.J. Neely, E. Modiano, and C.E. Rohrs. Dynamic Power Allocation and Routing for Time Varying Wireless Networks. *INFOCOM 2003*.

[NMR03]   M.J. Neely, E. Modiano, and C.E. Rohrs. Power Allocation and Routing in Multibeam Satellites with Time-Varying Channels. *IEEE/ACM Trans. on Networking*, 11, No 1, Feb. 2003.

[NMR05]   M.J. Neely, E. Modiano, and C.E. Rohrs. Dynamic Power Allocation and Routing for Time-Varying Wireless Networks. *IEEE JSAC*, 23, No. 1, Jan 2005.

[OSW94]   L.H. Ozarow, S. Shamai, and A.D. Wyner. Information Theoritic Considerations for Cellular Mobile Radio. *IEEE Trans. on Vehicular Technology*, 43, No.2:359–378, May 1994.

[OTGB08] D. O'Neill, B.S. Thian, A. Goldsmith, and S. Boyd. Wireless NUM: Rate and Reliability Tradeoffs in Random Environments. *Proc. Allerton Conference on Communication, Control, and Computing, UIUC*, 2008.

[Pak69]   A. G. Pakes. Some Conditions for Ergodicity and Recurrence of Markov Chains. *Operations Research*, 17:1059–1061, 1969.

[PDE]   J. Papandriopoulos, S. Dey, and J. Evans. Optimal and Distributed Protocols for Cross-Layer Design of Physical & Transport Layers in MANETs. *IEEE/ACM Trans. on Networking*.

[PED05]   J. Papandriopoulos, J.S. Evans, and S. Dey. Optimal power control for Rayleigh-faded multiuser systems with outage constraints. *IEEE Trans. on Wireless Comm.*, 47, no. 6, Nov. 2005.

[PGP83]   A.N. Philippou, C. Georghiou, and G.N. Philippou. A Generalized Geometric Distribution and some of its Properties. *Statistics and Probability Letters, North-Holland*, 1:171–175, June 1983.

[PM86]   A.N. Philippou and F.S. Makri. Successes, Runs and Longest Runs. *Statistics and Probability Letters, North-Holland*, 4:211–215, June 1986.

[Pra64]   J.W. Pratt. Risk Aversion in the Small and the Large. *Econometrica*, 32:122–136, 1964.

[Put05]   M. L. Puterman. *Markov Decision Processes: Discrete Stochastic Dynamic Programming*. Wiley & Sons, 2005.

[QCCW99] X. Qui, J. Chuang, K. Chawla, and J. Whitehead. Performance Comparison of Link Adaptation and Incremental Redundancy in Wireless Data Networks. *Proc. IEEE WCNC*, 1999.

[RBZ05]   M. Rossi, L. Badia, and M. Zorzi. On the Delay Statistics of SR ARQ Over Markov Channels With Finite Round-Trip Delay. *IEEE Trans. on Wireless Comm.*, 4, no. 4:1–11, Jul. 2005.

[Roc70]   R. Tyrrell Rockafellar. *Convex Analysis*. Princeton Landmarks in Mathematics, Princeton University Press, 1970.

[Ros96]   Sheldon M. Ross. *Stochastic Processes*. John Wiley & Sons, 1996.

[Rud64]   W. Rudin. *Principles of Mathematical Analysis (Second Edition)*. McGraw-Hill, 1964.

[Sch93]   M. Schael. Average Optimality in Dynamic Programming with General State Space. *Math. of Oper. Res.*, 18, no.1, Feb. 1993.

[Sha48]   C. E. Shannon. A Mathematical Theory of Communication. *The Bell System Technical Journal (reprinted with corrections)*, 27:379–423, 623–656, July-Oct. 1948.

BIBLIOGRAPHY

[Shi78] A. N. Shiryayev. *Optimal Stopping Rules.* Springer Verlag, 1978.

[Sin77] P. S. Sindhu. Retransmission Error Control with Memory. *IEEE Trans. on Communications*, COM-25, no. 5:473–479, May 1977.

[SMG02] C. U. Saraydar, N. B. Mandayam, and D. J. Goodman. Efficient Power Control via Pricing in Wireless Data Networks. *IEEE Trans. on Comm.*, 50, no.2, Feb. 2002.

[Sok39] I. S. Sokolnikoff. *Advanced Calculus.* McGraw-Hill, 1939.

[SR82] B. H. Saeki and I. Rubin. An Analysis of a TDMA Channel Using Stop-and-Wait, Block, and Select-and-Repeat ARQ Error Control. *IEEE Trans. on Communications*, 30, May 1982.

[SRK03] S. Shakkottai, T.S. Rappaport, and P.C. Karlsson. Cross-layer design for wireless networks. *IEEE Communications Magazine*, 41, issue 10:74–80, Oct. 2003.

[SWB09] S. Stanczak, M. Wiczanowski, and H. Boche. *Fundamentals of Resource Allocation in Wireless Networks: Theory and Algorithms.* W. Utschick, H. Boche, R. Mathar, Foundations in Signal Processing, Communications and Networking, Springer, Second Expanded Edition ed., 2009, vol. 3, 2009.

[TE92] L. Tassiulas and A. Ephremides. Stability Properties of Constrained Queueing Systems and Scheduling Policies for Maximum Throughput in Multihop Radio Networks. *IEEE trans. on Automatic Control*, 37, No. 12, Dec 1992.

[TE93] L. Tassiulas and A. Ephremides. Dynamic Server Allocation to Parallel Queues with Randomly Varying Connectivity. *IEEE Trans. on Inf. Theory*, 39, no 2, March 1993.

[TNV04] L. Tong, V. Naware, and P. Venkitasubramaniam. Signal processing in random access. *IEEE Signal Processing Magazine*, 21, issue 5:29–39, Sept. 2004.

[Top98] Donald M. Topkis. *Supermodularity and Complementarity.* Princeton University Press, 1998.

[TR99] J. N. Tsitsiklis and B. Van Roy. Optimal Stopping of Markov Processes: Hilbert Space Theory, Approximations and an Application to Pricing High-Dimensional financial Derivatives. *IEEE Trans. on Automatic Control*, 44, No 10, Oct 1999.

[Tun07] D. Tuninetti. Transmitter channel state information and repetition protocols in block fading channels. *ITW 2007, Lake Tahoe, California*, Sept. 2007.

[TVPH03] V. Tripathi, E. Visotsky, R. Peterson, and M. Honig. Reliability-based Type II Hybrid ARQ Schemes. *Proc. IEEE ICC*, 2003.

[URGW03] E. Uhlemann, L.K. Rasmussen, A. Grant, and P.-A. Wiberg. Optimal Incremental-Redundancy Strategy for Type-II Hybrid ARQ. *Proc. ISIT, Yokohama, Japan*, 2003.

[VTH] E. Visotsky, V. Tripathi, and M. Honig. Optimum ARQ Design: A Dynamic Programming Approach. *Proc. ISIT 2003*.

[VVTB03] F. Vacirca, A. De Vendictis, A. Todini, and A. Baiocchi. On the effects of ARQ Mechanisms on TCP Performance in Wireless Environments. In *IEEE Globecom*, 2003.

[Wil91] D. Williams. *Probability with Martingales*. Cambridge, 1991.

[XJB04] L. Xiao, M. Johansson, and S.P. Boyd. Simultaneous Routing and Resource Allocation via Dual Decomposition. *IEEE Trans. on Communications*, 52, no. 7, July 2004.

[Yat95] R.D. Yates. A framework for uplink power control in cellular radio systems. *IEEE Journal on Selected Areas in Communications*, 13, Issue: 7:1341–1347, Sep. 1995.

[YC03] E.M. Yeh and A.S. Cohen. Throughput and Delay Optimal Resource Allocation in Multi-Access Fading Channels. *Proc. ISIT*, 2003.

[YC04] E.M. Yeh and A.S. Cohen. Information Theory Queueing and Resource Allocation in Multi-user Fading Communications. *Proc. of CISS*, 2004.

BIBLIOGRAPHY

[YK05]   J. Yun and M. Kavehrad. Markov Error Structure for Throughput analysis of adaptive Modulation Systems combined with ARQ over Correlated Fading Channels. *IEEE Trans. on Veh. Tech.*, 54, no. 1:235–245, Jan. 2005.

[YL06]   W. Yu and R. Lui. Dual Methods for Nonconvex Spectrum Optimization of Multicarrier Systems. *IEEE Trans on Comm*, 54, No 7, 2006.

[YTH93] M. Yoshimoto, T. Takine, and T. Hasegawa. Waiting Time and Queue Length Distributions for Go-Back-N and Selective.Repeat ARQ Protocols. *IEEE Trans on Communications*, 41, no 11, Nov. 1993.

[ZR96]   M. Zorzi and R.R. Rao. On the Use of Renewal Theory in the Analysis of ARQ Protocols. *IEEE Trans. on Communications*, 44, No.9:1077–1081, Sept 1996.

[ZR97]   M. Zorzi and R. R. Rao. Error Control and Energy Consumption in Communications for Nomadic Computing. *IEEE Trans. on Computers*, 46, No. 3, Mar. 1997.

[ZV05]   H. Zheng and H. Viswanathan. Optimizing the ARQ Performance in Downlink Packet Data Systems with Scheduling. *IEEE Trans. on Wireless Communications*, 4, no. 2, Mar. 2005.

[ZW]   C. Zhou and G. Wunder. Throughput-Optimal Scheduling with low average Delay for Cellular Broadcast Systems. *EURASIP Journal on Advances in Signal Processing*, 2009, Article ID 762050.

[ZW00]   D. Zhang and K. M. Wasserman. Energy efficient data communication over fading channels. *Proc. IEEE WCNC*, 2000.

[ZW02]   D. Zhang and K. M. Wasserman. Transmission Schemes for Time-varying Wireless Channels with Partial State Observations. *Proc. INFOCOM 2002*, 2002.

Abbreviations and Nomenclature

$\mathbf{1}_C$	indicator function for set C
A	system action
$\mathcal{A}$	action space
$b(l)$	begin node of link l
D	delay cost (& number of destination nodes in MANET)
$\mathcal{D}$	set of destination nodes in MANET
$\mathbb{E}$	expectation
$\mathcal{E}_n$	measured interference level from user n
$e(l)$	end node of link l
F	fast fading path gain
$\{\mathcal{F}_n\}$	filtration
G	slow fading path gain
$\mathcal{G}$	non-cooperative game
g	goodput function
g_{l-t}	long-term goodput
g_{l-t}^{tr}	long term goodput for truncated ARQ
g_{s-t}	short-term goodput
h	channel gain
$\mathcal{I}$	information available from higher layers
J	cost-to-go (& payoff function)
L	Lagrangian of an optimization problem
L_{dual}	Lagrange dual function
L_{links}	number of links
$\mathcal{L}$	set of links in a network
l	link

$\mathcal{M}$	set of scheduling rates
$\mathbb{N}$	set of natural numbers
$\mathbb{N}_+$	$\mathbb{N}\setminus\{0\}$
N	finite time horizon (& number of users or nodes)
$\mathcal{N}$	set of users or nodes
N_{ACK}	number of retransmission attempts up to success
$\mathbb{P}$	probability measure
$\mathcal{P}_{out}$	outage probability
$\mathcal{P}$	set of feasible power allocations
P_{tot}	total power budget
p	error probability function
q	success probability function
$\mathbb{R}$	set of real numbers
$\mathbb{R}_+$	set of non-negative real numbers
$\mathcal{R}^r_{f(x)}$	absolute risk aversion coefficient of $f(x)$
R	reward
r	number of consecutive ACKs
S	system state
$\mathcal{S}$	state space (& set of network data flows)
S_k	time of k-th renewal occurence
T	optimal stopping time
T^{slot}	time slot duration
t	time (discrete or continuous)
U	utility function
u	queue length
V	Lyapunov test function
X	binary output (ACK/NACK) of the retransmission effort
Y_n	payoff (cost+reward) at slot n
Z	retransmission effort
α	arrival process
β	discount factor

Abbreviations and Nomenclature

Γ	network goodput region
γ	SINR threshold
Δ	dropped packets average
δ	dropping penalty
Λ	stability region
λ	expected data arrival rate
μ	transmission rate
Π	set of admissible policies
π	policy
$\pi_{m,n}$	price of interference from node m to n
ρ	allocated power
τ	time (discrete or continuous)
ϕ_n	common price of node n for all other nodes in MANET algorithm
$(\Omega, \mathcal{F}, \mathbb{P})$	probability triple
ω	weight

ACK	ACKnowledgement
ALO	ALOha-like ARQ protocol
ARQ	Automatic Repeat reQuest
a.s.	almost surely
CDA	Canonically Distributed Algorithm
CNR	Channel-gain-to-Noise-Ratio
CSI	Channel State Information
DLC	Data Link Control (layer)
FEC	Forward Error Correction (code)
GBN-ARQ	Go-Back-N ARQ
H-ARQ	Hybrid Automatic Repeat reQuest
i.i.d.	independent identically distributed
INR	INcremental Redundancy ARQ protocol
MAC	Medium Access Control (sublayer)

MANET	Mobile Ad-hoc NETwork	
MDP	Markov Decision Process	
MZT	Maximum Zero-outage Throughput	
MZT_{s-t}	Maximum Zero-outage short-term Throughput	
NACK	Not-ACKnowledgement	
NE	Nash Equilibrium	
NUM	Network Utility Maximization	
PHY	PHYsical (layer)	
p.d.f.	probability density function	
QoS	Quality-of-Service	
RTD	Repetition Time Diversity ARQ protocol	
r.v.	random variable	
SINR	Signal to Interference plus Noise Ratio	
SR-ARQ	Selective Repeat ARQ	
s.t.	such that (& subject to)	
SW-ARQ	Stop-and-Wait ARQ	
w.r.t.	with respect to	

I want morebooks!

Buy your books fast and straightforward online - at one of world's fastest growing online book stores! Environmentally sound due to Print-on-Demand technologies.

Buy your books online at
www.morebooks.shop

Kaufen Sie Ihre Bücher schnell und unkompliziert online – auf einer der am schnellsten wachsenden Buchhandelsplattformen weltweit! Dank Print-On-Demand umwelt- und ressourcenschonend produziert.

Bücher schneller online kaufen
www.morebooks.shop

KS OmniScriptum Publishing
Brivibas gatve 197
LV-1039 Riga, Latvia
Telefax: +371 686 204 55

info@omniscriptum.com
www.omniscriptum.com

Printed by Books on Demand GmbH, Norderstedt / Germany